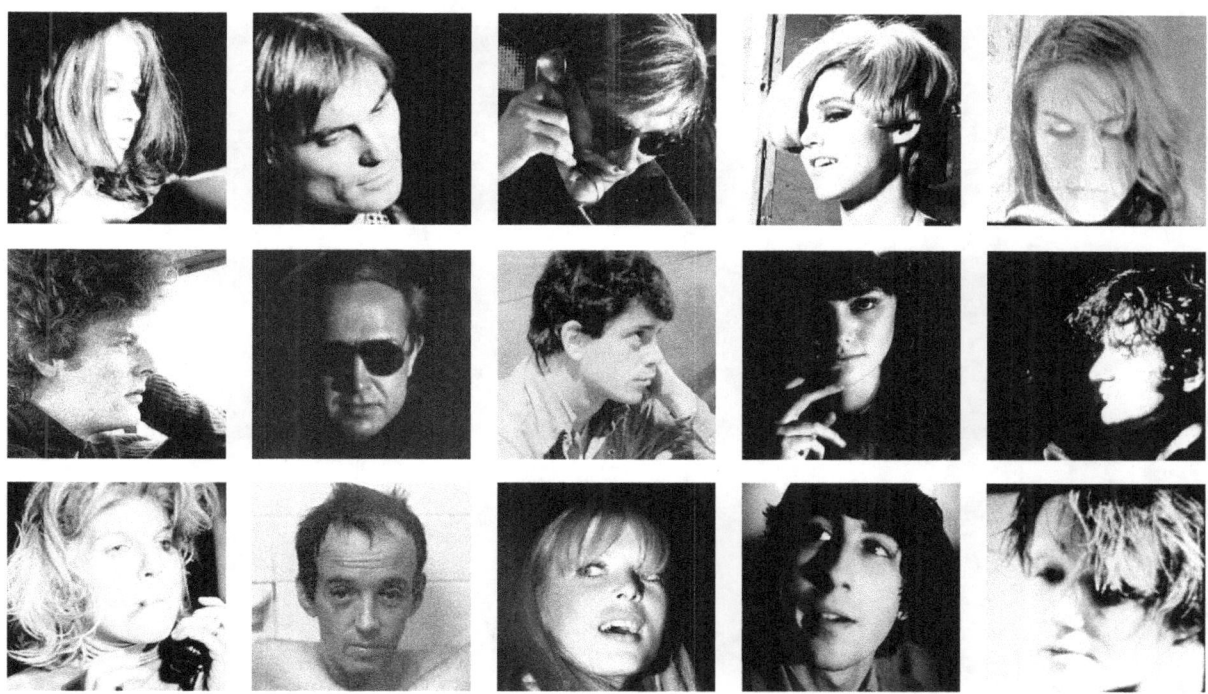

Andy Warhol's Factory People

Inside the 1960's Silver Factory. . . an Oral History

Book II Speeding Into The Future

Catherine O'Sullivan Shorr

Cover Photo & Portrait Montage on preceding page by Billy Name.
L. to R. from top: Ultra Violet, Allen Midgette, Andy Warhol, Edie
Sedgwick, Mary Woronov, Paul Morrissey, Robert Heide, Lou Reed,
Susan Bottomly (International Velvet), Ondine, Brigid Berlin, Taylor
Mead, Nico, David Croland, Ingrid Superstar

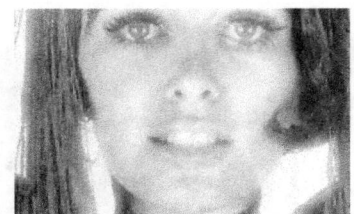

Poster design by Tom & Leo , Paris.

At right: Photo of author, taken in her formative, fringe-wearing
hippie days, 1966, in New York City.

Published by Planet Group Entertainment Ltd.

BOOK II

SPEEDING INTO THE FUTURE

If someone wants to be in movies, you can buy their life.
—Andy Warhol

CONTENTS

In the TV series, our intros offered a hint of 'cinematic sixties' excitement to come, as I hope they do here. Like the first part, our interviewed subjects, charming as they were, would not dominate screen time, since we'd unearthed so many photos, archive film clips, and art shots of, well, what they were talking about. Some French docu filmmakers, who still love Talking Heads (not the band) had a problem with that. Exit one more film editor. By now I was running out of ship hands and we were not even halfway across the straits. Should we turn back now before we lose our shirts? Shucks no. Inspired by Billy Name's vivid recall and his vast photographic collection, we forged ahead with Warholian abandon, three sheets to the wind. . .

We shot reels, and reels, and reels, of film which most people would say are boring or uninteresting, but people who curate his films know these films as art pieces.
——**Billy Name: Warhol Photographer, Factory Foreman**

I think the movies are non-commercial, and really have to be raw material in Andy's thinking, the basis for future (art) work.
——**Henry Geldzahler: Art Critic, Curator, Metropolitan Museum of Art, 1965**

He seems to prefer to do filmmaking to painting.
——**Leo Castelli: Famed Gallery Owner, Warhol Art Dealer**

Andy created his own Hollywood, based in part on having been rejected. He wanted to be taken seriously by a Hollywood that shut its doors on him.
——**Gerard Malanga: Warhol Factory Assistant, "The Prime Minister"**

You were a star! That was just great not to having to go through all the Hollywood producers, and banging and having the door close. If he chose you, you were an immediate star.
——**Ivy Nicholson: Warhol Superstar**

We were just shooting. There was no name. I mean, there was no *script*, how could there be a name? I never in my life believed that these would be considered films.
——**Allen Midgette: Actor, Warhol Star**

. . . The Screen Tests were murky, with poor contrast and focus. Except mine. The lens had been covered with debris and fingerprints (Andy didn't think it mattered!) and I spent two minutes cleaning it for him with my T-shirt.
——**Kip 'Bima' Stagg: Co-star of 'Beauty 1' with Edie Sedgwick**

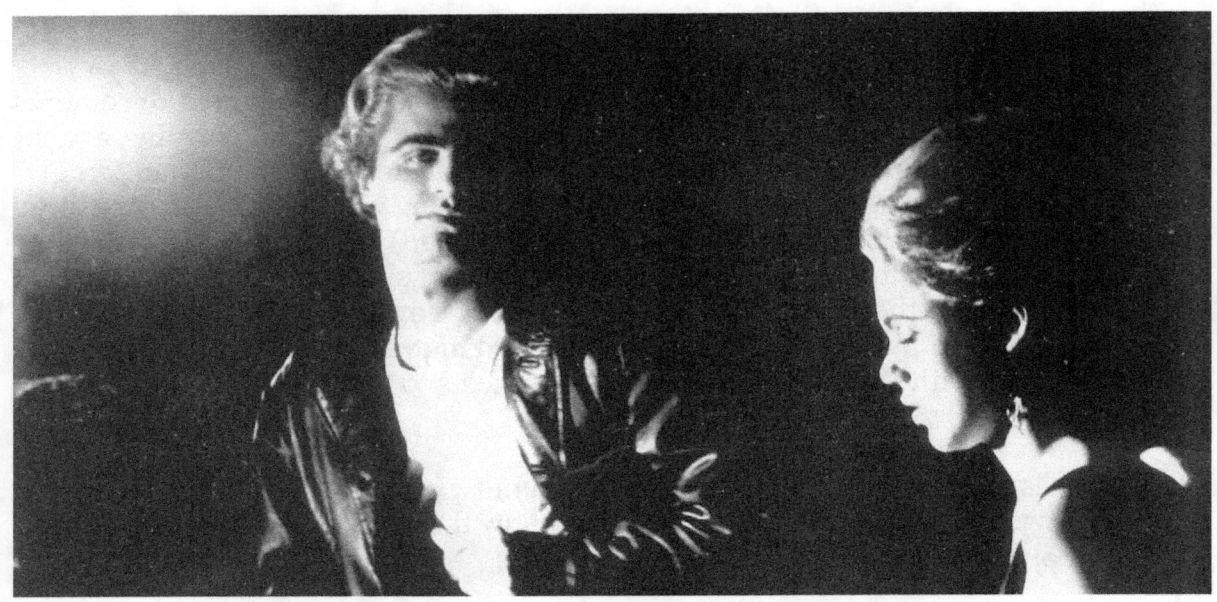

"Reels and reels of film!" Gerard Malanga and Edie Sedgwick act out in Warhol's 'Vinyl', 1965. (Photos: Billy Name)

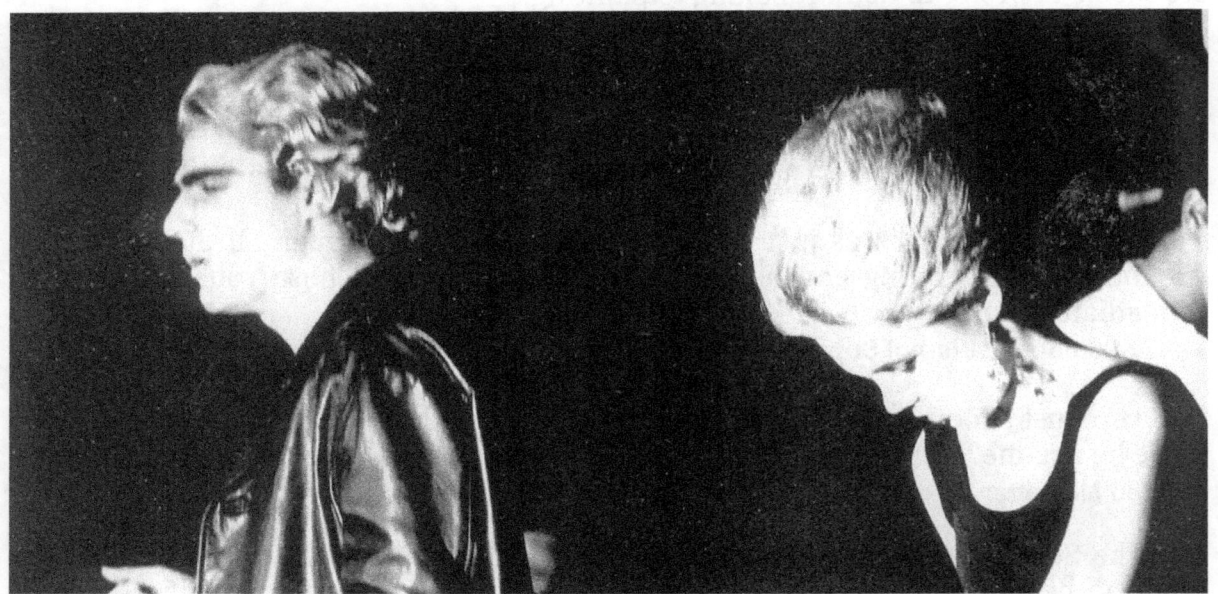

'Vinyl' was Edie's first role in a Warhol film. She did not have much to do, except look beautiful, even with hair teased into a beehive.

With a Warhol movie they would *carry* on, and they stopped when the film ran out. It was all improvisation. So they are real sleepers. The concept was extraordinary.
—**Ultra Violet: Socialite, Artist, Warhol Superstar**

I don't remember ever saying anything to Andy where he didn't say it was a good idea. He was so glad to have any ideas.
—**Paul Morrissey: Filmmaker, Warhol Co-Director**

Everybody loved Andy. People like Danny Williams, who got bumped because Andy thought it more valuable to work with Paul Morrissey.
—**Nat Finkelstein: Photojournalist with Black Star Agency, Warhol Chronicler, 1964-67**

Andy used to let other artists do their thing, too. There would be poetry readings, and people would do plays. He really was a very generous person.
—**Baby Jane Holzer: Socialite, Girl of the Year '64**

Edie was actually the second choice to star in 'Prison' with me. The first had been Jane Holzer. But there was some talk that the film would be salacious, and she was concerned about offending her family.
--**Bibbe Hansen: Youngest member of Warhol Family**

Edie, how does your family feel about your being in these movies?
—**Dave Dugan, CBS News Interviewer**

Agghhhh! They hate it! And they've decided I shouldn't have any money.
—**Edie Sedgwick: Warhol Icon, Girl of the Year, 1965**

Everyone gets to the point where the family trys to cut you off. Who could blame them? Why do you need this wild person going around and spending your hard inherited money?
—**Danny Fields: Edie Sedgwick confidant, Music Entrepreneur (The Ramones)**

Warhol had a goldmine in Edie, and he knew it. . . "We're going to make Edie the queen of the factory". At the moment Edie, literally, does her last film with Warhol, he brings the Velvet Underground in.
—**Victor Bockris: Biographer, Warhol, The Velvet Underground**

We introduced them to the Psychiatrist's convention. That's where the first public performance of the Velvet Underground took place!
—**Jonas Mekas: Founder, Film-Maker's Cinematheque, Anthology Film Archives**

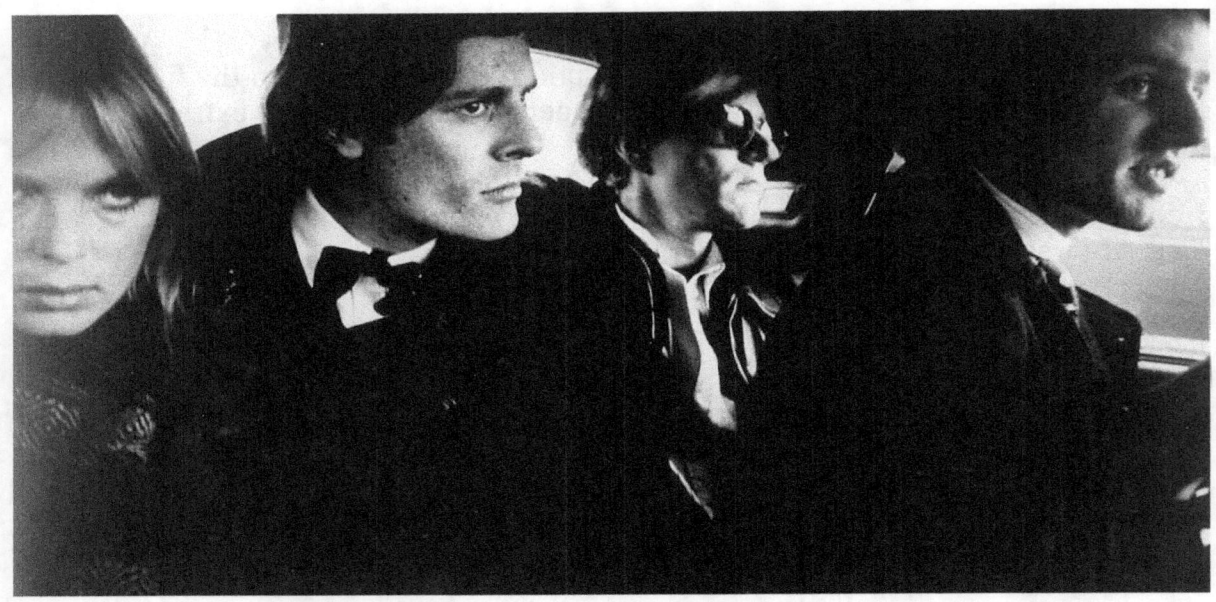

Nico, Paul Morrissey, Andy and Gerard Malanga share a limo, and good ideas, on the way to Philadelphia for a Velvet Underground gig. (Photo: Nat Finkelstein)

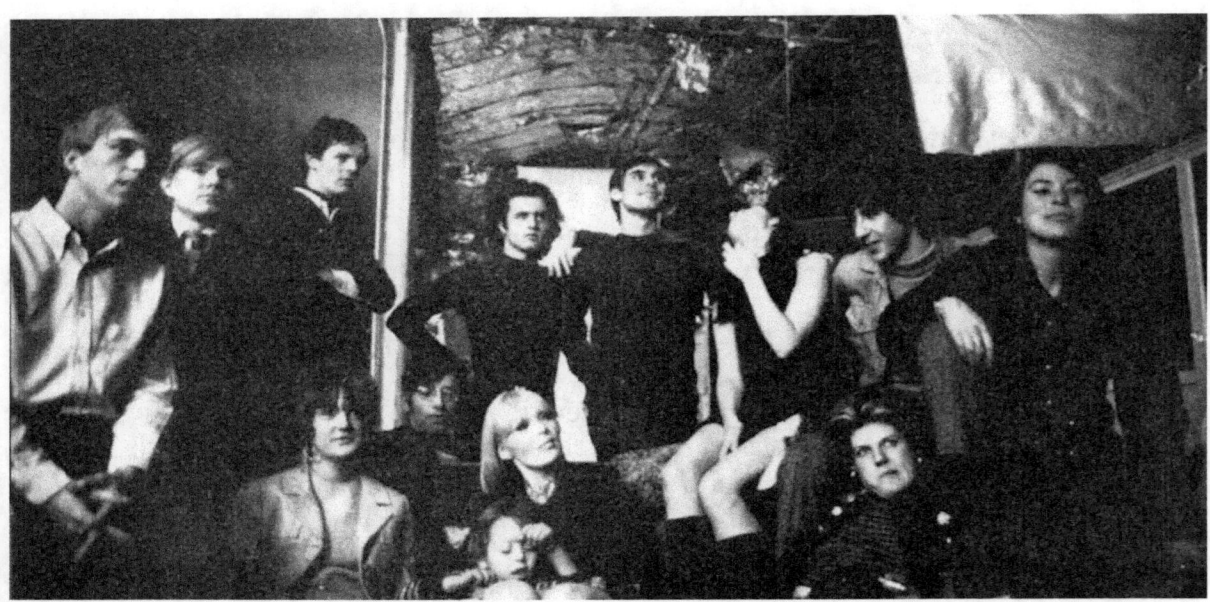

Factory Family get-together. See how many you can reecognize by now. (Photo: Billy Name)

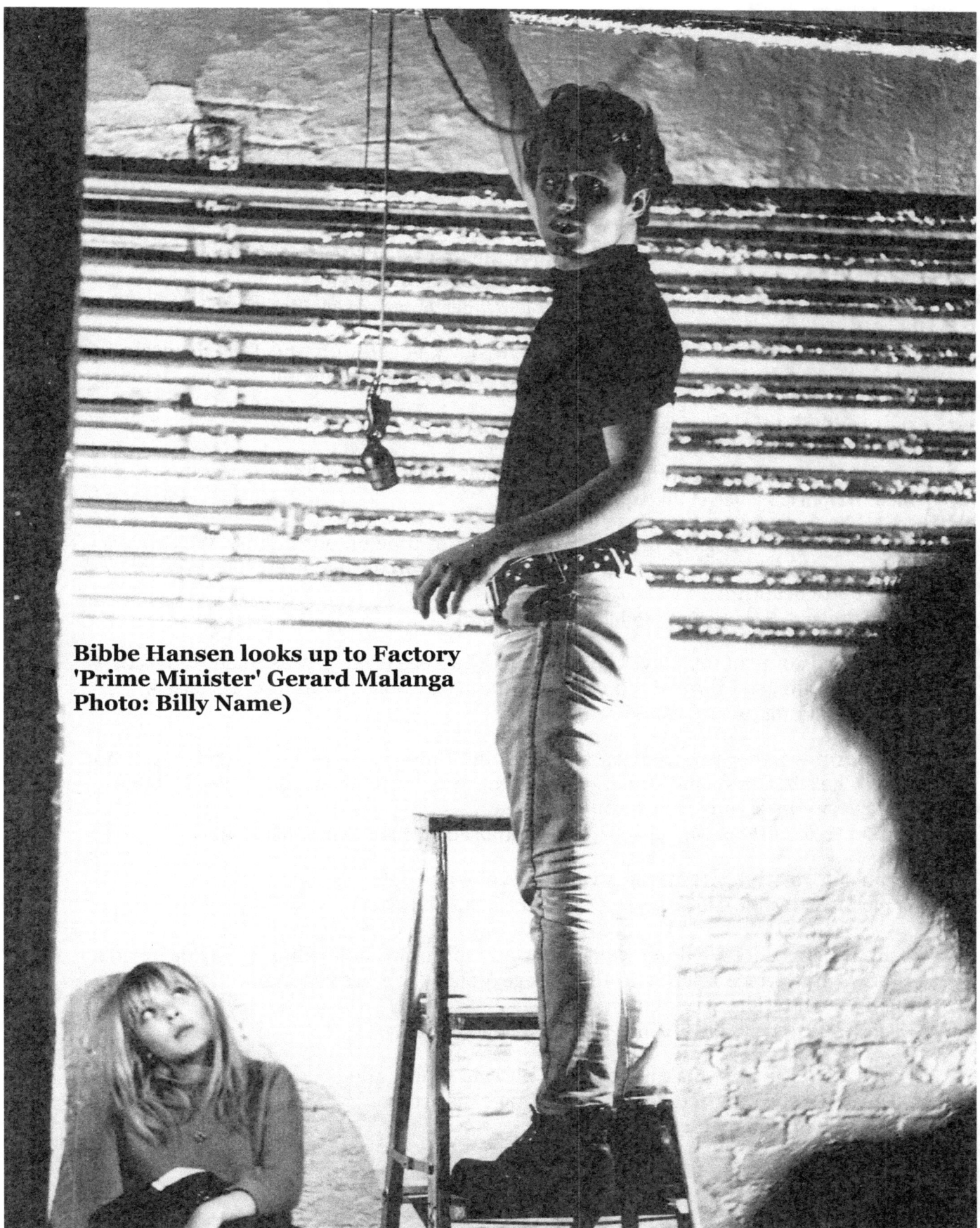

Bibbe Hansen looks up to Factory 'Prime Minister' Gerard Malanga Photo: Billy Name)

This is not nuclear physics; this is three chords: I'm, waiting for my man, twenty-six dollars in my hand.
—**Lou Reed: Rock Legend, Founder of The Velvet Underground**

The Velvet Underground. . . I didn't know at first what 'Waiting for the Man' was about. I kind of thought it was something vaguely homosexual.
—**'Leee' Black Childers: Factory Acolyte, Photographer, Former Music Mgr. (Bowie, Iggy Pop)**

The Velvets would dress in black with their black goggles on and I would dress in black with my black goggles. And we would arrive at these people's houses looking like the death crew!
—**Mary Woronov: Writer, Artist, Cult Actress, Warhol Star**

Andy was in the shadow, standing in the shadow, always behind the camera.
—**Nico: Warhol Icon, Velvet Underground Star**

They didn't show 'Chelsea Girls', so we had a lot of time on our hands. We drove to St. Tropez with Nico driving. I'm thinking, "Okay, you have to keep your eyes on the road. You're beautiful, but I want to *live*!"
—**David Croland: Factory 'Boy', Publisher, LID Magazine**

Andy spliced some of my play 'The Bed' into 'Chelsea Girls'. It was to be Andy's first split-screen film, so I think it did influence the style, those rooms at the Chelsea.
—**Robert Heide: Playwright, Warhol Confidant**

Brigid Berlin's father ran the Hearst Publishing Empire, so, to have a daughter who was in 'Chelsea Girls', and underground film, was quite shocking. You are talking about a very conservative background.
—**Vincent Fremont, Founding Director Andy Warhol Foundation for the Visual Arts**

Oh, you'd do anything, thinking it would never come out.
—**Brigid Berlin: Warhol Muse, Movie Character, and Confidante**

The art critics said, "We don't want to see any more two hour films of Taylor Mead's ass." So Andy wrote a letter to the Village Voice: "We are *rect*ifying this oversight with all the materials at our command."
—**Taylor Mead: Poet, Underground Personality, Warhol Star**

Art was *dead*. We were making movies! We said it over and over, "If Andy offers a painting, take the hundred dollars. Don't take his art."
—**Louis Waldon: Actor, Artist, Warhol Star**

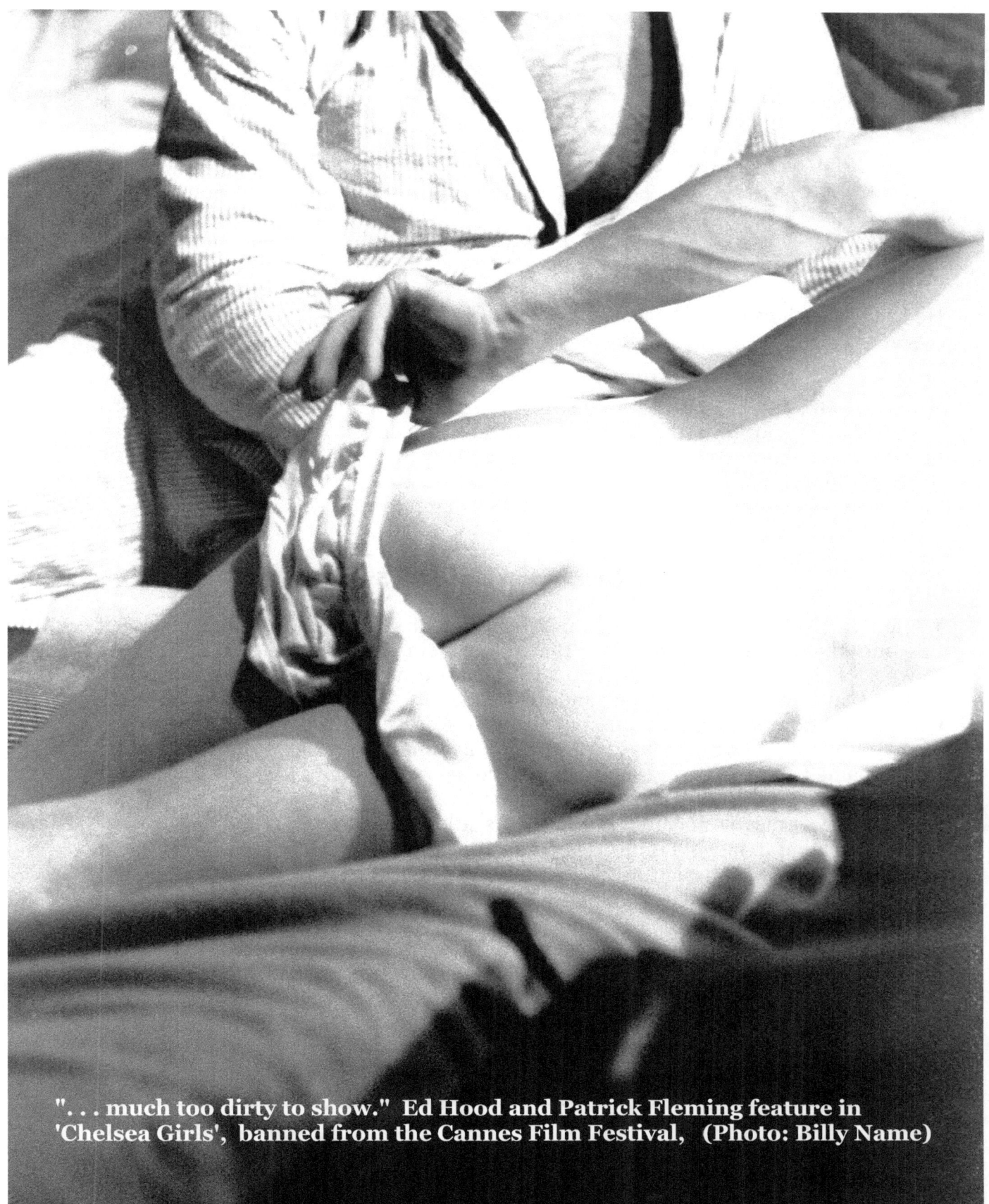

". . . much too dirty to show." Ed Hood and Patrick Fleming feature in 'Chelsea Girls', banned from the Cannes Film Festival, (Photo: Billy Name)

Andy, why are you doing these movies?
—Interviewer, CBS News

Um, it's just easier to do; it's easier to do than painting.
—Andy Warhol

He just wishes it were all *e-e-easier*.
—Brigid Berlin

So did we-e-e. It was, alas, not to be. Not even half-way through editing, and we'd already blown the initial budget and were not even close to making our French broadcast deadline. You know the feeling—should we give up and chalk up our loss, or plough ahead into risky territory? We took a page from Warhol: "You can give up, but it won't get easier." So, dive, dive, dive, and damn the torpedoes. . .

Breaking News, New York 1965-1966

While Warhol "gives up" painting to put his Superstars—and anyone else who shows up—into the movie spotlight, Bob Dylan is causing his own 'electricity' at the Newport Folk Festival by giving up his signature acoustical guitar. The Rolling Stones 'Can't Get No Satisfaction', and the Beatles are here, there, and everywhere—which soon prompts Warhol to promote his own discovery, the dark and edgy 'Velvet Underground'. Unfortunately, Lou Reed and his unmerry band of musicians don't get the same welcome, except in the dank recesses of downtown New York. In L.A., Cher, no slouch in the Goth department, was heard to mutter, "They will replace nothing, except maybe suicide." Luckily, she's still around, and so is Lou, but I doubt they get together to talk old times. No matter; we found archival footage for it all and threw it together to entertain ourselves. History out of context will always make the purists purple with rage, but who cares? So, while the Velvet's John Cale madly fiddles, Vietnam is being bombed into oblivion and soldiers search for their own oblivion in dope and Saigon hookers with antibiotic-resistant clap. The draft, naturally, is protested, while the Civil Rights war gets heated and the marches all wind up mixed together. Black Power gets publicity, and Betty Friedan and some pissed-off women found the National Organization for Women. We will agree with them well after they've done the hard work, but for now the rest of us wear miniskirts and dance madly, because so much is going on. Though the Silver Factory is but a factor in what is rapidly becoming a tumultuous global era, Warhol's world and its self-contained clubhouse of misfits and miscreants prove to be an integral part of . . .

... THE SIXTIES IN NEW YORK CITY

Every moment was the right moment.
—Ondine

Victor Bockris: Allen Ginsberg once said to me, "I know this sounds strange, but I think Andy Warhol created the sixties, single-handedly. He had the vision and actually made it happen." I think in a certain sense he was right. If you take the sixties seriously, trying to really change the basis of life-styles and the way we live and think, the Factory would be the place to go get your instruction manual. There was no other organization, nor group of people that had a stronger hold on the communal idea of it all. Even though Andy is most known as a painter and a filmmaker, he was in those days doing many things... The tentacles of the Factory spread into many different places—the fashion world, the rock and roll world, the world of interviews and the magazines—so by '65 he was overtaking most of the people in those worlds. I suppose the most fascinating thing about it is the sense in which it was kind of a teenage gang. These guys started dressing alike. They had this uniform that consisted largely of black jeans, black T-shirts, black boots, black leather jackets or something akin. They didn't walk around looking like the Ramones, but it does become a costume.

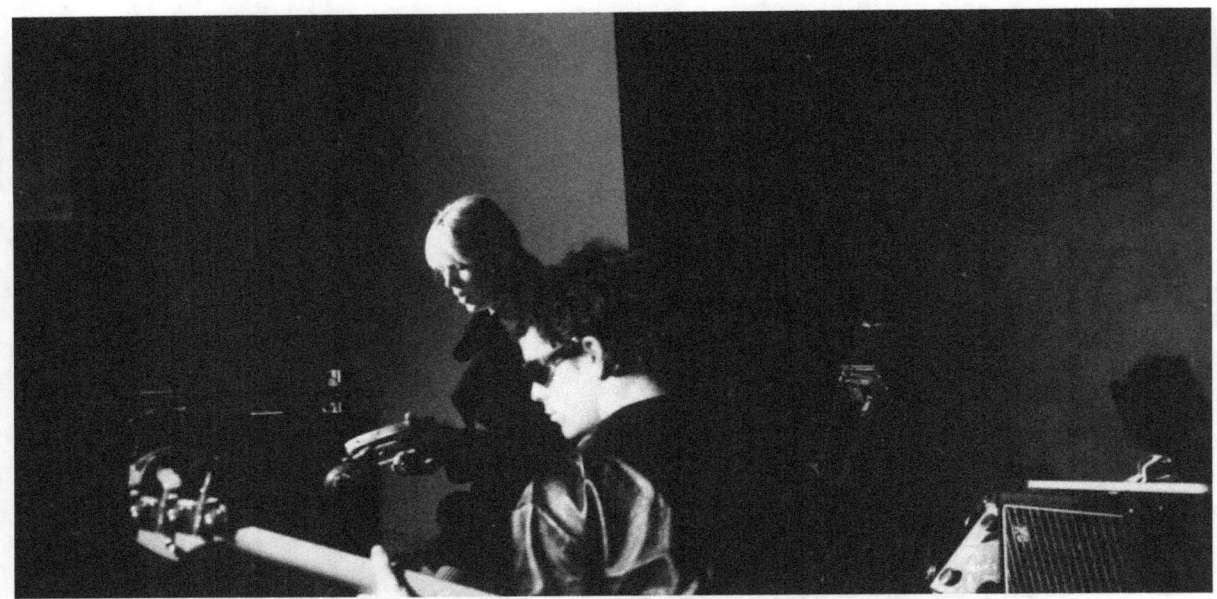

Boy in Black.   Lou Reed and the Velvets with Nico, play in the West Village.

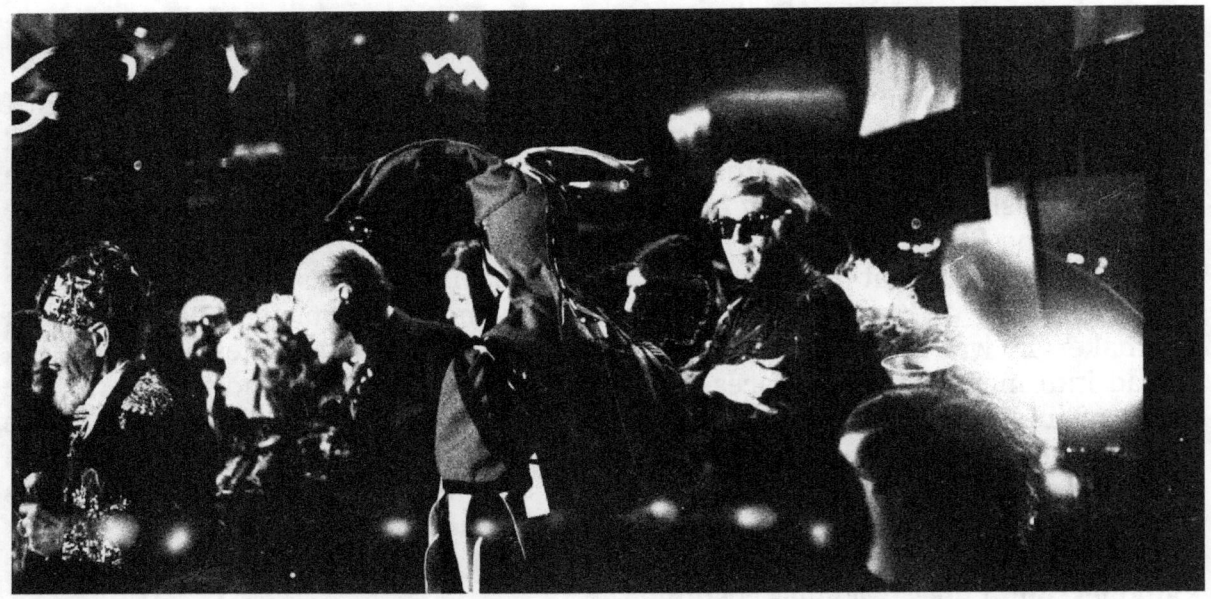

Boys in Black. Andy and Friends at the Cheetah Disco. (Photos: Billy Name)

Nat Finkelstein: We all frequented the same places in the West Village. There was the Café Society downtown, Steve Paul's The Scene. That was basically the hangout. There was La Luna, down in little Italy, where you went at three in the morning to get a decent Italian meal. And of course, the Kettle of Fish. There was a co-mingling there of the Dylan crowd and the Warhol crowd. It was an open bar, owned by the Mafia, and thriving during that period when Carmine De Sapio and that old guard still ruled Greenwich Village before NYU took it over and demoralized the area. Old country Italians, which meant that they were socially very liberal, so Allen Ginsberg and all sorts of people could come and mingle there. The Kettle also was adjacent to the Gaslight, where the Beat Poets got their start. Bleeker and Macdougal were the center of West Village society.

Billy Name: It was no longer this macho thing at the Cedar Bar, where you just got drunk and started fights. This was a new world, a younger generation of artists who succeeded their elders. Pop! It's art! And, it's American-oriented. It's New York-oriented. . . In some European cultural centers, they were hearing about Warhol, but it was still the inner art world, so you would just work with the people you interacted with, because they were fabulous!

Ultra Violet: About Warhol's repetition, you know the silk screen, Number One Electric Chair? There are eight. Again, that has to do with the sixties, where East met West. . . All of this actually came from way beyond, the gurus that came from India, Indian art, sacred art, the Buddha. You don't have one Buddha, you have six hundred and seventy Buddhas. And then Warhol took that and he did six hundred and seventy Coca Cola bottles.

Oh, Ommm, and blessings to Ultra. I would never have thought of comparing a Buddha to a coke bottle—I am but a poor Buddhist, not a rich artist. . . Ultra Violet had been Salvador Dali's mistress and muse for a number of years, and later was the paramour of sculptor John Chamberlain. Though proximity to artists does not necessarily make one the next Warhol, Ultra, née Isabelle Collin Dufresne, who happily bossed Warhol around when commissioning a custom artwork, is today a successful artist in her own right. She was interviewed in her studio in Chelsea, preparing for an exposition.

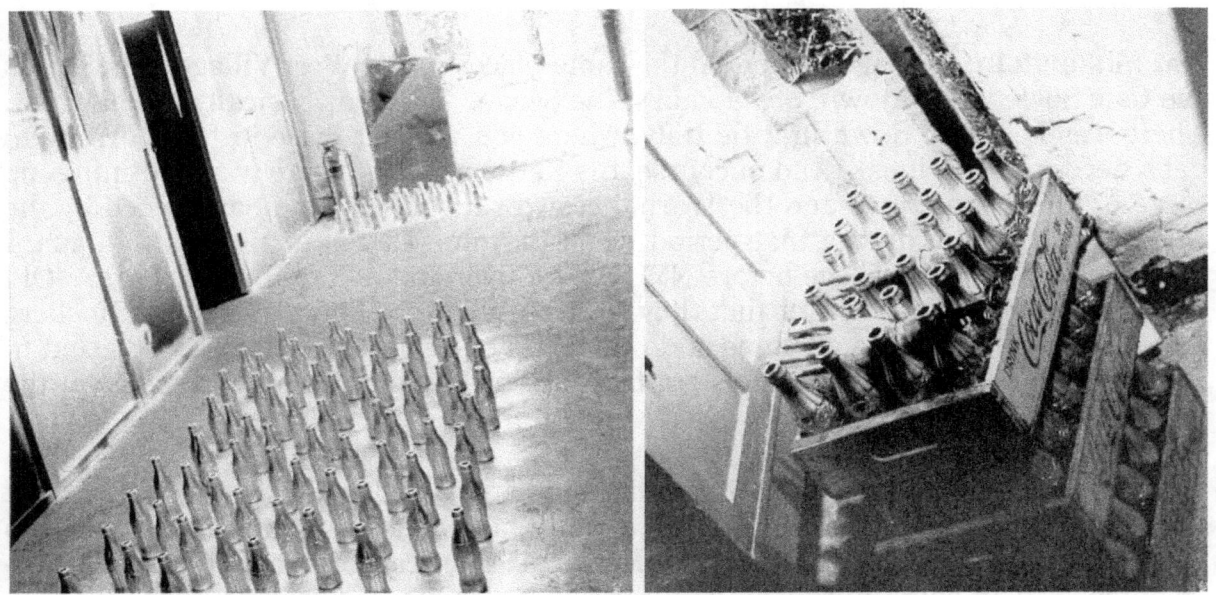

Billy Name's inspired Factory instillation inspires Warhol's Coca Cola craze.

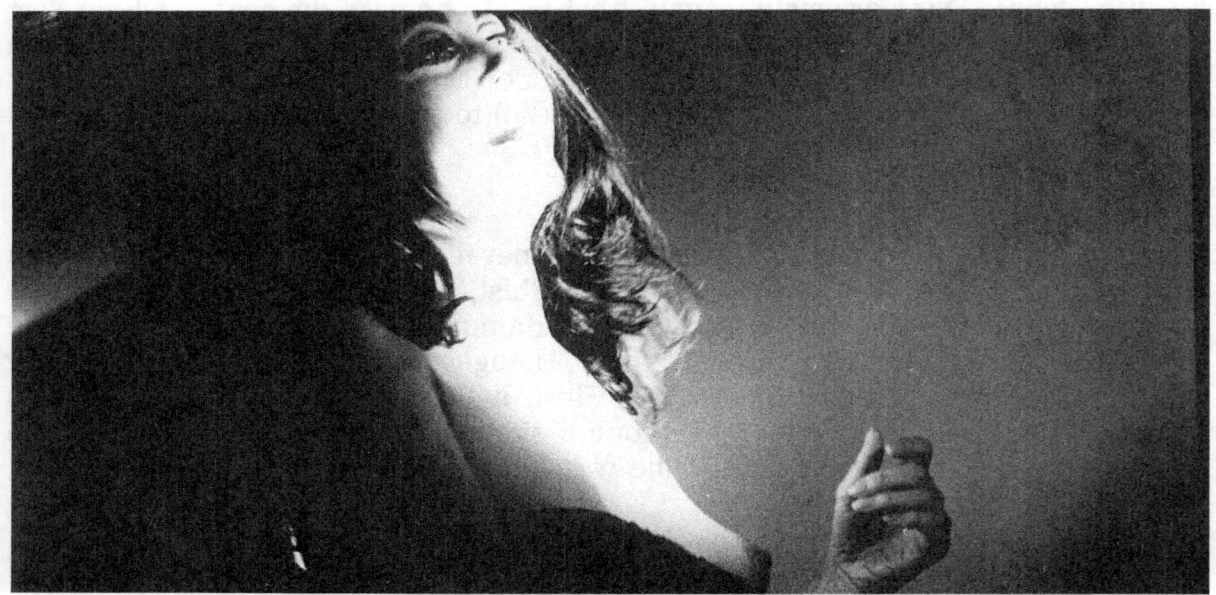

Ultra Violet in a Zen mode, has a wardrobe malfunction. (Photos: Billy Name)

Vincent Fremont: There are certain artists that wouldn't be working today if it wasn't for Andy breaking ground. As Ivan Karp put it, and Henry Geldzahler, Andy looked back to artists that he appreciated and was influenced by when the Pop movement started. He could be put down easily, because he was coming from the commercial side. Well, that doesn't make you *not* an artist! I think Andy personified and became the Pop Pop. He actually lived and breathed it. He was the most visible. He took the most chances. And he took the most heat because he was also doing other things. The films, for example. . .

Jonas Mekas: Almost all of the films, before they were shown at the Cinematheque or any other place, were first screened at the Factory, just for the actors, stars, and Andy himself, on a piece of fabric. Just a big space, a big piece of white fabric and some chairs, people around munching on something. It was very casual, nothing formal. Nothing formal *ever* took place at the Factory.

Gerard Malanga: There was no such thing as 'Superstar'. Andy invented the term. The idea was that our stars were not just Hollywood stars; they would be bigger than Hollywood stars. They were Superstars. So the underlying emphasis would be on the 'Super'. Actually, Andy's repertory of actors, or real people, initially came from Jack Smith's studio. When Andy shot Dracula, basically it was a Jack Smith movie, even though Andy was behind the camera. So, I think Jack was a major influence on Andy's filmmaking at the time, in terms of the people that were being used.

Robert Heide: Two movies I hadn't remembered being in; that tells you something about the Factory in those days *(laugh)*. Both were with Jack Smith. One of them was 'Dracula' slash 'Batman', and the other one was called 'Camp'. . . Ron Tavel was for a while called the "Factory playwright", and there was some kind of falling out, and this idea that I would be the new Factory playwright. That was being bandied about. I *do* remember a party at Grand Central Station, way underground, and one of the great moments with Edie (Sedgwick). She had dyed her hair to match Andy's hair, his wig. Diane Vreeland (Editor of Vogue Magazine) was there. Finally when they arrived, they came out of the train, Andy wearing black shoes, black pants, black leather jacket, black everything. And there was a big hole in his behind. His ass was sticking out! So he was making a fashion statement. . . We had to be cool; there was an idea of not saying too much. Gerard was always cool. Nico was cool. Lou Reed was cool. Andy became cool.

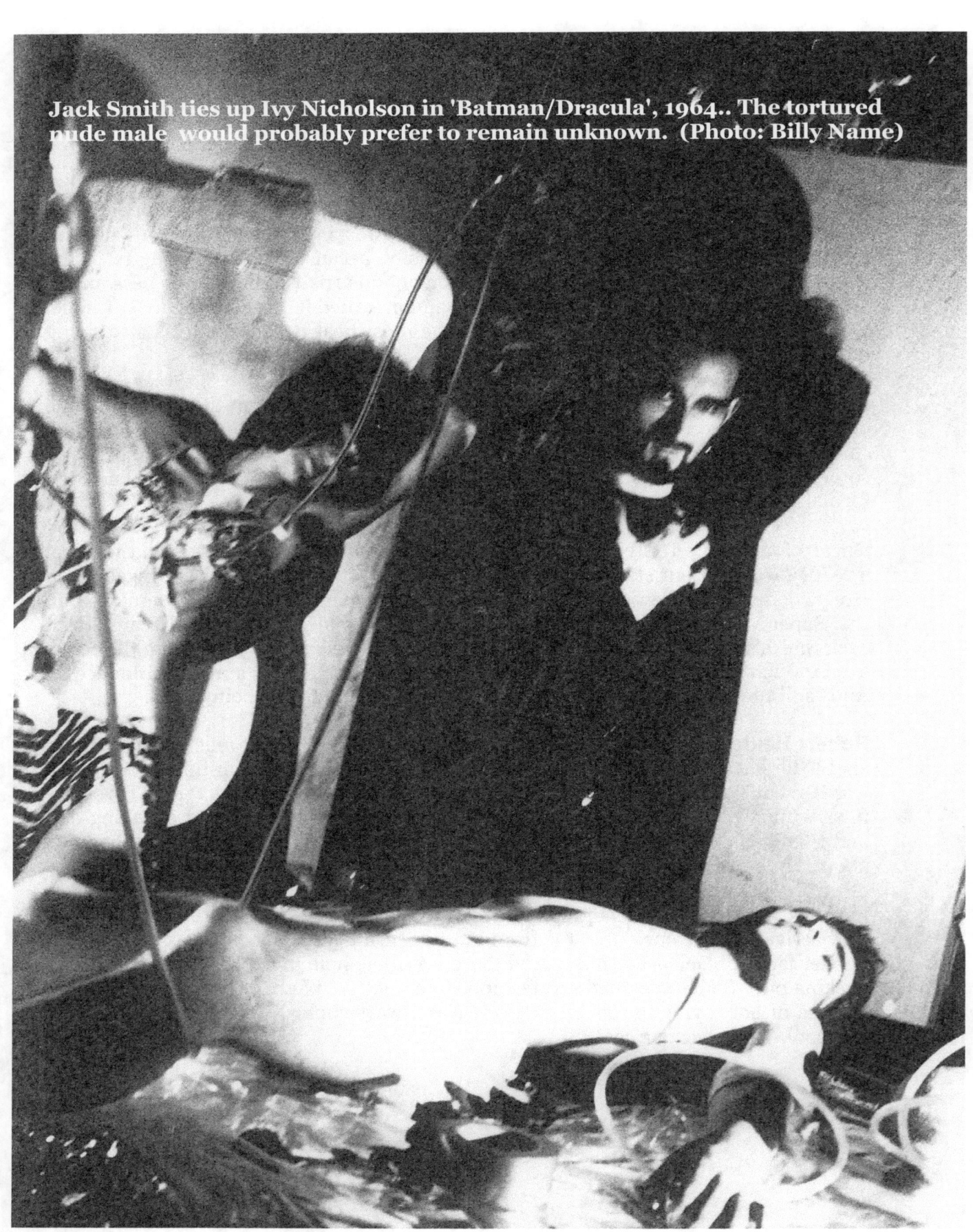

Jack Smith ties up Ivy Nicholson in 'Batman/Dracula', 1964.. The tortured nude male would probably prefer to remain unknown. (Photo: Billy Name)

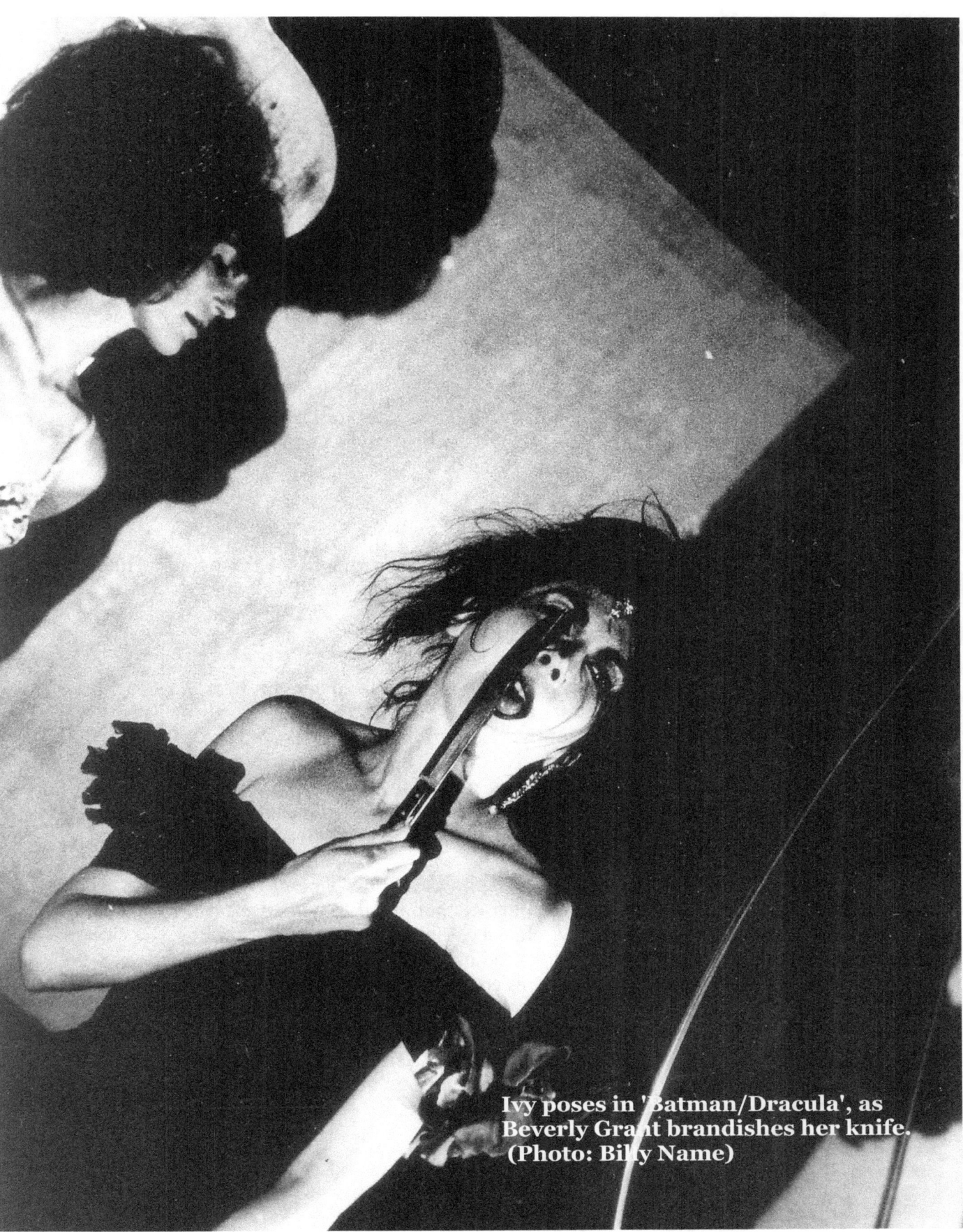

Ivy poses in 'Batman/Dracula', as Beverly Grant brandishes her knife. (Photo: Billy Name)

Though Heide appeared in Warhol films, his focus was the written word. His play 'The Bed', about gay existential angst, got raves from critics looking for something to be depressed about, and played to a packed coffee house in the Village. It wasn't just any coffee house; it also presented early works by the likes of Sam Shepard and John Guare, and was acknowledged as 'The Birthplace of Off Off Broadway'. Warhol was there, later interviewed by Kenneth Goldsmith for his '65 book, 'I'll Be Your Mirror'.

Andy Warhol: My newest film is 'The Bed', from a play by Bob Heide that played at the Caffe Cino, in which we'll use a split screen, one side static, of two people in bed, and the other, moving, of the lives of these two for two years. All my films are artificial, but then, everything is sort of artificial.

Warhol filmed 'The Bed' in artist Richard Bernstein's loft, after which it made its way to Jonas Mekas' Cinematheque on 41st Street, the only theatre in the neighborhood without sticky floors. Warhol's grungy "filmmaking universities" were avoided by the peace and free love brigade. Nobody ever gave it away in Times Square.

Ivy Nicholson: We weren't the only ones who had fun! Flower children were part of the sixties culture. It was such a great period. I miss it. Even though I wasn't really into the drugs thing, I was still part of the decoration and the fun and the wildness. I have no idea what the cops were doing. No one ever saw them. Nowadays we live in a world where people take pot smokers and put them in jail. Who ever died of pot? Why not eliminate cigarettes, the most dangerous drug in the world.

By 1965, the words 'Superstar', and 'Girl of the Year' had become synonymous with Warhol and the Silver Factory. Exotic, erratic superstar Ivy Nicholson made more movies and continued to pursue the elusive object of her affection, while the first Warhol favorite, Baby Jane Holzer abdicated her throne to newcomer Edie Sedgwick, whom Ultra Violet dubbed, "Andy's precocious puppet." As far as Warhol was concerned, "Every day is a new day," and though "the war and the bomb worried" him, he didn't feel there was much he could do about it. Except make his movies. Warhol's and Ron Tavel's film about the Cuban Crisis, 'The Life of Juanita Castro', was considered by the Village Voice to be a "serious statement", but for the most part, the 'breaking news' of the sixties had little influence on. . .

...FACTORY LIFE

I always say, "One's company, two's a crowd, and three's a party."
—Andy Warhol

'Leee' Black Childers: The Factory in those days was a great mixture. Nothing was asked of you, you could do as you pleased. You could come and do nothing, in which case nothing happened to you. You were just there like a bump, and a lot of people did that. Or you could participate and end up in movies. You could take drugs, lots of pills; anybody who says they didn't take pills up there was at some other factory, because they certainly took pills at that one. And you never knew what they were. You could go up, down, and then up again.

Billy Name: One fall day we were all up on the roof of the Factory. Andy was working with Billy Kluver, who had worked on the original Telestar satellite, the first satellite for Bell Labs. An artists-scientists collaboration called EAT, 'Experiments in Art and Technology', was at the Armory, so Andy and Billy Kluver made these silver balloons. The first one we made was long, about forty feet, and we took it up on the roof. Who was there—Billy (Kluver), Andy, me, Gerard, Harold Stevenson, a painter, Binghampton Birdie, Fidel Castro's cousin, Danny Williams, Pontus Hulten, who was the curator of the first Warhol Retrospective, the Flower Catalogue, at the Moderna Museet in Stockholm. He called it, "The first art sent into space."

Andy Warhol: I'm doing some things called 'Clouds', because it's called 'Up Art'.

Robert Heide: They were making silver Mylar pillows which were floating around in the air. I said, trying to be logical, "Well, would anyone buy these?" And someone said, "Well, Andy will sign them!" So many people wanted to be close to Andy, and I wonder if they did because of the price tags. "Andy will sign them!"

Warhol considered his "floating sculptures" to be his grand farewell to art. When that first silver balloon, all forty feet of it, was launched from the roof of the Factory, Warhol worried about helicopters flying into it, or police investigating all the hoopla. Since the police rarely showed up for any of the other drug-fueled shenanigans that went on, it would seem he had little cause for concern.

Taylor Mead: I'm drifting away. . . In America it's called Quaalude, in France it's called Nuvaran, in India it's called Revenol, in England it's called Mandrax—I know it in all the countries. I was on it for years. And I'm still on drugs. Drugs come from the earth, give me a break. And our ancestors, from the grasses they ate, they had drugs, coconuts. . . Anyway, as sophisticated as I am *(laugh)*, Andy loved it. Andy was only on a tiny mild speed, Obetrol, but he was sympathetic to everything. And he loved the odd behavior, of course. Anyone who was out of it, because I think in his childhood he was totally out of it—St. Vitus Dance, Epilepsy or whatever.

Victor Bockris: It was a feeling prevalent among those people, particularly those who had been there for a while. If you were there for a year or so, big deal—you were playing. But if you were involved, as Taylor Mead was, from the beginning, or Gerard, Ondine, Billy, etcetera. . . Ondine put it so well when he said "Andy completed us."

Andy Warhol: Employees make the best dates. You don't have to pick them up, and they're always tax-deductible.

Brigid Berlin: I was never an Andy Warhol groupie, and yet I saw him every single day. I certainly was fine without him; I didn't have to be part of the group every night. And you know, um, it was the only job I ever had.

Gerard Malanga: Brigid was not really part of the Factory in the sixties, of the Factory scene itself. Some days it would be quiet, where nothing was happening. Billy would still be playing opera records, but people have the impression there was an ongoing party. . .

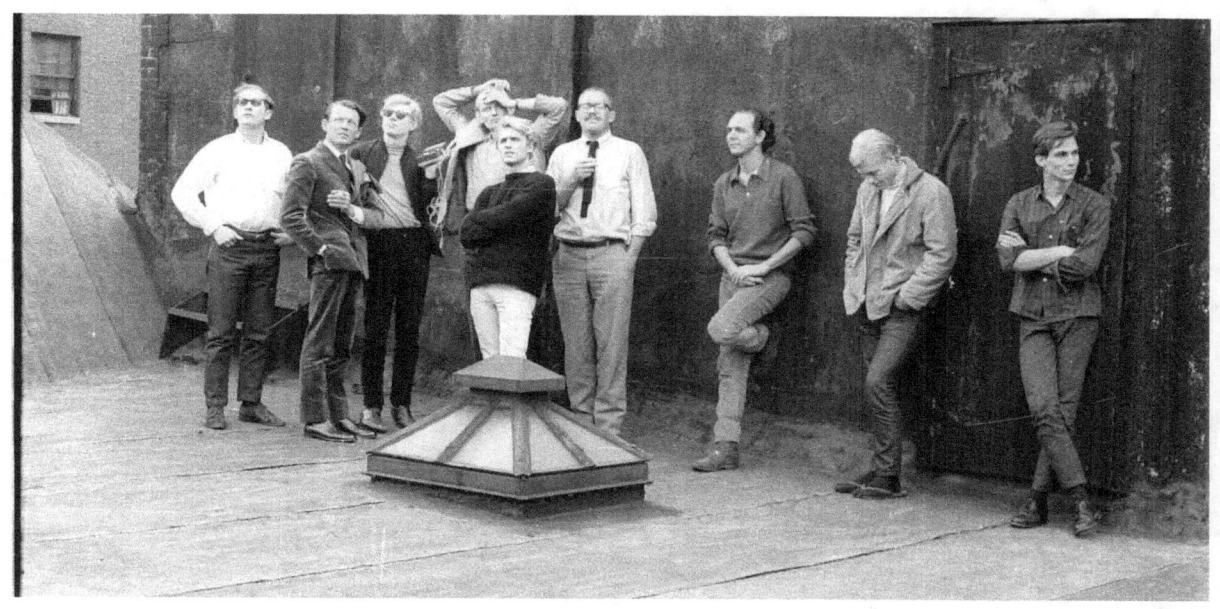

Baloon launching! Danny Williams, Harold Stevenson, Andy, Billy Kluver, Gerard Malanga, the curator at the Musette Moderne, Sweden, Castro's cousin, Paul America and Binghamton Birdie.

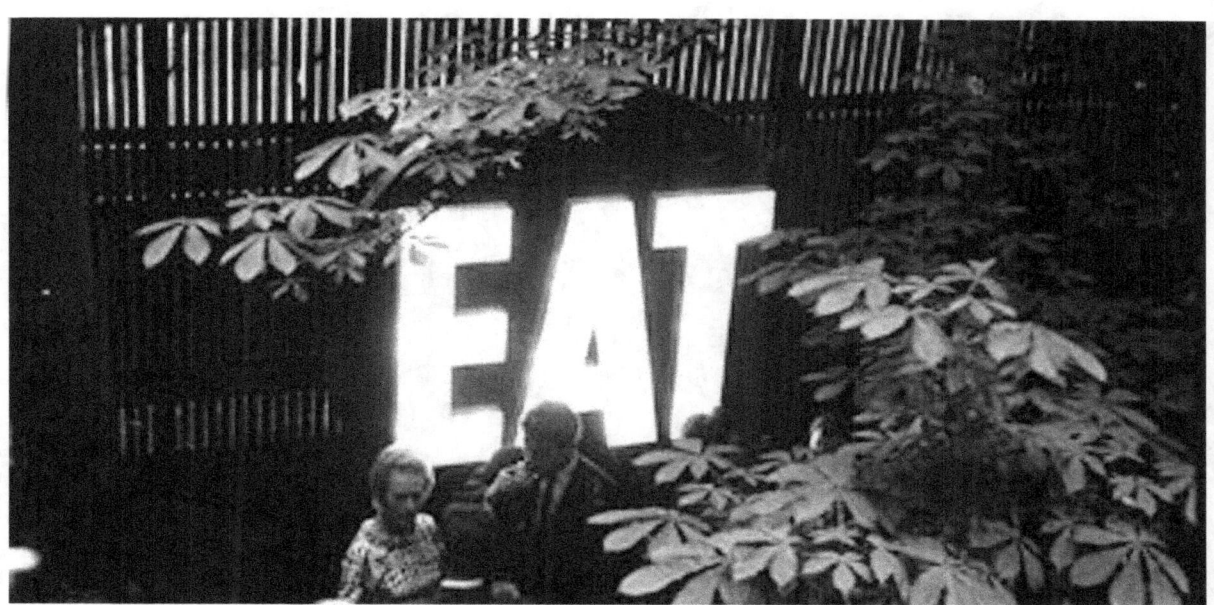

Art , science and partygoers meet at EAT (Experiments in Art and Technology) at the Armory. (Photos: Billy Name)

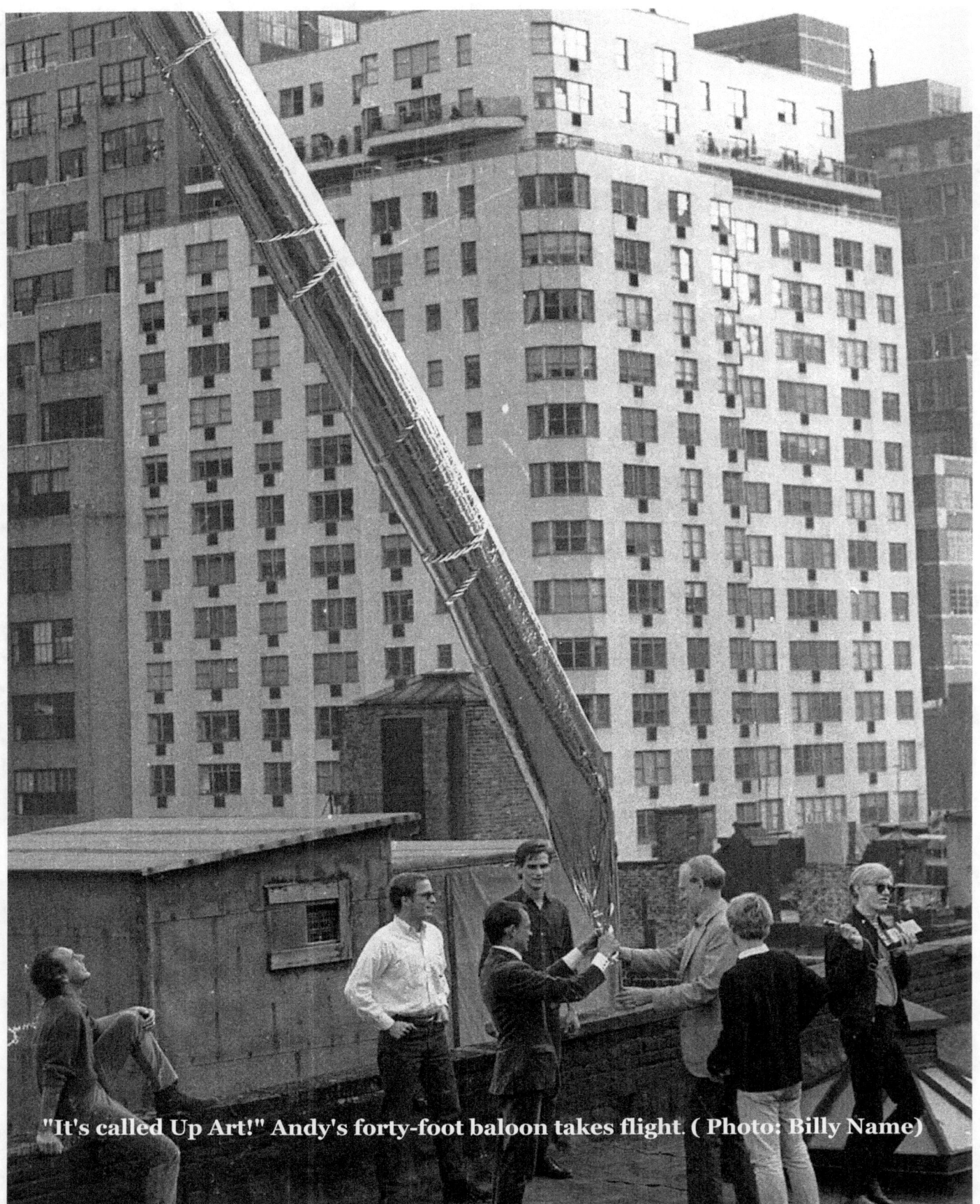

"It's called Up Art!" Andy's forty-foot baloon takes flight. (Photo: Billy Name)

Billy Name: Brigid Berlin came through me because Ondine and I had the same amphetamine connection. His name was Rotten Rita, he was an interior designer who lived on the Upper West Side, and he and Ondine were like the two greatest Maria Callas fans in all the world. . . The people in the New York art slash drug world were not sleaze bags. We just used methamphetamine for fuel, to keep things going.

Many of the character who wandered about the dusty, musty silver-foiled Factory were Billy's underground friends. With nicknames like 'Ondine' (Robert Olivo), 'Rotten Rita' (Kenneth Rapp), 'The Duchess' (Brigid Berlin) and 'The Sugar Plum Fairy' (Joe Campbell), the motely group of talents who made up the 'Mole People' sounded to biographer Victor Bockris as if "they'd woken up in a novel by Genet or Burroughs and crept off its pages." Warhol's much-beloved nickname, 'Drella', culled from a thoughtful combination of Dracula and Cinderella, spoke volumes of his own literary persona. . .

Victor Bockris: To have such an extremely bizarre group of people from such disparate walks of life and such different forms of work, brought together and forged into one group—the Factory was an idea of a way of being, a communal way of living and working, which yes, I would say is essential to the real pulse of that time.

Danny Fields: I looked out on the deserted street. Now, of course, it's a trendy neighbourhood, but it was nothing on a Sunday. . . A taxi suddenly pulled up and Ondine and Rotten Rita and Brigid got out. She was wearing nothing but a flower print sarong wrapped around her, completely topless, with a plastic stethoscope and a fake alligator doctor bag. Brigid opened up her little fake doctor kit, and in there were some real doctor's substances. It was about having the doctor show up, the best doctor in your life. I recognized those bottles; you don't just get them anywhere. She made a concoction, and I almost lost my crotch. It was sixty a poke. Ondine was encouraging people to let Brigid poke them, so she went up to them, and with one hand pulled down their pants, with the other hand shot them in the ass. What did she call it—Desoxyn. The prime ingredient of Desoxyn was an extremely powerful amphetamine that she would let soak until the liquid would turn the color of technicolor urine, this fabulous color, and then she would mix it with Nembutal and Black Beauties. It was not actually scientific, but she really got her mixtures down pretty good.

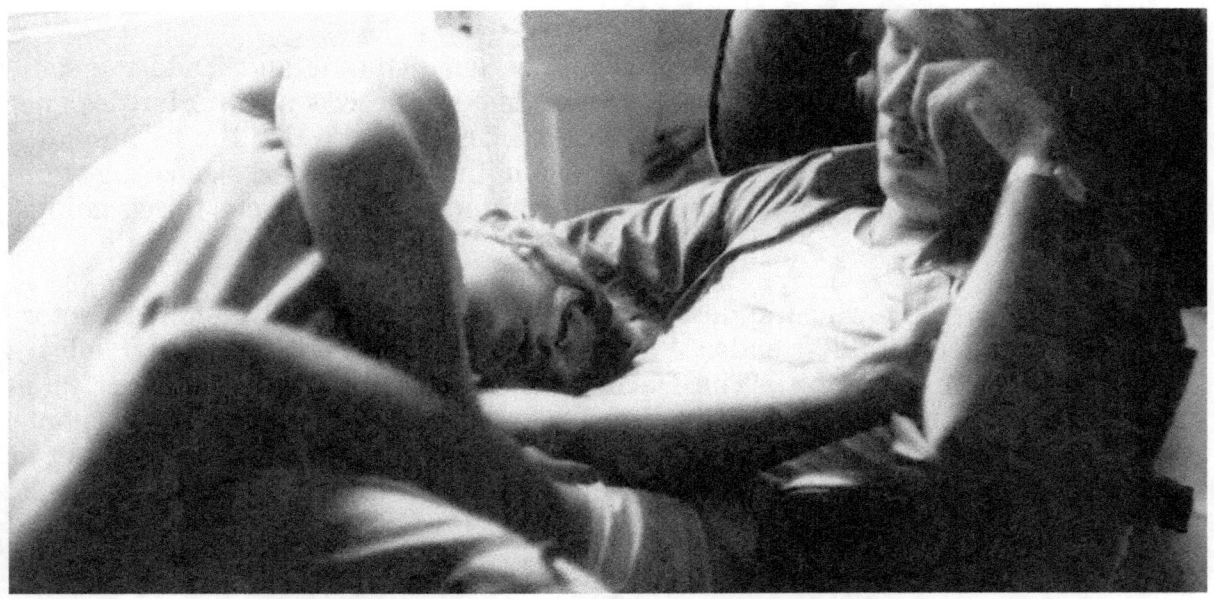

Brigid Berlin takes a nap on Rotten Rita in Henry Geldzahler's Eames chair. (Photo: Billy Name)

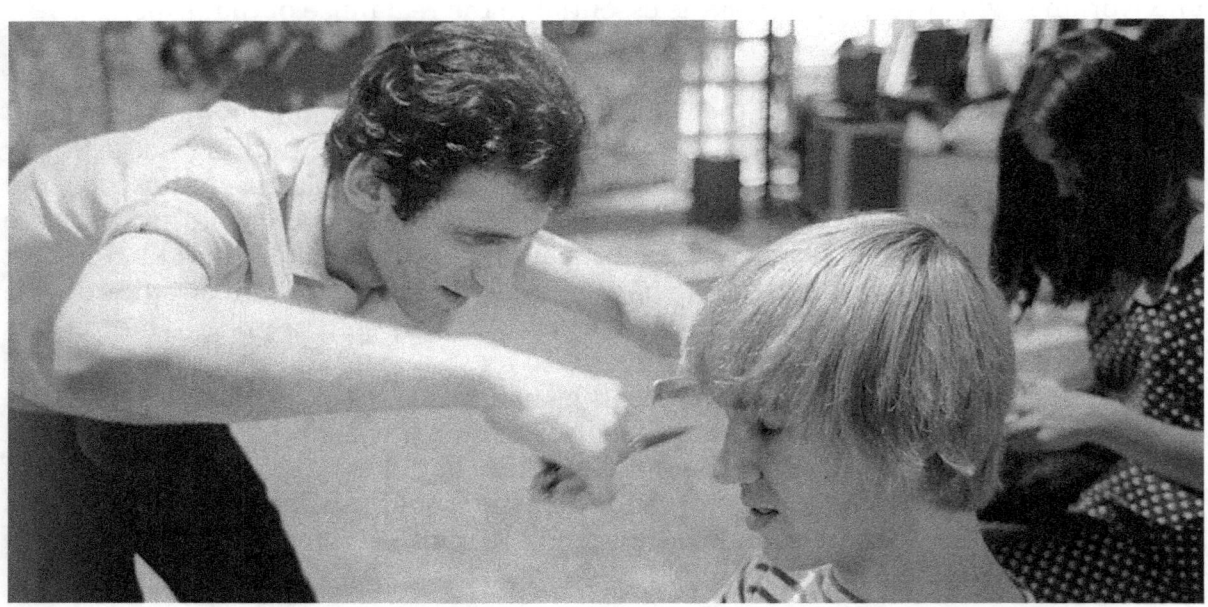

Billy Name snips Chuck Wein's hair. His talent with the scissors inspired Warhol's early silent films 'Haircut No.1', No.2 and No.3 (Photo: Stephen Shore)

Brigid Berlin was also known as Brigid Polk, for her talent with a hypodermic needle. Though she injected herself three or four times a day with a guaranteed appetite suppressant, she also loved to eat, and was often grossly overweight. A former debutante whose father headed the Hearst publishing empire, Brigid spent much of her time with Warhol on the phone, gossiping about everyone from the Factory denizens to those famous in society. She adored Warhol, and became one of his closest friends. Brigid appeared in 'A Walk Into The Sea, Danny Williams and the Warhol Factory', recounting the suicide of Warhol's lover. Danny's niece, director Esther Robinson, licensed us a bit of Brigid's interview which did not appear in her film. . . An entertaining documentary was made about Brigid, entitled 'Pie in the Sky', produced and directed by her friend Vincent Fremont and his wife Shelly.

Vincent Fremont: We are not going to have an interview with Brigid, unless you have ten thousand dollars *(laugh)*. Brigid was very intimidating when I first came to New York.. She was a major presence, both physically and with her mouth. She was very bright, very creative. She did a lot of what you'd call 'trip books', all done on amphetamines, and she talked about it in the documentary I did with her, that my wife and I did. . . There was a lot of amphetamine running around, though Andy never really overdid. There was amphetamine, but the craziness also energized everybody. People threw out ideas all the time. A lot of crazy people were at the Factory, who were considered crazy but they were also very creative.

Ivy Nicholson: Everyone was high. The cops were probably high because nobody ever got arrested—I mean, it was extremely rare. I remember I did take a trip because my ex-husband told me he wouldn't give me a divorce unless I took a really heavy duty one, where I could see my blood running through my veins. He wasn't even there! Well, he was there, but where? I didn't see him. At one point I lay on the ground, which looked like a mosaic. I spread my hands out, and I am saying, "Now I know the meaning, the connection of man and the world!" Can you imagine?

Yup, Ivy, we sure can. . . In the sixties, filmmaker Hillary Harris made an award-winning short called 'Organism', depicting 24 hours in the frenetic life of New York City. Using time-lapse photography, Harris brilliantly compared the living city to the inner workings of the body, the snaking traffic becoming blood corpuscles flowing through veins, buildings rising and being demolished within seconds, you get the idea. The busy inner workings of Ivy's mind reminded us of that movie. . .

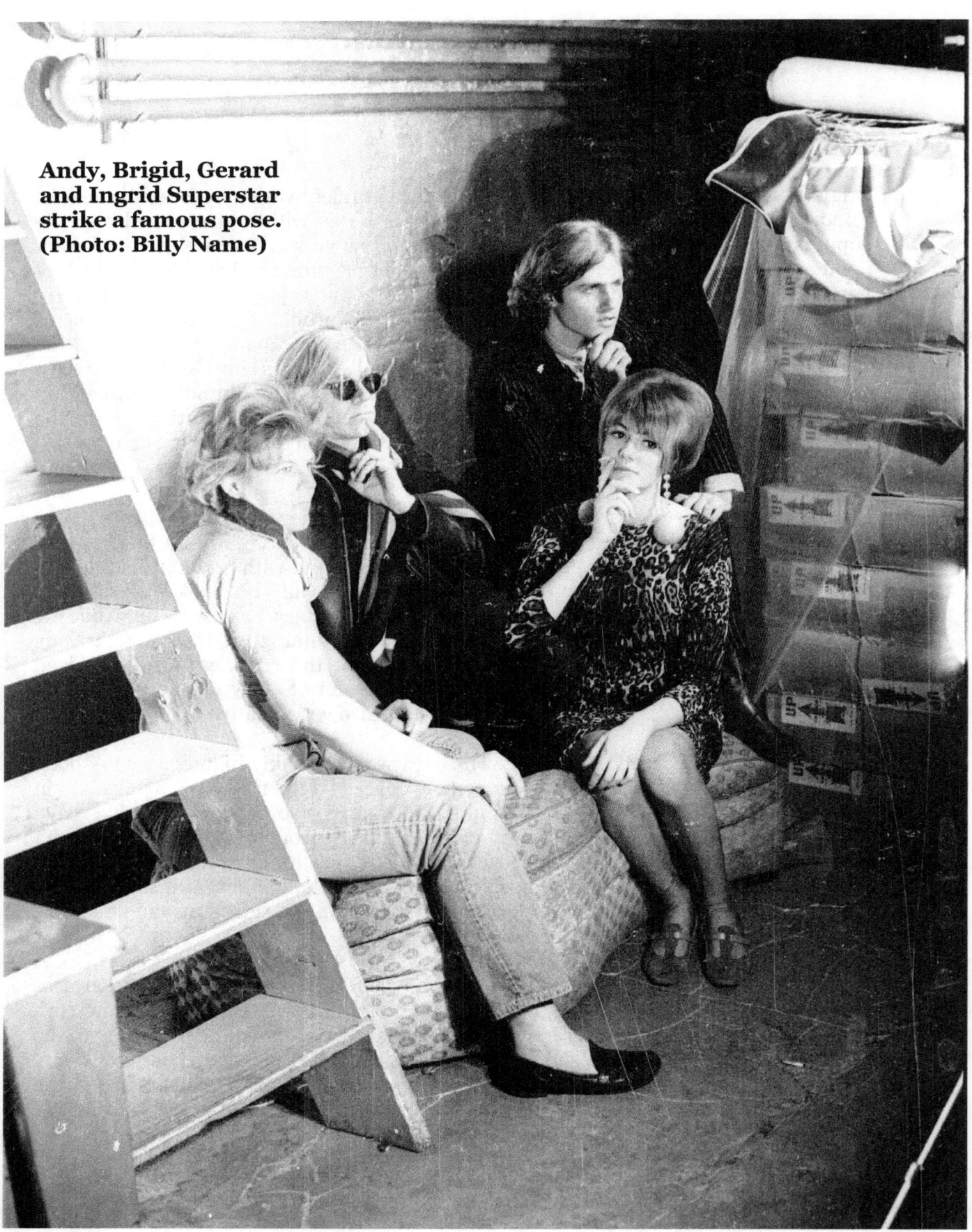

Andy, Brigid, Gerard and Ingrid Superstar strike a famous pose. (Photo: Billy Name)

. . . Hilary Harris' time-lapse footage in 'Organism' was so original for that era that we added a bit of it here, there, and throughout our series, hoping to contribute to the often manic energy in Warhol's Silver Factory, where supplicants arrived, made a big splash, and then disappeared with dizzying suddenness. . . Considerably quieter, David Croland was a fresh young newcomer to the Family, so he was still a bit dewy-eyed and in awe of the jaded veterans. Or maybe not.

David Croland: There was always a party at the Factory. It wasn't like, here comes a party—it *was!* I went there after school just to meet Susan (Bottomly). I was a schoolboy then. But people who would hit on us didn't have a chance. She was like, "Get your hands off my boyfriend!" and I was like, "Get your eyes off my girlfriend, let alone your hands." So I went after school and there were always six to twelve people there. That's a party in itself, and that's just the regulars.

Mary Woronov: A party is where you have Hors d'Oeuvres, and a hostess saying "How do you do," dancing. I never saw a party there. It was this weird holding tank where people came in, and other people were deciding to eat them alive or not. It was always a battle about who could come in and who couldn't. The only vague kind of parties were when Andy would show his movies. Geldzahler and others would be there, kind of uptight, not really having a good time, and Warhol wouldn't give a shit. He would just show the movies anyway, because he loved them so much.

Mary Woronov and Dave Croland had differing opinions of just about everyone at the Factory, including Warhol. But she held paticular antipathy for Dave's girlfriend, the delicate, porcelain-skinned Susan Bottomly. A sixteen-year-old Boston debutante when she entered the Warhol stable of stars, Susan had been dubbed 'International Velvet' because she reminded Warhol of a teenaged Elizabeth Taylor in her film about a racehorse, 'National Velvet'. Warhol's own 'Horse' film (1965), delved into later, had more to do with young male hustlers than Elizabeth's equine glory.

David Croland: My favorite was, of course, Susan. But Nico and I had a very good friendship, because she was very cool and she understood life. She was quiet and sophisticated, and cool. Paul Morrissey, who I loved and I still do, because he liked to laugh. I liked Ingrid Superstar, because she was such a victim, but so sweet, and very nice. But a victim of her own insecurity, being around the other girls who were so beautiful. Ingrid wasn't bad-looking, but she wasn't Susan or Nico or Edie.

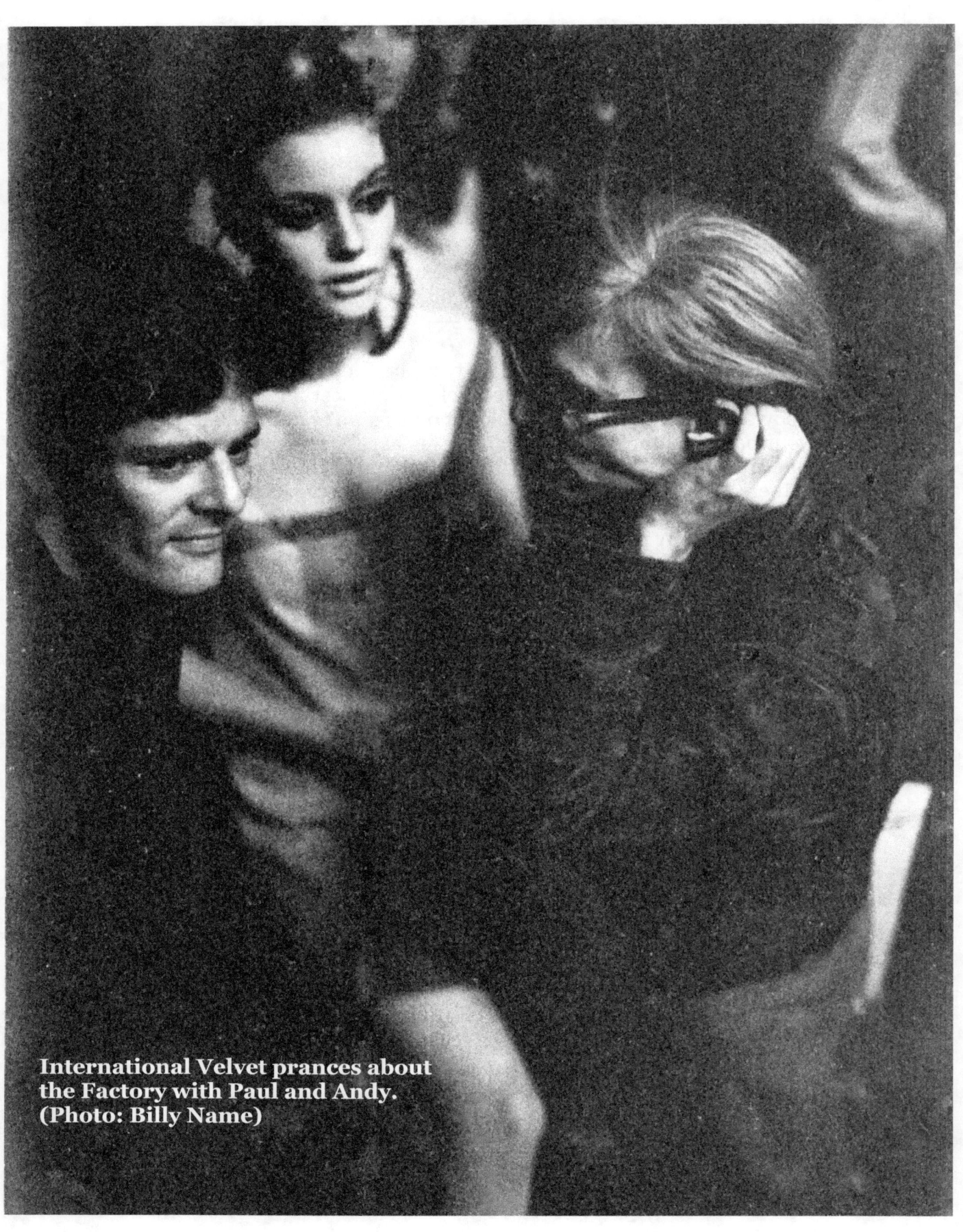

**International Velvet prances about
the Factory with Paul and Andy.
(Photo: Billy Name)**

Mary Woronov: Something like Ingrid, she was invented as a dark mirror to Edie. She looks like Edie. But Edie's rich, she's poor. Edie's classy, she's trashy. So Ingrid was always encouraged to *bark* up and say stupid things and disrupt things, and I didn't want her around. For the first part of my famous scene in 'Chelsea Girls' we tried to tie her up, put her under a desk. I thought that was a good idea *(laugh)*. I didn't mind saying "Hi" to her. No, I didn't even like saying "Hi" to her.

Ingrid Superstar, whose real name was Ingrid Von Schefflin, was the 'ugly duckling' of the Factory who never became a swan. Big-boned and gawky, with a harsh braying voice, she had little talent, but a good heart. Picked up in a 42nd Street bar by the Warhol people to "teach Edie a lesson" over her diva antics, Ingrid tried desperately to fit in. She would perform certain feats refused by the other girls, giving excellent blow jobs on camera, usually naked. Ingrid worked diligently in Warhol films until 1968, and disappeared from the world at the age of forty-two. She had been battling heroin. . . As for young Warhol star Bibbe Hansen, her street-smart past, born of necessity, may have saved her from the same fate.

Bibbe Hansen: The drugs at the factory were free, what I remember, speed and pot. They were both my drugs and the drugs of my mother, the drugs of my group. So I was comfortable with them. That was not anything unusual for me. I was like, "Hey, got any pills? Got a joint?" I just wanted to get high.

Ultra Violet: I don't know if it was my background, but I always knew that drugs were dangerous and I did not want any part of it. Andy and the whole group; they were willing to give you drugs, they thought it was okay. . . I did go to this doctor, not the Doctor Feelgood, but another criminal, who would give me supposedly Vitamin B12 or B15 shots, and I learned much later that it had amphetamine in it, which is so criminal. He went to jail. Those people should be on the electric chair!

Ultra and I shared a doctor on the Upper East Side. We'd visit for a little 'pick-me-up'. He was older, wiser, avuncular. I doubt the good doctor realized these 'vitamin shots' might be addictive, since he himself was taking them. His hands were a bit shaky, the needle a bit old, but once that initial rush hit, you could stay up for days. In the sixties, in New York, you didn't want to miss a thing. Speed did not carry the onerous 'meth-head' moniker it does today—everyone used it, rock stars, artists, and Warhol, who felt it brought him closest to his ultimate goal: "To be a machine."

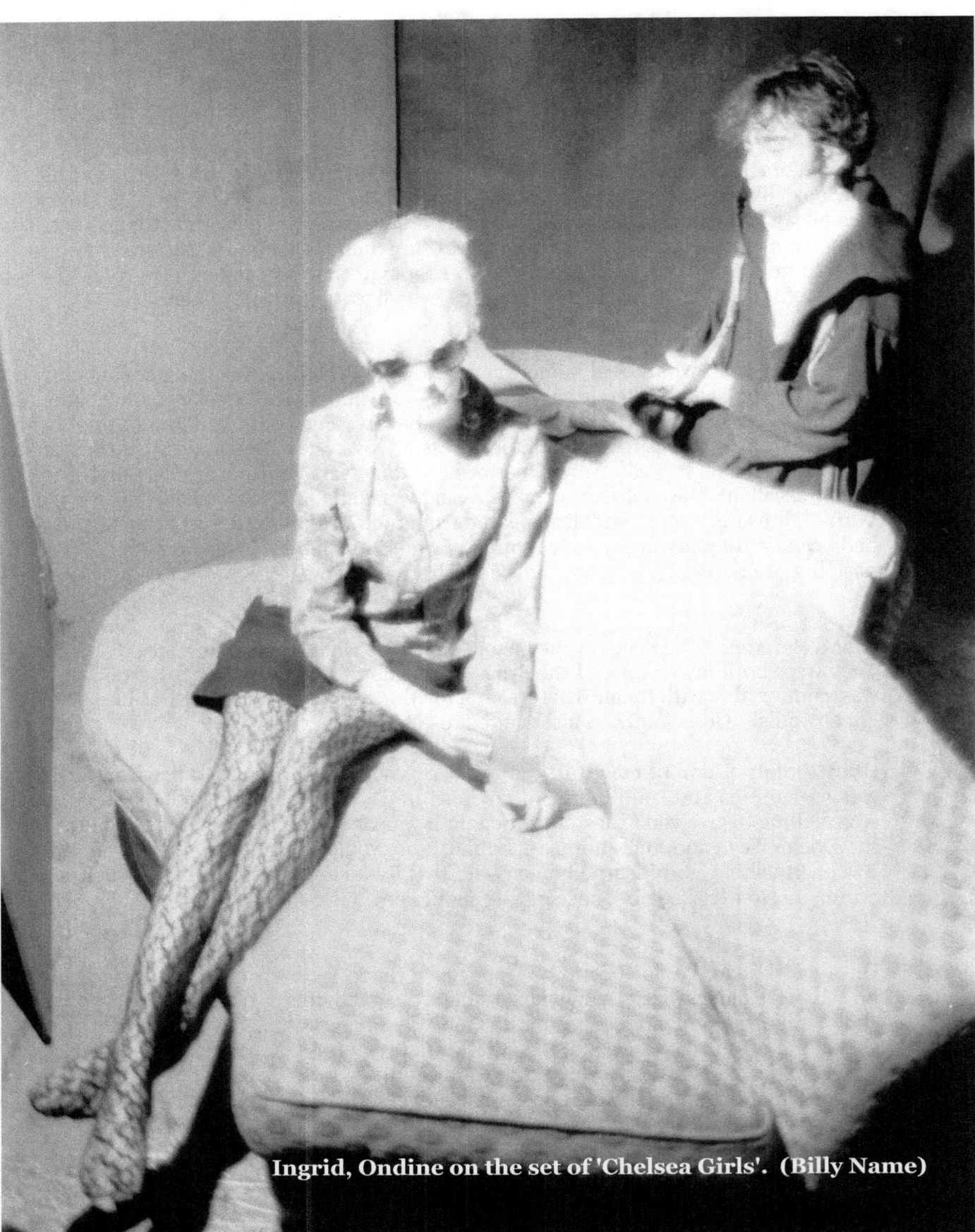

Ingrid, Ondine on the set of 'Chelsea Girls'. (Billy Name)

Andy Warhol: I would go home and sleep for an hour, then somebody would wake me up and I would go back to work.

Nat Finkelstein: One day I'm in my home and I get a call from Andy. "You have to meet me at the Café Society, something important is going to happen!" Now, today was August 8, 1965, the first of the big demonstrations against the Vietnam War, when Martin Luther King's people were forced to ally with us left-wing people. . . That night I was kinda stoned on acid, but I pulled myself together, and made it downtown. I ran into an editor of mine who said, "Hey Nat, great spread in the New York Times Magazine." So I stopped at the newsstand and sure enough, there were six pages showing the first violent demonstration in D.C. I run into the Café Society, and there's Andy sitting with his coterie, and a couple of black people, which was rare for Andy. I open up the Times and say "Look Andy, isn't this great?" Andy could care less. He looks up and says, "Nat, I want you to meet the Chambers Brothers."

Nat Finkelstein often spoke of Warhol's lack of interest in politics, the Vietnam War, civil rights, or, for that matter, gay rights. But he also may have been disgruntled that Warhol didn't seem impressed with his grand spread in the Times. Warhol was probably much more interested in recruiting the Chambers Brothers, who'd been playing their rock and roll hits ('The Time Has Come Today') in the Cheetah Club, a favorite Factory haunt. Warhol was looking for his next foray, into music, and the recent notoriety of the Chambers Brothers at the Newport Folk Festival, along with the newly 'electrified' Dylan, probably had more to do with Warhol's interest than the fact they were black. Louis Waldon, however, had a different take on Warhol's aversion to politics. . .

Louis Waldon: Andy lived on the edge. Andy's people, most of them are insane and he's living right there among them. And Andy didn't like politics. No. He wouldn't let politics be spoken. *(mimicking Warhol)* "Oh, don't do that." Basically he knew nothing about politics, wasn't into it at all. The reason? Politics *dates* the project. He was trying to make his movies everlasting. He wanted them to belong to no period. They did talk a little bit about the Vietnam War, but they wouldn't push it at all or bring it up. And Andy didn't say it, but everybody in the Factory hated hippies. They just hated them! Poor Allen Midgette got the brunt of that because he was a hippie, a stone hippie. He was into that free love and the whole hippie thing. . . "That's boring," they kept saying, especially Andy. "That's boring." Hippie? Not even exciting.

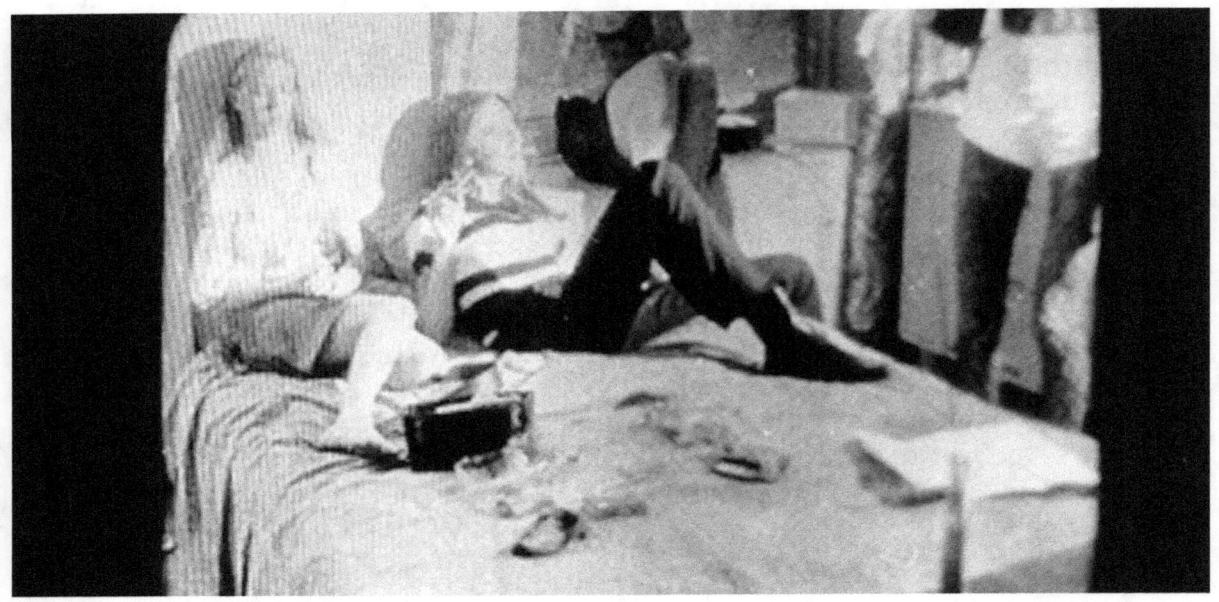

Pepper Davis lies next to Mary Woronov, as 'Hanoi Hannah', prepares to demolish her costars in 'Chelsea Girls'. (Photo: Billy Name, taken from monitor)

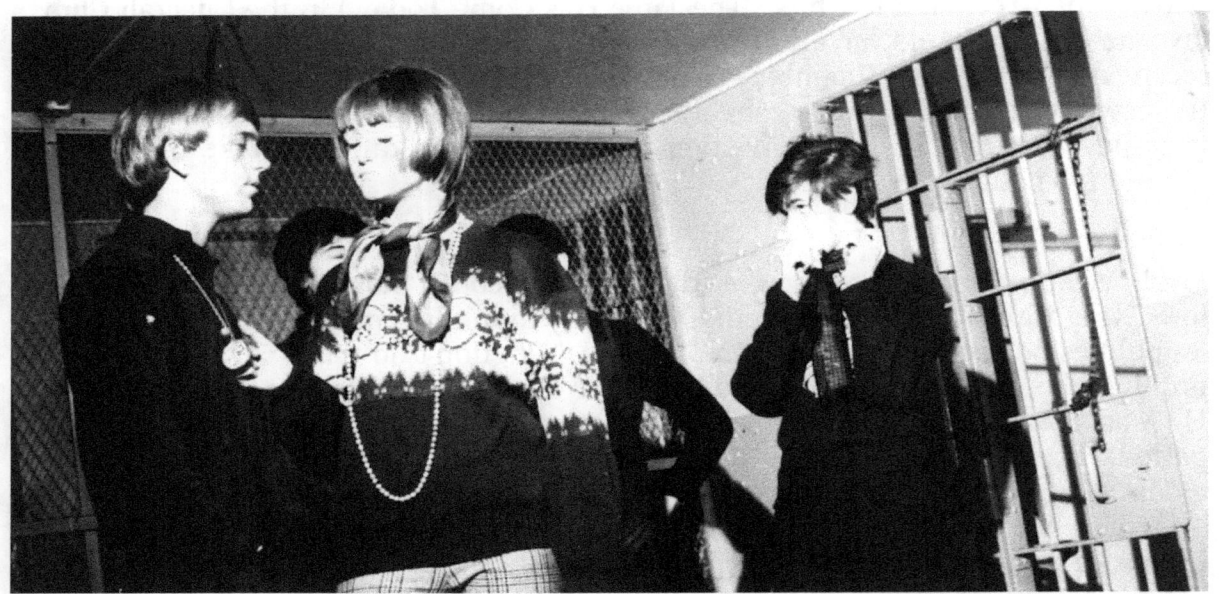

Allen Midgette and Ingrid Superstar, 'Jailed' for not fitting in. (Photo: Billy Name)

As one of those hippies who was into LSD but also into speed, I managed to fall, often and rather sloppily, between the two camps—which made it a joy all these years later to interview Allen Midgette where he once used to live, at the Chelsea Hotel. He now resides in Woodstock, making leather goods and gardening. Throughout the interview, Allen nonchalantly rolled his homegrown from the bottomless stash in his lovely leather purse, by which time everyone, including the camera crew, were thoroughly stoned. Luckily, there was room service for snacks.

Allen Midgette: I would just sit down and wait quietly, and if somebody talked to me, I would be happy to speak to them. But I wasn't going to go over and say "Hi kids, what's going on?" It wasn't that kind of scene. Brigid comes over and calls me a flower child, which I knew didn't mean anything; it could just be my look. I didn't mind. It's better than being a speed freak or— It's not that I want to put any of it down, but there was definitely a division. I'm sorry, there's no way to really talk about it, because, oh yeah, they're one big happy family.

Mary Woronov: But Billy Name was responsible for that. First, they all met in some café somewhere—this is way before me. Then Billy brought them into the Factory, and it became the place where they met. Brigid was there because she gossiped with Andy; they could talk forever about a fucking hangnail. And Andy was a tremendous star fucker. I mean Brigid would talk forever about it. Ondine, the only star he ever cared about was Maria Callas, and that was it. To him the rest of it was bunk.

Vincent Fremont: Brigid exchanged ideas with Andy. They were like a married couple. Brigid was the only one who could yell at him. They would really torture each other in a very loving manner. She always said that she didn't like his work. She'd never take a print or a painting as a present. She'd rather have a vacuum cleaner, a part in a film. Anything but the artwork.

Taylor Mead: There was constant work going on . . . Gerard helping make the silk screens and Andy filming, or walking away from filming. I guess I did a great many movies, ten at least, but with Andy it was all so easy. You just wandered in and sat down. The filming would start, and Andy would sometimes just walk away from the camera. He was so low key. He operated on all kinds of levels. And all the famous people coming through. I had no idea who I met, I guess Jim Morrison, the Beatles, Rolling Stones, famous people coming in, and then realizing if they weren't contributing to the scene, they should leave.

Gerard Malanga: Andy always felt, one of his philosophies was that he always felt to make decisions was hard, and he always liked to take the easy way out. I think Andy would say to himself, "Gee, it seems right. I'll just go along with it."

Andy Warhol: Gee. . . (*long pause*) I don't know.

Gerard Malanga: So in the end, other people started making decisions for him. Barbara Rubin was involved in that to a certain extent. She was a dear friend who was also a filmmaker who was hanging about in the Factory. Barbara was basically a strong intellectual force on Andy, in terms of her spontaneity, and she was a real catalyst, who brought some interesting people to the Factory, like Bob Dylan.

Jonas Mekas: And of course, it was Barbara who changed Bob Dylan after the motorcycle crash, converted him, for good or bad, into Judaism.

Bob Dylan: Do we change planes anyplace?

We used footage of Dylan at an airport heading to Heathrow in London with Bobby Neuwirth, legenday folk singer/activist Joan Baez (his love life was complicated) and an impressive contingent of keepers for a 1965 concert. Judging by his interviews there, he could be as clever as Warhol at putting on the clamoring press.

Victor Bockris: The relationships between the different entourages that dominated the sixties, like Leary's entourage, Ginsberg's entourage, Warhol's entourage, or Dylan's—a lot of them had to do with drugs, and people's attitudes toward drugs. For example, some people would think that people who shot amphetamine were inhuman reptiles who should not be allowed in the house. Others would think that anybody who *didn't* shoot amphetamine was a fool, and shouldn't be encountered. And then there were people who felt that heroin was a terrible thing, and so on and so on. And they formed groups.

These groups, when brought together, were like oil and water, even when they shared a peace pipe of marijuana, as witnessed by Billy Name, Gerard Malanga, Nat Finkelstein, and Robert Heide, who happened to be at the Factory when Dylan came calling, and wound up in a Warhol screen test. All had conflicting memories, but luckily, photographs were taken. . .

DYLAN VISITS THE FACTORY

Warhol is a cultural figure, but not an artist.
—Bob Dylan

Gerard Malanga: Barbara brought Bob Dylan over to the Factory with his sort of sidekick roadie Bobby Neuwirth. Andy was thinking of the idea of getting Bob to be in a movie. Bob was a really hot item at that point already. And so Andy's way of wooing Bob was giving him a Double Elvis Presley painting (a 'Flaming Star' silk-screen portrait). Bob was a bit of a punk in those days, nice, but real cocky.

Nat Finkelstein: Each one of them was looking for pretty camp followers. Each one had their own image—Dylan's image was hairy, masculine, super-super macho, Andy's image was exactly in the other direction. Barbara was the catalyst for those things. She had this elitist idea that if you brought geniuses together, the world would be a better place. So, she made this arrangement. On Warhol's side this was a promotion. On the Dylan side they were doing a follow-up on the 'Don't Look Back 'movie. Each one wanted to use the other one, but when they got together they did not like each other at *all*.

We licensed footage from the great D.A. Pennebaker's 'Don't Look Back', of Dylan doing his promo 'card trick', while Allen Ginsberg saunters across the screen. Sublime. Ginsberg could certainly be considered part of Dylan's circle, though Nat Finkelstein was convinced that Dylan loathed gays. Nat was present in his official capacity as photojournalist to record Dylan's momentous first (and last) visit to the Factory. According to Nat, "Warhol wanted to get all of the weirdoes out—people like Billy Name and Ondine—those people were not invited that day, because Dylan was coming." Billy remembers the Dylan scenario somewhat differently. . .

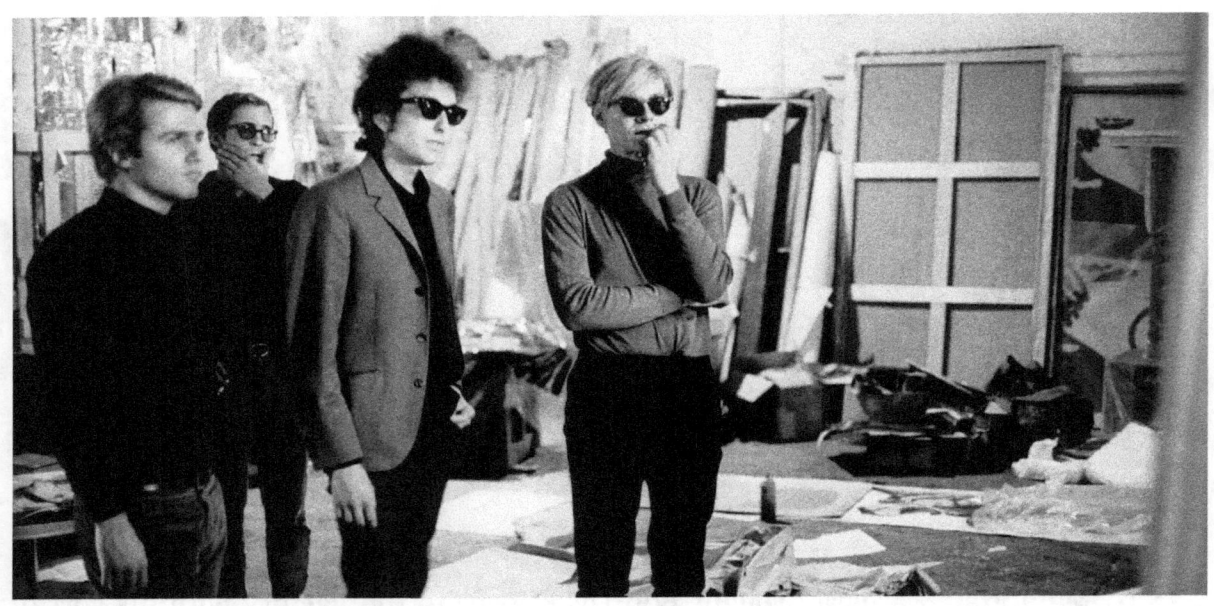

Gerard Malanga, Bobby Neuwirth, Dylan and Warhol in the Silver Factory.

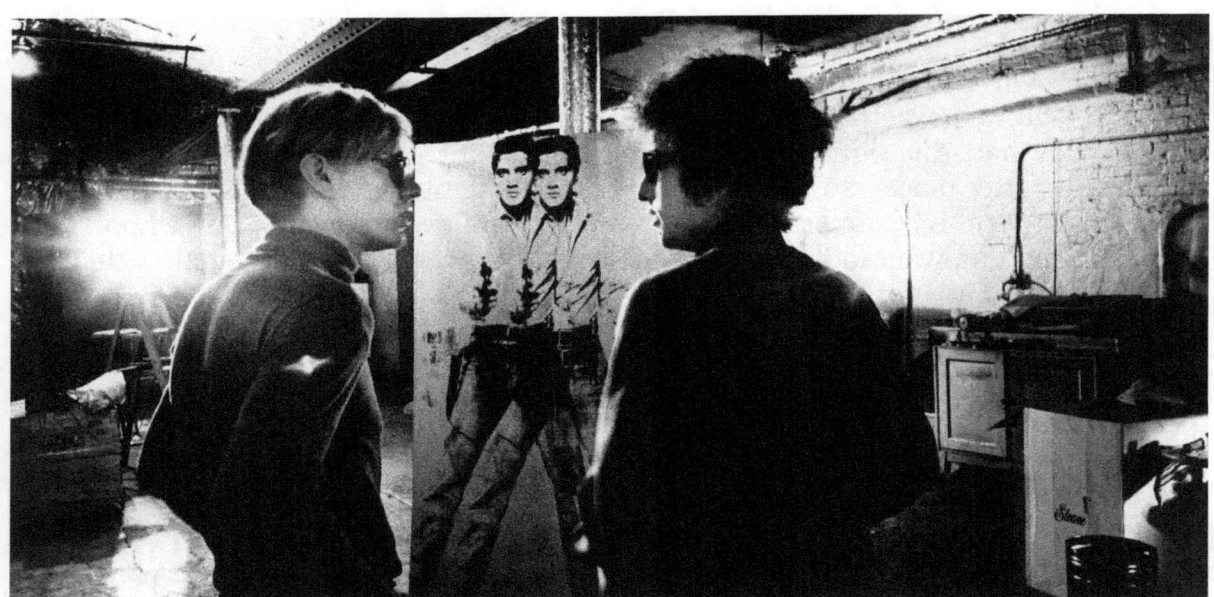

The boys chat about art, music, and the efficacy of sunglasses. (Photos: Nat Finklestein)

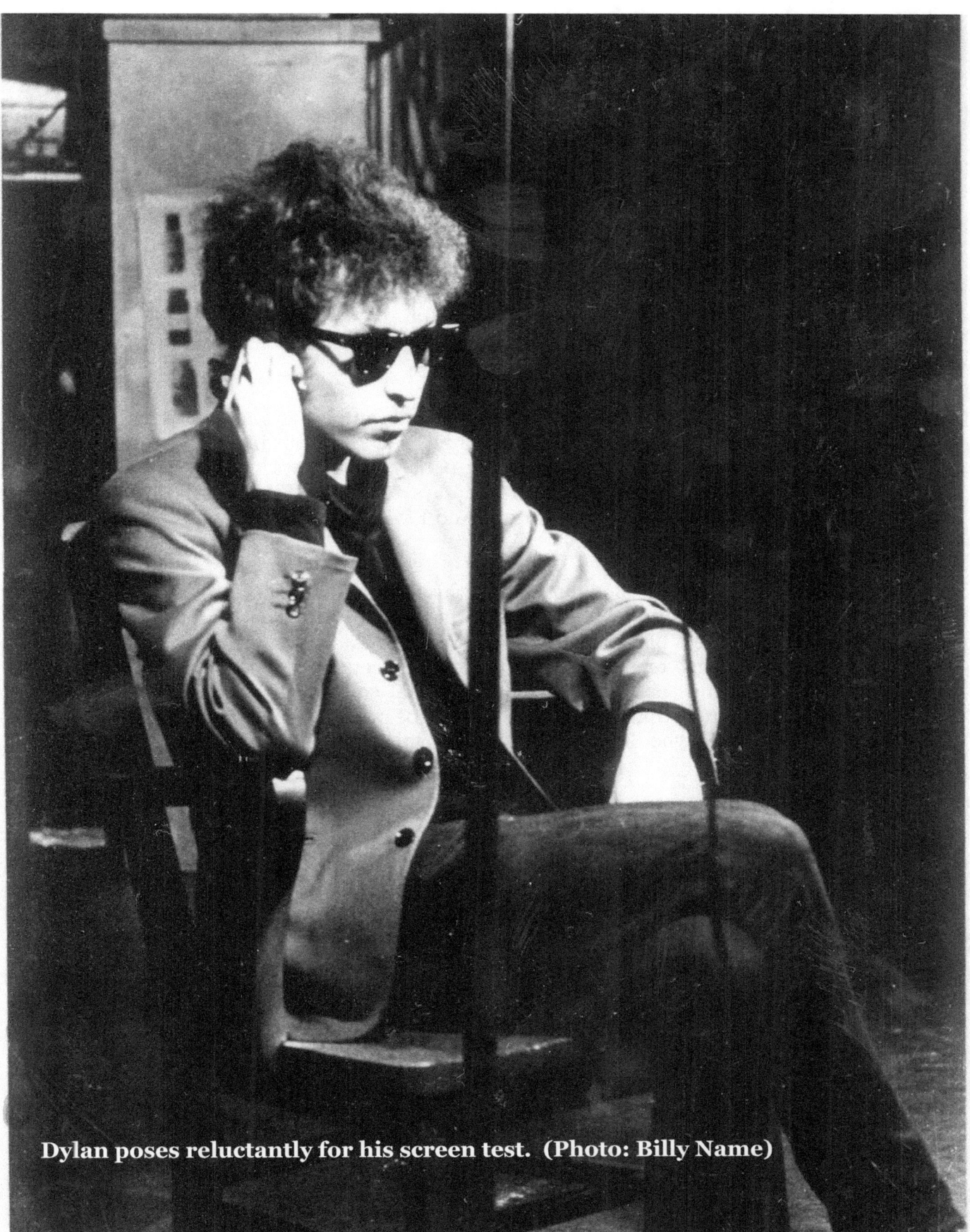

Dylan poses reluctantly for his screen test. (Photo: Billy Name)

According to Billy Name, who actually *was* at the Factory for the Dylan visit and also took photos: "Dylan was so insulated, it was like he was almost not there, or he really didn't care to be there." Billy and Ondine decided they didn't want to be there either. Dylan for his part had nothing but contempt for the 'Napoleon in rags'. He wrote 'Like a Rolling Stone' shortly after, and the lyrics, with lethal accuracy, sum up the darker side of the Silver Factory. . . "Look at him, he calls you, you can't refuse. When you ain't got nothing you got nothing to lose."

Robert Heide: Andy was doing one of his screen tests, and Dylan was sitting there, looking really bored and uncomfortable. Then he said, "I'm splitting." Dylan heads for the elevator, and he sees one of these big panels of Elvis with the gun and the cowboy hat, in silver. He turns around and says to Andy, "I'll just take this for payment, man." He goes on to the elevator. And I swear to God, Andy's face turned tomato soup red.

Gerard Malanga: In the end Bob just carried this gigantic painting down the freight elevator. I went to the window and watched them tie it to the roof of their station wagon. And they drove it back to Woodstock. Word got back at some point that Bob had traded the painting for a piece of furniture (a couch) with his manager, Al Grossman, so Bob, in essence, didn't take Andy that seriously. I don't think they really liked each other. I think Bob found Andy to be pretentious, because Andy was behaving peculiarly. Maybe Bob felt a bit put off by that. So Bob ended up not being in any major film of Andy's.

And I'm sure Bob was just crushed about that. He just may, however, have later had second thoughts about trading in his Elvis for a used couch (funny how an old couch figures into so many Warhol intrigues). In 2008, a twelve-foot wide painting entitled 'Eight Elvises' sold for over $100 million. . . Meanwhile, back at the Factory, while Warhol was still smarting over Dylan's 'cruel' snubs, life went on as usual. In a clip from Bruce Torbet's film 'Andy Superartist', we see handsome young Billy Name, the Factory foreman, working harder than a one-armed paper hanger, putting away paint cans and organizing his extensive camera equipment for an upcoming shoot. He takes a moment to galantly light the enormous cigar of Henry Geldzahler (then assistant curator at the Met) before rushing off to another Warholian chore. . .

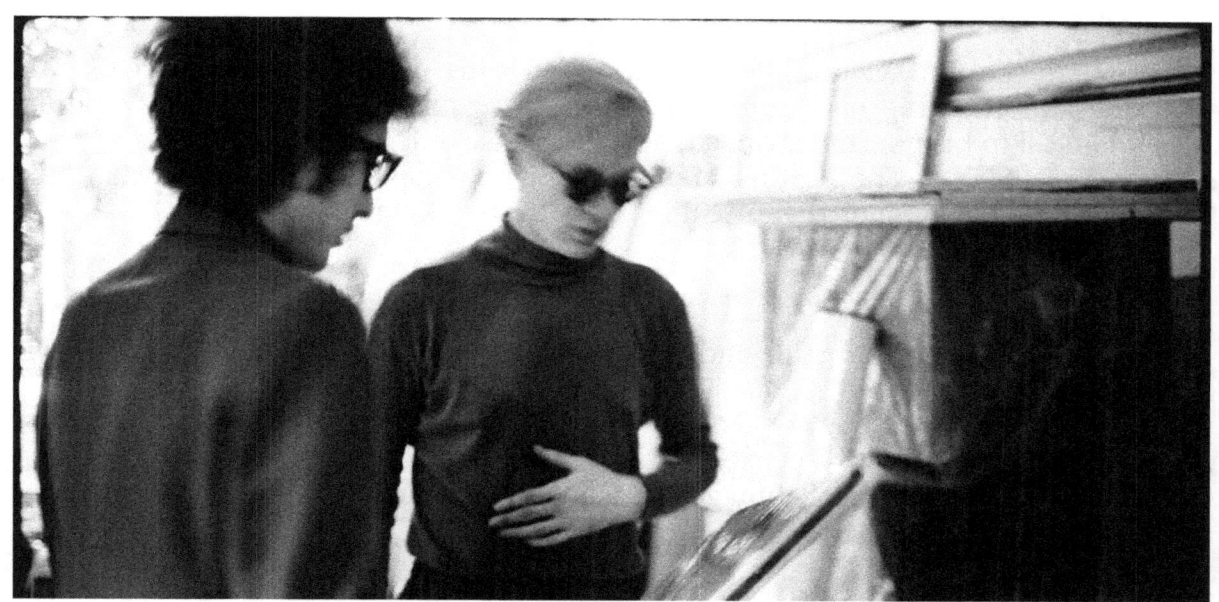

Warhol offers Dylan a painting.

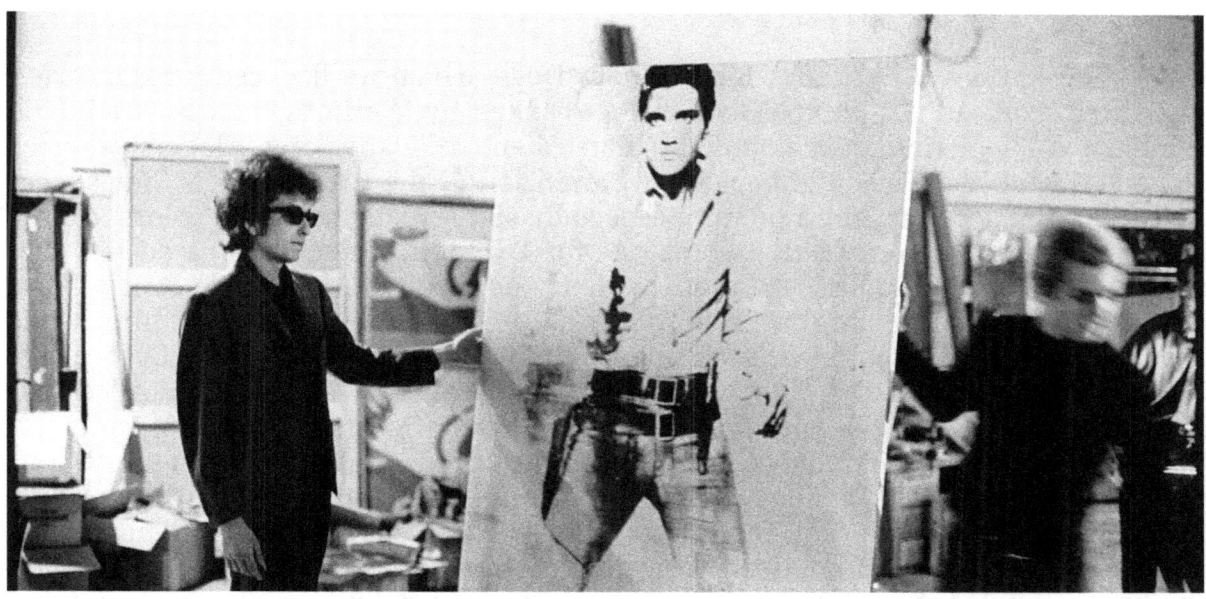

"I'll just take this, man."   Photos: Nat Finkelstein)

. . . Later in the film, Geldzahler is interviewed with Warhol perched next to him, fidgeting and checking his fingernails, which have just been polished by Ondine. Warhol is still in his nautical striped boat-neck phase, but he and pal Bob Heide were soon to pay a visit to The Leather Man down in the Village, in vain hope of decking 'Drella' out in custom duds that might make him look as macho as Dylan.

Henry Geldzahler
I think he (Andy) can find stills and images in his own movies that will be the basis for future (art) work.

Andy Warhol
Oh, Henry, do you think social imagery is going to come in, you know, like Bob Dylan singing his funny songs?

Henry Geldzahler
Your Birmingham Dog picture is just as interesting as anything Bob Dylan is doing.

Andy Warhol
Yeah, but what does that all mean? What does that all mean?

Geldzahler shrugged. Warhol's Birmingham Dogs, which we licenced for the series, was lifted from an AP photo (Book 1, P.56) taken by Warhol's then boyfriend Ed Wallowitch, depicting police and German Shepherds attacking Alabama's black citizens during the Civil Rights riots—we even found the live footage! Songs were written of the account, but a picture, especially silk-screened in vivid colors, can be pretty effective, so Henry had a point. As for Dylan, he could have cared less that among the "Factory squirrels" (another Henry euphenism), he was known as 'The Creep'. The hardcore amphetamine heads wanted nothing to do with him, while Dylan's people were coldly contemptuous of gays, unless they were Beat poets. Warhol did get back at Dylan in his own inimitable way by making a film called 'The Bob Dylan Story' in 1966, with Paul Caruso, Susan Bottomly, Susan Pile, and John Cale. I doubt Dylan took note of it, since he'd dropped from radar after a mysterious motorcycle accident in Woodstock (I seem to recall the Factory mascot motorcycle being a major prop). Warhol, Dylan and accompanying entourages were encouraged to despise each other, and not just because the heterosexuals were into acid and pot, the homosexuals into amphetamines. No, there was a definite choice of drug to be made if one was to fit into the carnal life of the Silver Factory, even vicariously. . .

. . . FACTORY SEX LIFE

Sex takes up too much time.
—Andy Warhol

Victor Bockris: Andy purposely created an entourage of highly sexual people, who were. literally, very active sexually. But also, it bounced off them. They were beautiful, but the way they walked, the way that they looked at you was always sexual. It also was challenging. You know, particularly the gay thing. If someone's not gay and you walked up to them back then, they got nervous, wondering what you were going to do. So he really had a sort of frightening sexuality around him. He referred to himself as "AW, all witch, all woman." And that is how he saw himself.

Mary Woronov: Andy was not a sexual object for me. I could not understand his sexuality at all. I mean he had many, many lovers in the beginning, when he was an advertising guy—fag advertising guy with a lot of lovers. And then I remember that he seemed to have none. I know that he and Gerard played games, and he was into torturing Gerard, like he would say, "We all have plane tickets to go home but you don't have one." And I know that Gerard would get hurt. For some reason Andy would keep Gerard powerless, like why didn't he use him in the movies more? I don't think Gerard knows. He was more necessary in a different way. Gerard moved on a sexual level. That was his place. He was responsible for bringing girls in.

Gerard Malanga: Mary Woronov, of course. She was a girlfriend of mine, International Velvet, whose real name is Susan Bottomly—those are my two stars that I brought to the Factory. It went something like, "Do you want to be in a movie?" *(laugh)* I made movies of them, and then brought them to the Factory, so I could claim saying, "I made the first movies of Mary and Susan." They're early films of mine.

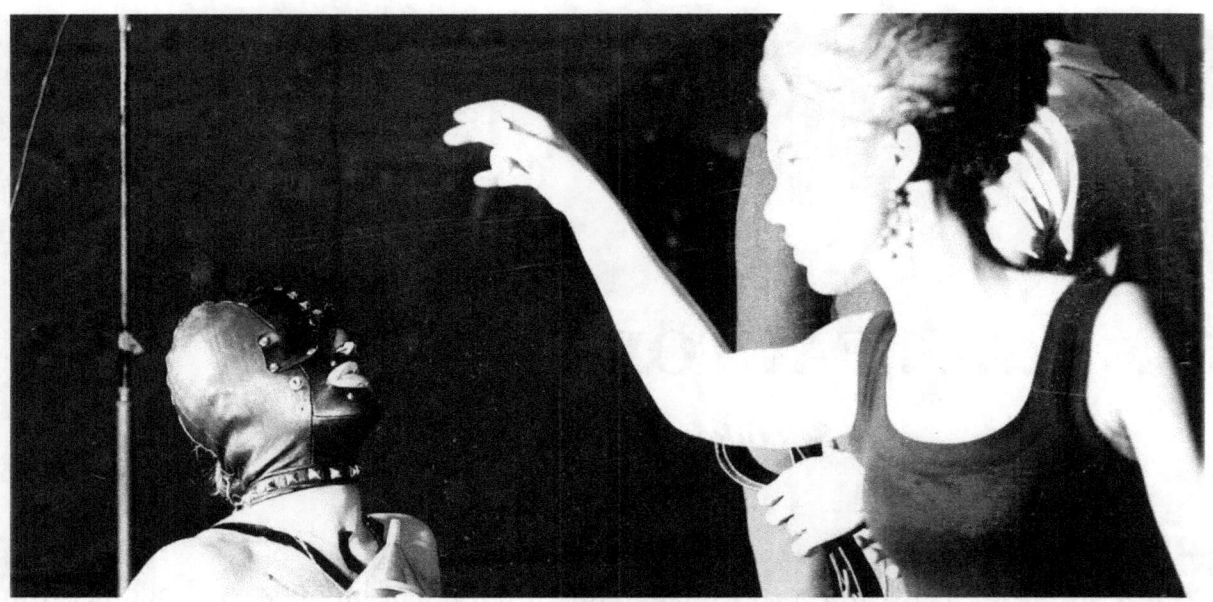

Edie teasing Gerard yet again, in 'Vinyl'.   (Photos: Billy Name)

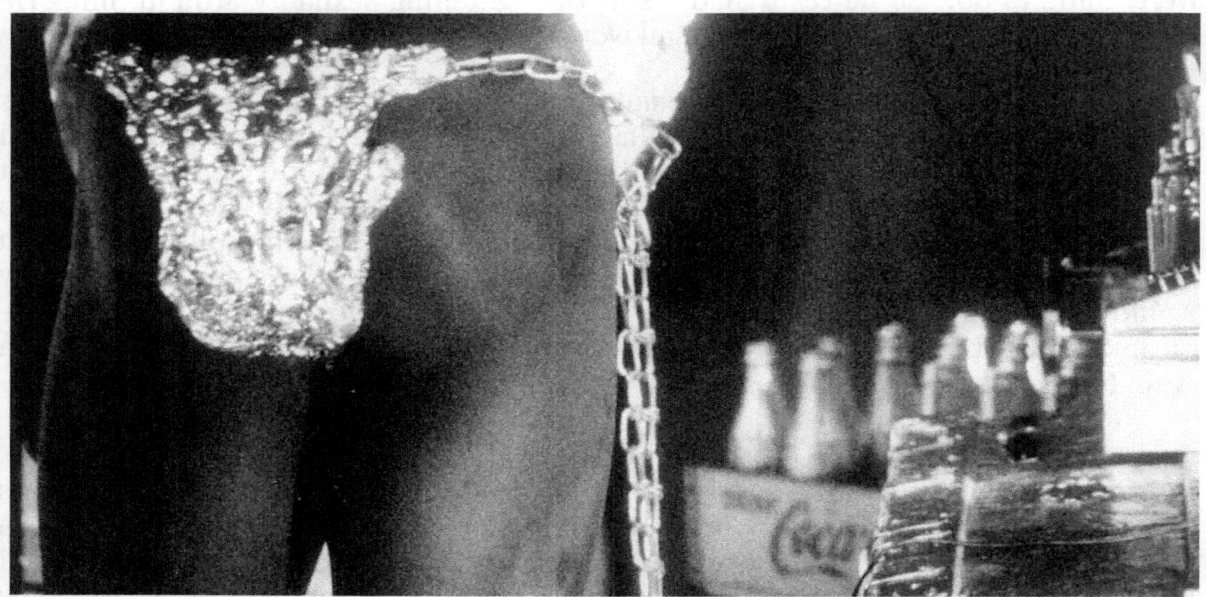

A star of the film 'Couch', dancer Rufus Collins, in silver foil finery, contemplates a favorite Factory beverage.

Mary wondered why Gerard himself wasn't that often in front of the camera. He certainly had movie star looks, so it could have been a ploy on Warhol's part to get back at him for some perceived slight. Warhol seemed to enjoy making his devoted assistant miserable. Gerard finally got his chance to star—as a juvenile delinquent—in 'Vinyl', along with Ondine. Written by Ron Tavel, the 'story' was based, loosely, on the Anthony Burgess novel 'A Clockwork Orange' (Kubrick later made a film rather more faithful to the book). This Factory-made film, as in the others to come, would revolve around sex in all its unlovely permutations, the more unorthodox the better, while Warhol watched avidly. In one sado-masochistic scene, Gerard is tied up to a chair, blindfolded and tortured, which would seem to fit with what was going on in his own relationship with Warhol. . . Factoryite music producer Danny Fields, Edie Sedwick's sidekick, remembered Warhol had kept Gerard out late the night before his big film shoot, so he would be exhausted and have no time to learn his lines.

Danny Fields: I never thought Gerard was happy. I thought he was very serious, very attentive to Andy. But that he was a happy, jolly thing? He was a seducer of beautiful women, but he was loyal to Andy, and I thought of them as a couple, not a sexual couple, but as a companion to go out with. He was really like a body slave to the Emperor. He worked hard for Andy, doing whatever it is that artists do—I don't think pimping exactly, but Gerard made it easier. Along with models and actresses and girls who . . . well, it was possible to be successful just by being that. What do you call it when you both . . . symbiotic? Andy wanted the beautiful girls, but he wanted them on *film*. Gerard mainly wanted them around because he wanted to be romantically and sexually in love with them, or poetically or whatever.

Victor Bockris: Mary didn't really get close to Andy because she was first of all Gerard's creature. She had an affair with him, the beginning of that working together period, and she wouldn't let Andy change her name—that was the key point. He wanted to call her 'Mary Might', and she didn't want it, because she wanted to become known as an actress. So Andy realized, well, she's not playing the game.

Mary Woronov: Gerard had no place. I never saw an apartment. He was attractive, but it was more like we were brother and sister. I mean, he would put his hands all over me, but he never came on to me. He made movies with me through the Warhol system, but Andy started using me and not him. By that time, I knew these, I called them fags, and with love, okay? We got along fabulously. I was way beyond Gerard by that time. . .

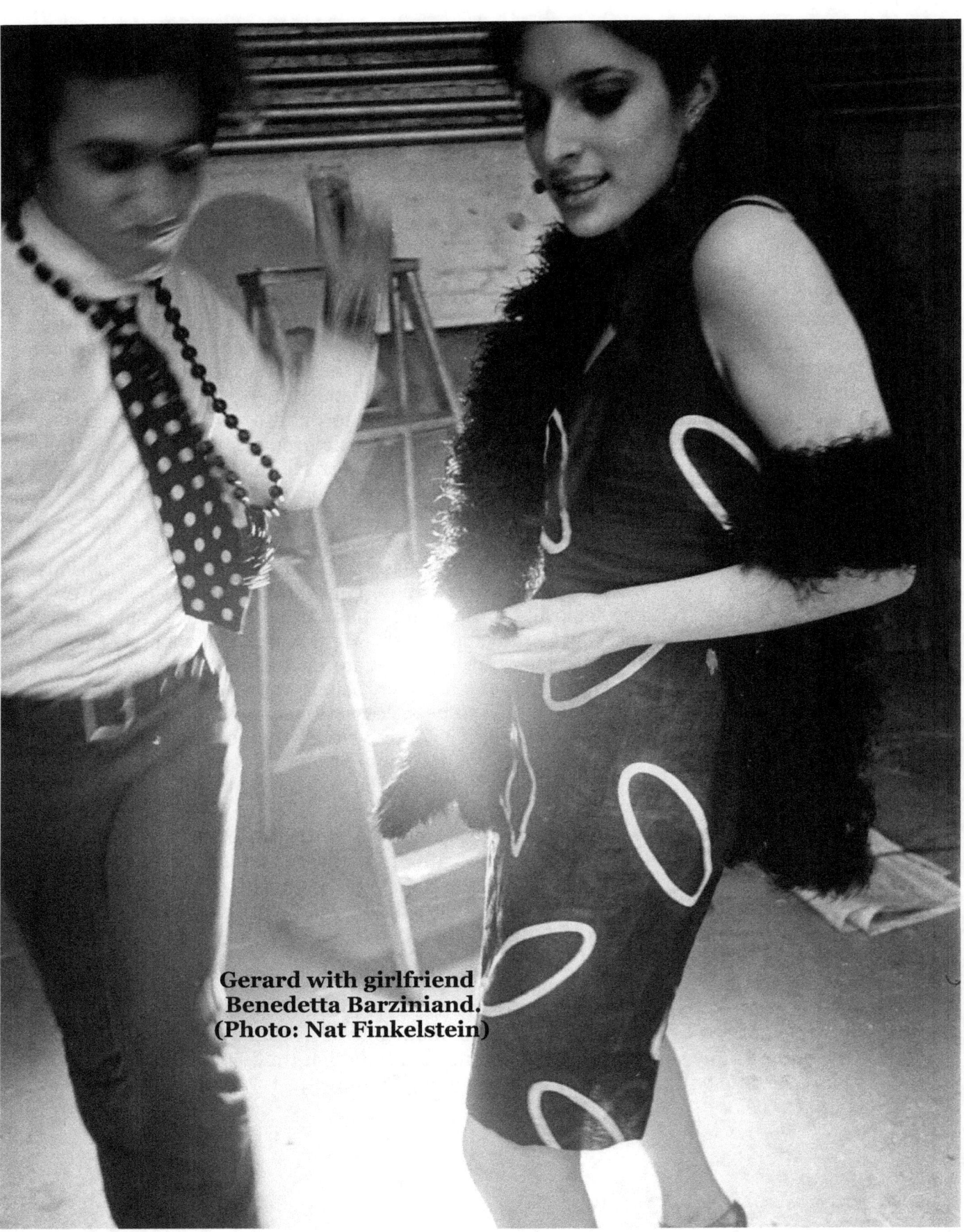

Gerard with girlfriend
Benedetta Barziniand.
(Photo: Nat Finkelstein)

. . . It would be simplistic to call Mary a fag hag. Edie was one, as was I. They taught us how to attract men! I landed a Peabody (where are you now, Rob?) when they sprayed my hair silver and glued foil circles over my nubile body. Of course, dancing made them all fall off. Fags made you feel fabulous. I'm hanging on to them—and maybe, fab name or not, jettisoning the husbands, like Mary. She refused to allow the boys to change her style (which was dressing like one of them), and projected this tough S&M act in her films, where she was encouraged, like all Factoryites "to be herself." No wonder Roger Corman ('Women in Chains') loved her. . .   At the other end of the feminine wiles spectrum lay, like a foreign spider who'd flown in on a fruit salad, the French coquette Ultra Violet, whose romantic conquests rivalled those of her doppelganger, Hedy Lamarr. But even she could not land Monsieur Warhol. In her frank and funny book, 'Famous For 15 Minutes', Ultra's bold advances sent Warhol running for the Factory fire escape, "actually shaking."

Ultra Violet: I think Andy realized that we had some kind of value. The women were so very beautiful. Beauty has power, and Warhol was drawn to beauty, with women— with men it's not so essential. So, Andy had power, surrounded by a court of beauties. We were quite few (laugh). He used to tell me, "Leave Dali, Dali is too old." Well, I eventually left Dali, because I realized Surrealism was going to end up in an impasse, as a fish tail (I think she means Dali's famous Lobster telephone). But Andy was extremely subtle in his manipulation. He had extraordinary charisma. Magic, he had magic! People were drawn to him like a magnet, zoom! Was that manipulation?

Taylor Mead: Andy manipulated people, did things consciously, subconsciously—a mixture there of playing games. And he loved his power. He knew he was important to them. But on the other hand, he made them all famous, semi-famous. I am one of the most semi-famous people in the world except for Ultra, of course. Is she up there? Ultra, are you there?

Taylor refers to our downtown studio 'holding pen' above the interview stage, where we had corralled our stars while they awaited their calls, munching on cartloads of organic fodder, troughs of designer water and, yes, sorry, buckets of expensive booze. This, of course, was the master footage that got stolen in France. We flew back to New York to do it all again, and actually got some better stuff. (Now you guys know the truth). It was easier on the budget this time, not counting the bar bills, also more in-depth because we knew everybody better, except for cranky Nat Finkelstein, whose photos of Dylan we'd been trying to license, but he kept firing his agents.

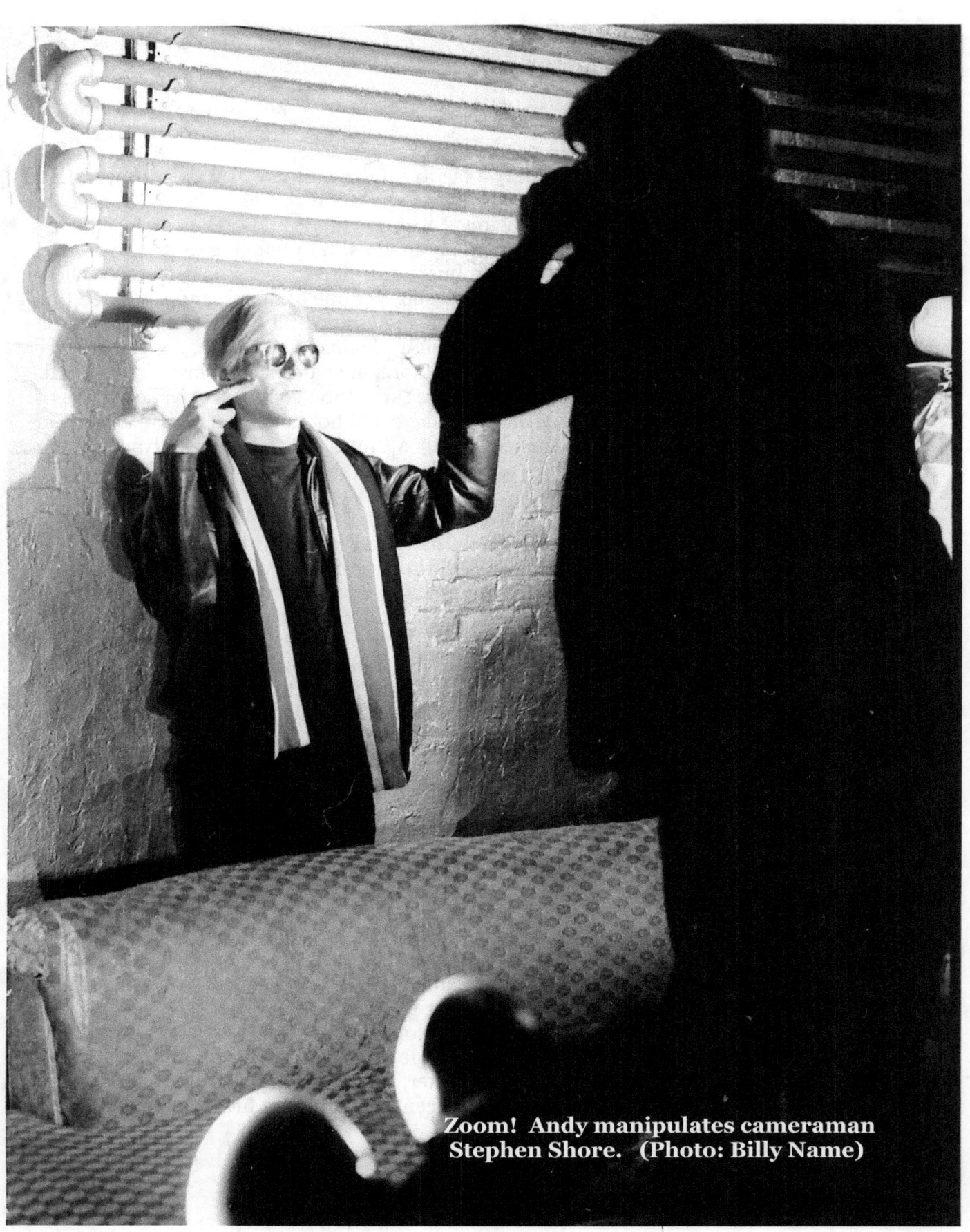

Zoom! Andy manipulates cameraman
Stephen Shore.   (Photo: Billy Name)

Nat Finkelstein: Andy was a user. Andy was a homosexual. He was not a 'woman lover'. He was a woman 'be-friender' and a woman manipulator, but the aspect of being with a woman? No, that wasn't Andy. He had a mother fixation, but Andy didn't love women. He sued them like everyone else. . . Incredible manipulator, and everybody loved him! Except of course, those who hated him.

Nat, though considered an outsider by the Factory family (with good reason), was close to Nico, Edie, Mary, and Andy's lover Danny Williams, who created the wild strobe lighting for Warhol's multi-media extravaganzas. As I mentioned, we caught up with Nat in Paris, at the opening of his one-man show in a storefront venue in St. Germain de Près. He had plenty to say about, well, everyone. No love lost there.

Nat Finkelstein: I'm hetero, so certain things were kept away from me, things I didn't want to bother with, because I don't believe that someone's sex life is really my business. But I did go out cruising with Andy a couple of times. There was this place on Second Avenue which had telephone booths so that you could call people at the other tables and pick them up. And there was an ice cream parlor, Serendipity, further uptown that had the French moviolas.

Stephen Bruce: Andy was becoming more and more outrageous, and much more accepted. . . Usually Andy came at night (to Serendipity), because he was a notorious night person. He was out at every club, every opening. I think the saying was, he would go to the opening of a door.

Stephen gave us one of his wide Cheshire cat grins, and clammed up, as if fearing reprisal for his previous revelations. Knowing the Warhol Foundation's legal team as we now do, this may have had some merit. According to biographer Victor Bockris, "Serendipity was one of Warhol's first factories. He created works of art right at the table in exchange for meals."

Billy Name: So there was Andy and Stephen, everybody was what now you may call gay, but it wasn't overt. I think the Factory was one of the arenas which allowed the cultural life of the homosexual world to integrate into the mainstream. Andy's allowing everyone to demonstrate their own talents freely, without the inhibition of "He can't do that, that's taboo," put a big zero on taboos.

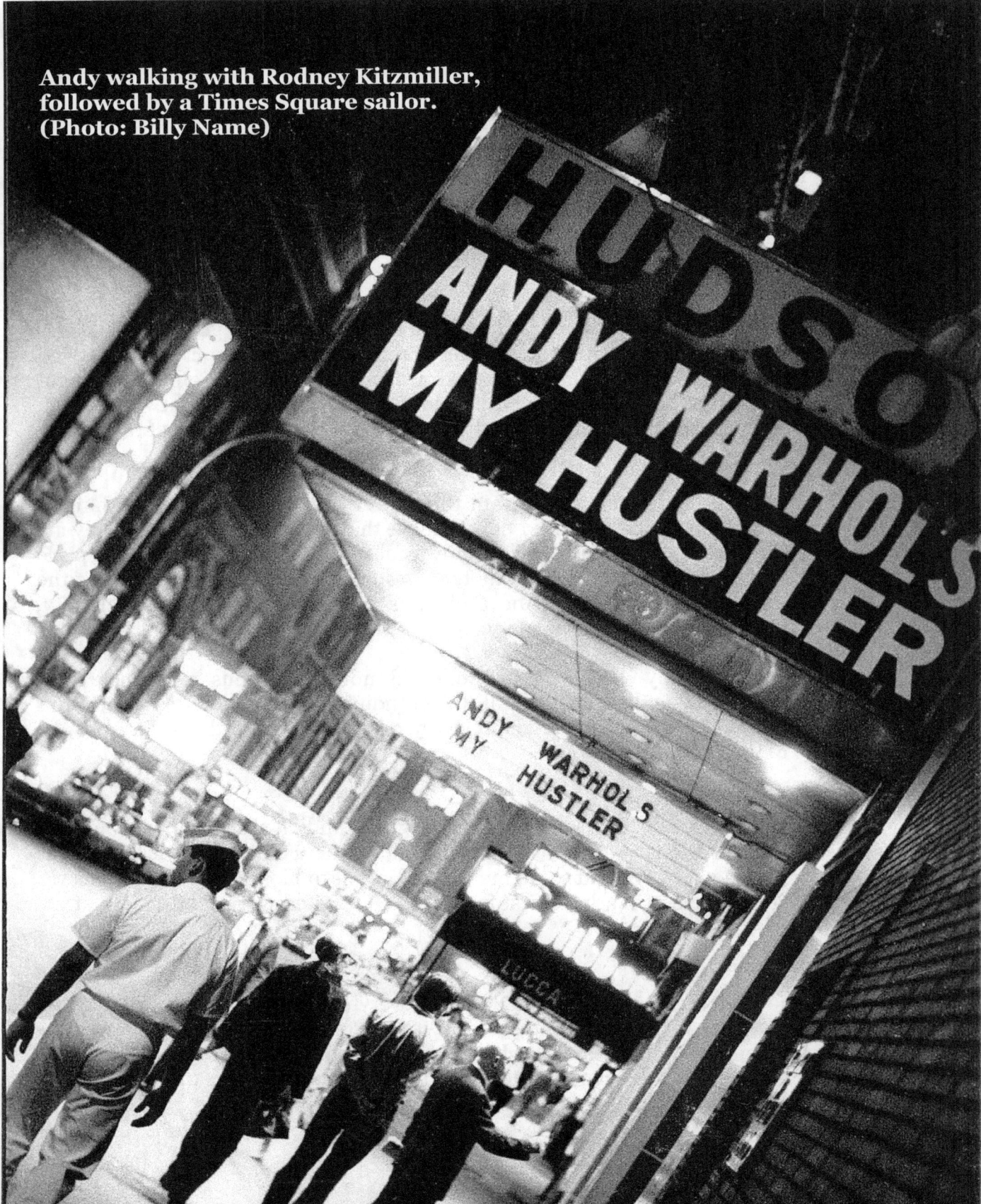

Andy walking with Rodney Kitzmiller, followed by a Times Square sailor. (Photo: Billy Name)

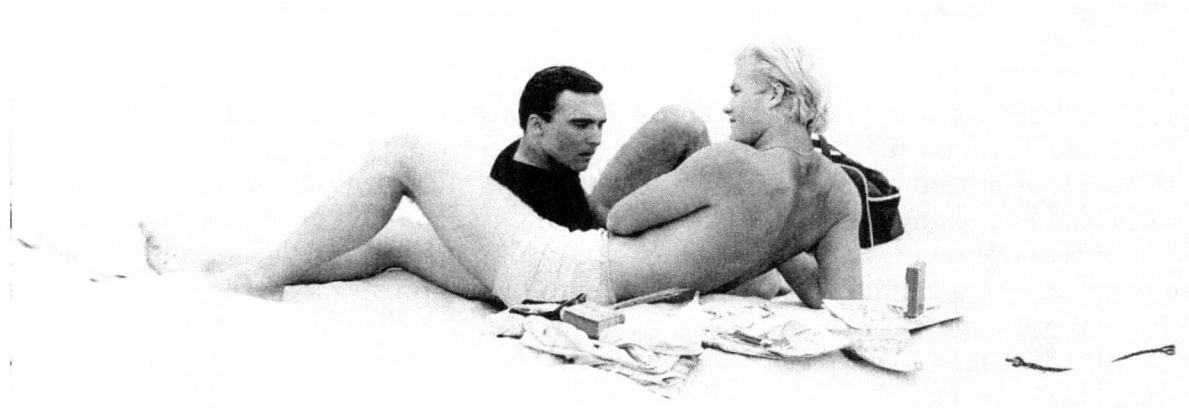

Joe Campbell (aka Sugar Plum Fairy) and movie-star handsome Paul America, on location in Fire Island for 'My Hustler'. The picture was used for the marquee poster. (Photo: Billy Name)

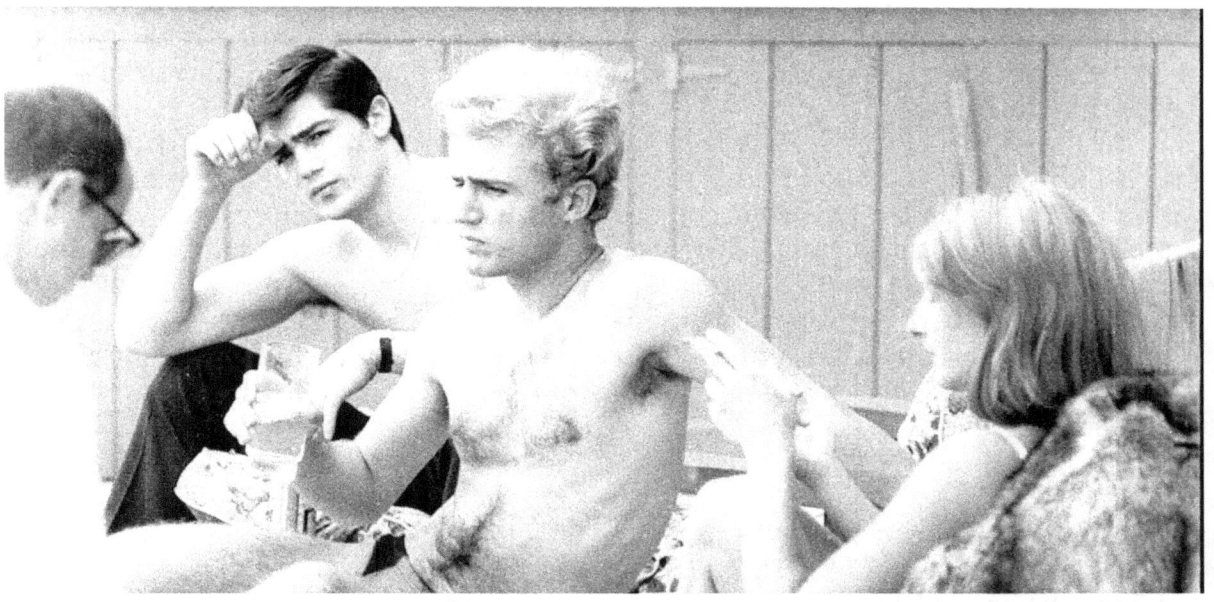

Ed, Joe, Gerard, and Edie Sedgwick's French roomate Genevieve Charbon enjoy a break on location for 'My Hustler'. (Photo: Billy Name)

Bibbe Hansen: Andy and Gerard and the rest of us went to a tiny little restaurant on Astor Place, and Andy delighted us all by showing a sex change operation. . . He drew it all out on napkins for us—how it worked—how the operation worked and how you take the penis and make it into a vagina. That was fascinating.

We thought so too, when we came across a drawing Warhol had made, anatomically correct. He'd copied it from an old-fashioned medical illustration, just as he'd also faithfully reproduced old medical ads for nose bobs and hernia trusses. Was Warhol considering sex change surgery? Doubtful, in light of his horror of hospitals—which was to prove prescient. Because he himself felt so unattractive, Warhol often took on the persona of his glamorous Superstars, carefully applying make-up and assorted wigs, and prancing about. Look-alike transference, the shrinks call it. Later photos show him flirting in full drag, looking strangely schoolmarmish. But one Factory *femme fatale* seemed always in a bit of denial. . .

Ivy Nicholson: Andy not only asked me to marry him, but he had quite normal reactions when I showed up in a miniskirt. He had no time to put a banana down there *(laugh)*. Well, I do have good legs.

Brigid Berlin: I thought he was totally asexual. Nobody has come back from the dead to tell you they slept with Andy. I mean just take one look at Andy. Who would sleep with him?

Brigid Berlin made a moue of disgust, as if her old friend would return momentarily with a callow young lad in tow just to prove her wrong. Those closest to Warhol did sometimes behave as if "Andy has just left the building." Ironically, 'Brigid and Andy' would prove to be the longest lasting couple. . . Filmmaker and Warhol co-director Paul Morrissey, speaking with biographer Victor Bockris, remembered Brigid as doing all the talking and Warhol as being very quiet, but imploring people to "Come to the Factory" every day. It was not just for the company. He wanted to film them.

Paul Morrissey: Andy himself was not a very exciting person. But it was fun to go there, because people like Brigid Polk and Ondine, in those days they were considered not well-behaved. They'd come around a lot and just talk and were extremely funny. Andy was there to hold open house.

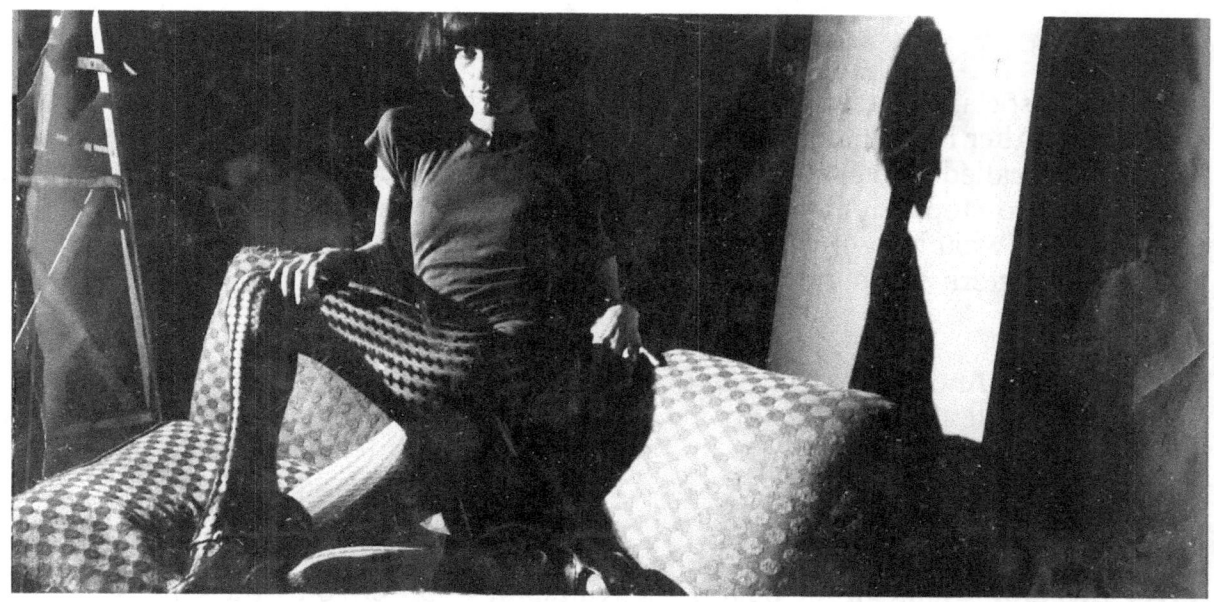

"I do have good legs." Ivy strikes a sexy sixties pose in the Silver Factory.

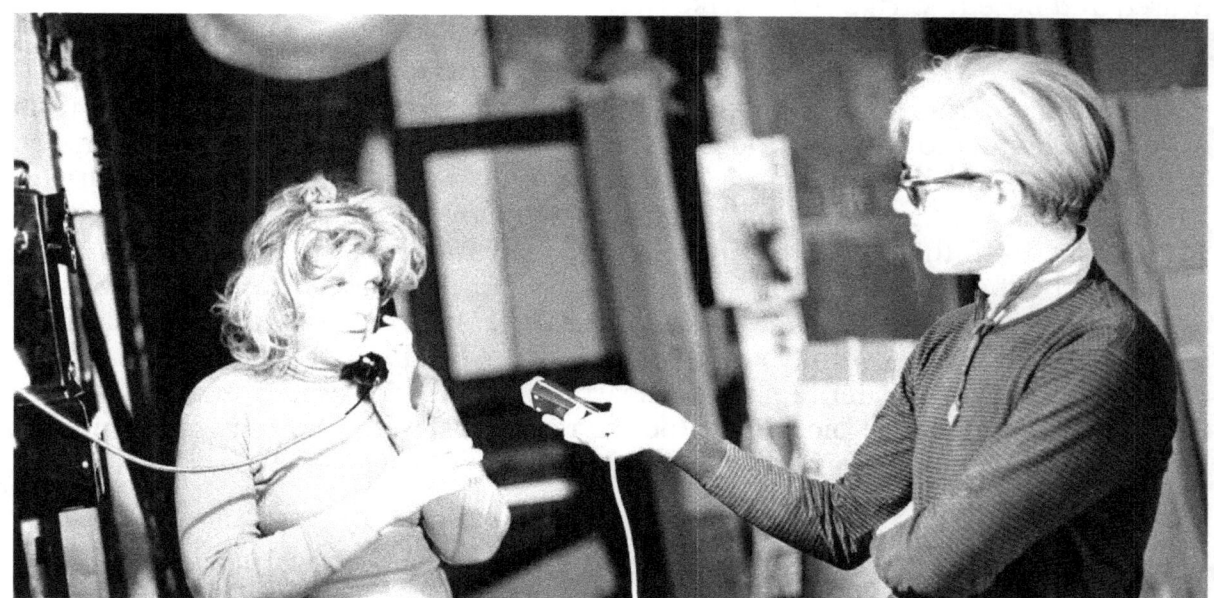

"It's for me." Andy constantly records Brigid Berlin's every word. (Photos: Billy Name)

As Warhol's social calendar filled up, time spent in his own house dwindled, leaving his lonely mother in the gloomy basement. She was not allowed to answer his phone, and Brigid recalled when she rang up with the latest salacious gossip, Warhol would yell at "Ma" to stop listening in. But she persisted, since it was the only way she could find out what her son was up to. Ma was also kept in the dark about the good-looking youngsters who periodically moved in, then out again.

Taylor Mead: Andy always loved young people. He said the young people are the ones that we will all be talking about. But I think he loved young people, ah, more than was legal to think about. He was a voyeur to some extent, but not to the extent that people make him out to be, because he had his affairs, and he was quite aggressive sometimes sexually. Well, not my type *(laugh)*.

David Croland: Some of the people who came in, who were only there for a month or two, scared me because they were not really a part of it. They wanted to be part of it. Certain boyfriends of Andy's scared me. Rod La Rod—how about that for a name? I don't know his real name, but he was scary. Scary and boring at the same time. I'm never bored, so when people bore you and scare you, that's a shitty combination. Scared *and* Bored? Strike one! Strike two!

Rod La Rod, Warhol's latest boyfriend, a rangy nineteen-year-old who hailed from Alabama, claimed to have two Gods, George Wallace, then Alabama's governor, and Warhol, "the Great White Father." Though no one else was allowed to touch 'Drella', La Rod was always grabbing him. Croland was only a year younger but a cultural world apart from the redneck oaf who had won Warhol's heart, and Croland, along with just about everyone, loathed the guy. Victor Bockris acknowledges that Warhol and his Rod would regularly get into bizarre fights, but "it appeared to be a strangely loving relationship." Warhol ignored the clamors of his disgusted Factory family, but he expected sooner or later to have his heart broken, as with other romantic liaisons. Sadly, we only have one picture of Rod, or rather his crotch, to remember him by. He's standing next to a Warhol self-portrait on the following page. . .

Andy Warhol
Fantasy love is much better than reality love.

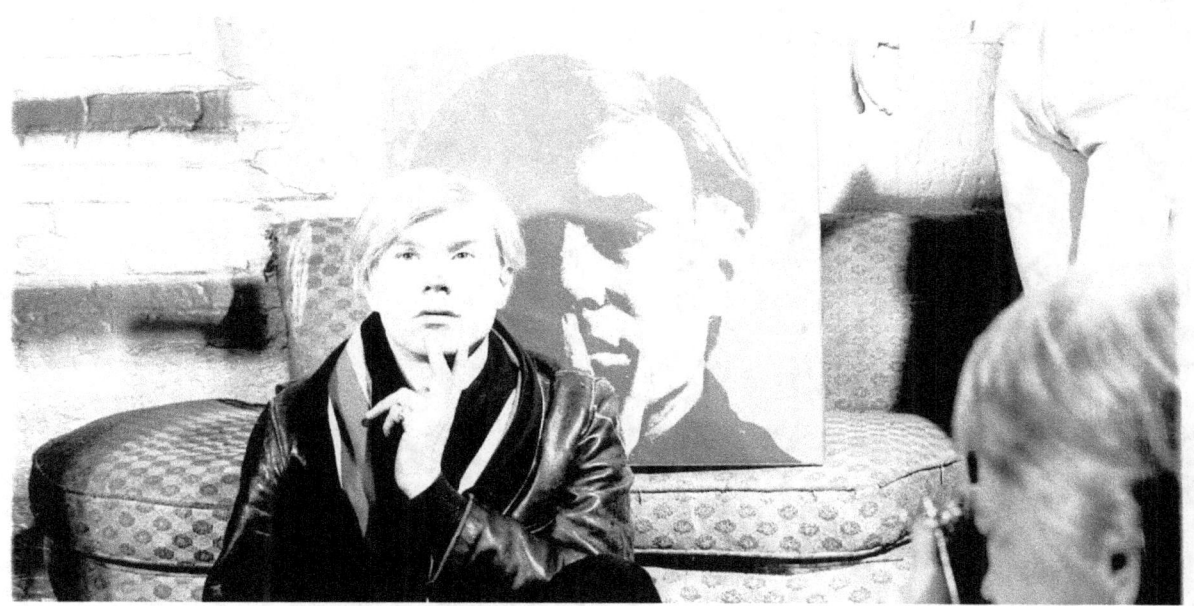

Andy and self-portrait. The bottom half of Rod La Rod stands at right in white jeans.

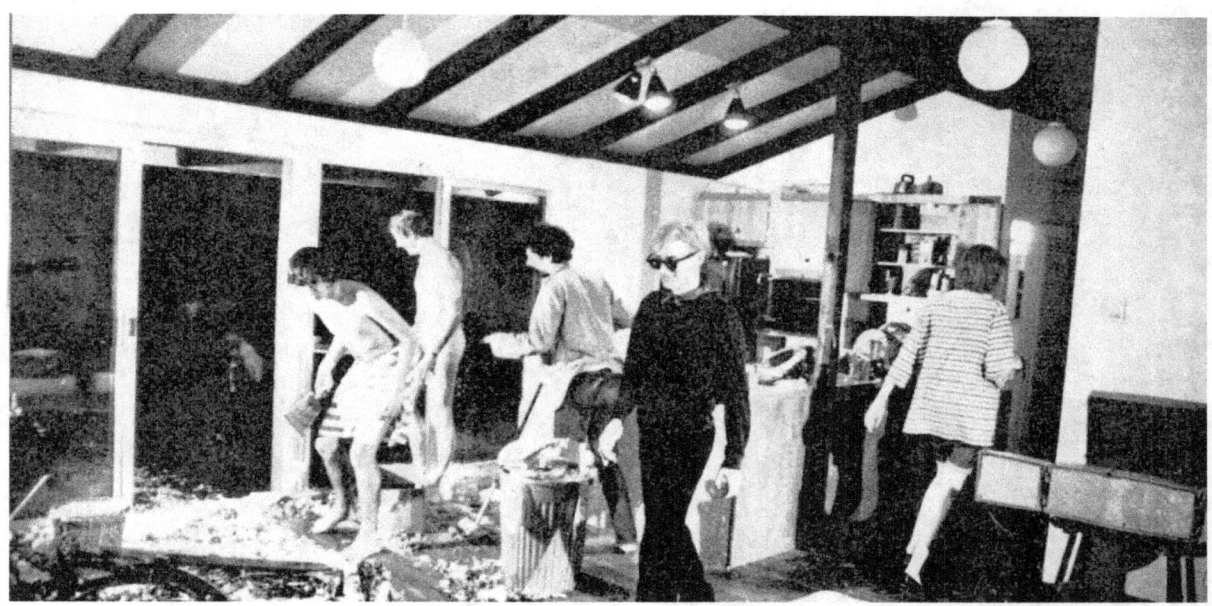

'Where the Boys Are'. Warhol films at a beach house on Fire Island. (Photos: Billy Name)

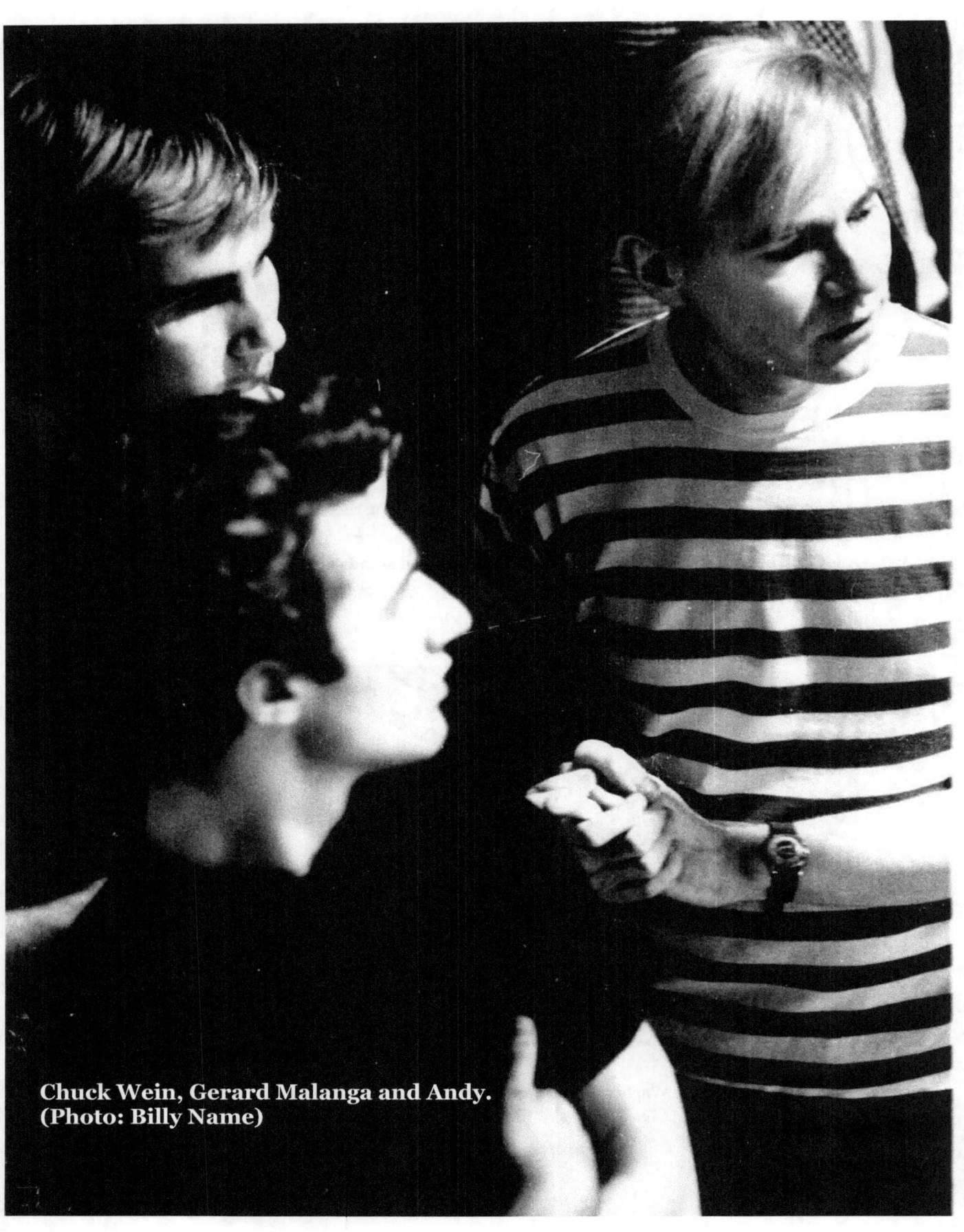

Chuck Wein, Gerard Malanga and Andy.
(Photo: Billy Name)

Victor Bockris: The extreme division between gay and straight men still existed very strongly in those days. Now the gay, I'm sorry, the *Beat* Generation were, in fact, very influential on Warhol. He had been influenced by the movie made by Alfred Leslie and Robert Frank in '59, 'Pull My Daisy' and he'd been in one of the recording sessions when Kerouac was laying down the sound track, and of course he'd read Ginsberg's 'Howl' and Burroughs' 'Naked Lunch', and don't forget that was a very gay thing. . . Allen Ginsberg used to drop by the Factory sometimes to see if he could pick up some cute boys, but he just wasn't their style, so he didn't fit in that well, although Andy did put him in that movie 'The Fifty Most Beautiful People'.

The Fifty Most Beautiful People' (64-66) was, I think, also called 'Fifty Fantastics', and included Ginsberg's boyfriend Peter Orlofsky, who actually was quite handsome. At about the same time, Warhol was busy filming 'Thirteen Most Beautiful Boys', and we included some of that footage in our series, which featured the tragic, talented Freddie Herko (who would later dance his way out of a window on Cornelius Street), and the indefatigable Gerard Malanga. In 1965, Gerard accompanied Warhol to Paris for his Flower Paintings opening at the Ileana Sonnabend Gallery. Warhol also brought along Edie Sedgwick and her confidant/'advisor' Chuck Wein. Edie and Andy quickly became 'The Couple', appearing in Paris Match and Vogue, and hitting all the nightclubs, while Gerard may have stewed about his precarious financial situation in a foreign country, among other things. . .

Gerard Malanga: We went to Paris together, Chuck Wein, me, Edie, Andy. Andy paid for our plane tickets. We stayed in the best hotel on the Seine. Andy had a big show of the Flower paintings, and I gave a poetry reading at the Sonnabend Gallery. It was an eventful two weeks. Andy was thrilled by the whole thing. The first night we arrived in Paris, we went to Castel's, a disco as they called them in those days.

According to some of our other interviewees, the Factory's 'Prime Minister' was actually none too happy with the turn of events both at home and abroad, since his position as Warhol's nightime club-hopping companion was being usurped by the enchanting Edie. And he did not trust the sly, opportunistic Chuck Wein for one New York minute, with good reason. But, it seems he managed to have a good time anyway. Memories are like that.

Gerard Malanga: We had a wonderful opening, a glowing review of Andy's show, so it was an exciting period in Paris. I mean, I was just a kid from the Bronx, and here I am socializing with all these rich and glamorous people. I started writing poems about fashion models getting killed in car crashes and things like that, so it was a very inspiring, momentous time.

Warhol enjoyed manipulating his traveling companions against each other, as much as he relished the laissez-faire French and their "yummy" food. He may have told Gerard he paid for the tickets, but Sonnabend, knowing Warhol hated to fly, had offered him a round-trip by sea, and he'd bravely asked for four plane tickets instead. Since Gerard arrived in Paris penniless, it must have been a bit frustrating for him. Luckily, many parties were planned around *Le Roi de Pop art'*, and the French have always known how to have a good time. There would have been unlimited and inventive Hors d'Oeuvres and vast quantities of vins rouge et blanc, champagne, and 'digestifs'. We can attest to this as poor film people accustomed to French freebies. So, I'm pretty sure that Andy, despite his aversion to travel and preference for living vicariously, loved being an honored guest of France.

Andy Warhol: I'm the type who'd be happy not going anywhere as long as I was sure I knew exactly what was happening at the places I wasn't going to. I'm the type who'd like to sit home and watch every party that I'm invited to on a monitor in my bedroom.

Warhol calmly announced his famous 'retirement' from painting surrounded by the swooning French, safely on the other side of the pond from his apoplectic New York art dealers. He then skedaddled off to England to see a gallery owner and attend a reading by Allen Ginsberg. When Warhol returned to America he was true to his word. The only paintings he now produced were copies of paintings he had already done, or an occasional portrait to make money—to make more movies. . .

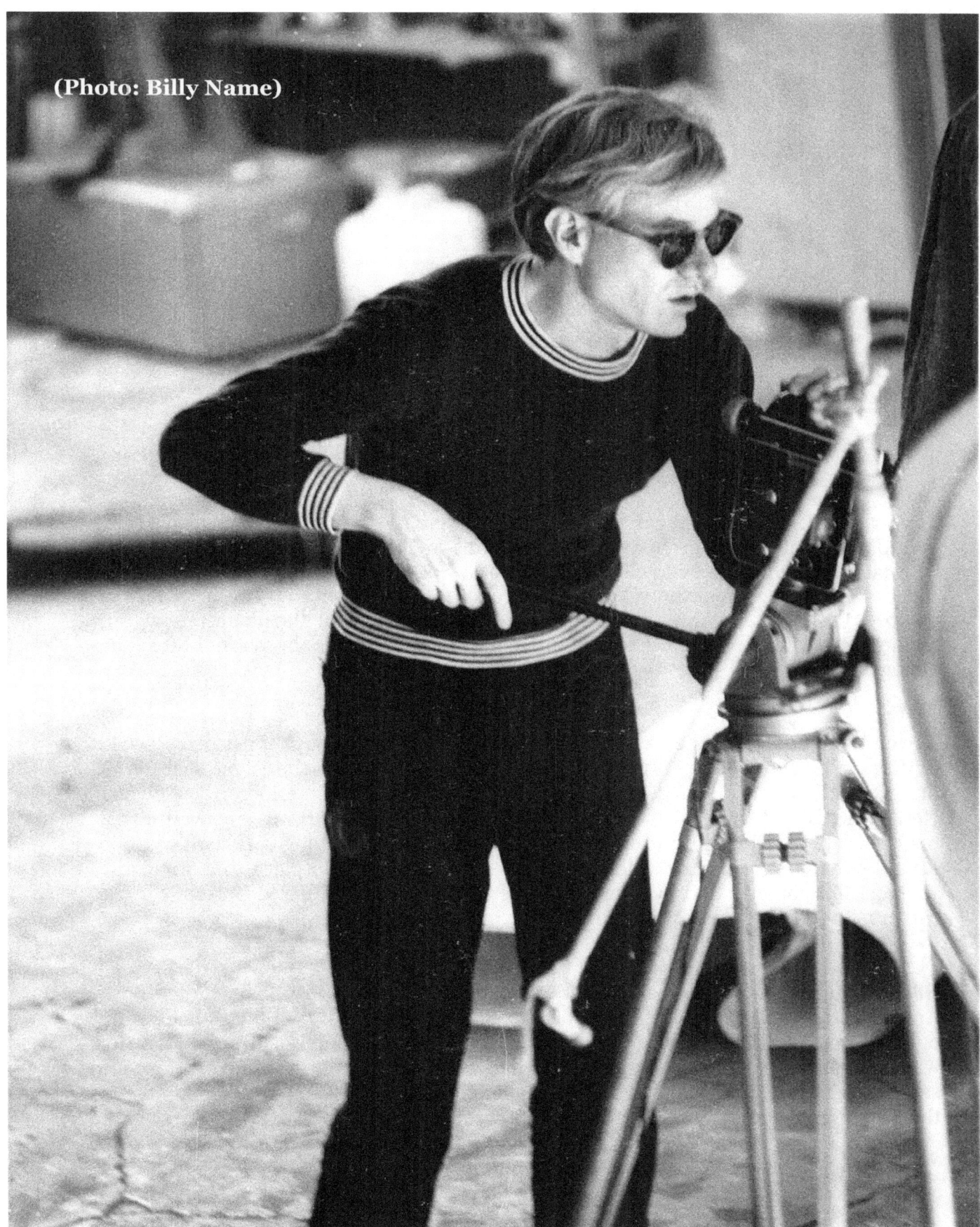

ANDY MAKES A MOVIE
... EVERY TWO WEEKS

Warhol can't paint anymore, and he can't make movies yet.
—Henry Geldzahler

Taylor Mead: After a screening of 'Tarzan and Jane Regained', the art critics said, "We don't want to see any more two hour films of Taylor Mead's ass." My sarong kept falling down while I was climbing the trees. So Andy wrote a letter to the Village Voice: "I have searched the vast Warhol archives, and can find no two hour film of Taylor Mead's ass. We are *rect*ifying this oversight with all the materials at our command." And we did two hours of my ass. The last show at the Warhol Museum, I sang 'Moon River'.

Taylor Mead had made the Tarzan film with Warhol in '63 , though it wasn't screened until later, by which time Warhol was busy with the creation of the Silver Factory. It did get publicity, mostly negative, but fun for a first effort. It's periodically shown at New York's MOMA, where you can find Taylor basking in the front row, waiting for his close-up. . . Here in a downtown bar, his rendition of Henry Mancini's 'Moon River', playing an imaginary violin with his cane, brought the place to a standstill. Perhaps the patrons were waiting for our star to bare his withered bottom for the camera, but we had already licensed the original footage.

Billy Name: Artists are creators, and once creators meet facility they start to flow. Andy had this facility, the Factory. The space had three arches. In each I had set up outlets for spotlights, where Andy could make films, and I would make sets. I'd order wood sheets from a hardware store and hinge two of them together and we'd have a set. We added straw and made a movie called 'Horse'. We brought a live horse into the Factory. We were making a cowboy movie, so we thought we 'd have a horse in it.

At this point in our interview, Billy let out a great whinny, which found its way into the film, along with a real horse whinny, a cat's yowl, some birds chirping, and a couple more cows mooing their opinion of Warhol's 'Cow' wallpaper. (After twenty years in L.A. creating sound designs for major motion pictures, this is what I wind up with.) The 'Cows' had been supposedly suggested by Warhol's art dealer Ivan Karp, although according to Robert Heide, Billy Name was responsible. It's safe to assume that most of Warhol's associates quite reasonably thought he needed to do something "bucolic" with his art after all the Death and Disaster paintings, the electric chairs and car crashes. In Bruce Torbet's film 'Andy Superartist', we found footage of the grand opening at the Castelli Gallery, with bemused patrons and their children wandering among cows and silver floating clouds. One little boy was heard to giggle, "He calls them floating sculptures!" Only a couple of things sold, but what fun was had by all. Except Leo Castelli one supposes. And the horse, of course.

Victor Bockris: With Andy's silent presence behind the camera, Gerard Malanga and Ron Tavel held up cue cards that said, "Approach the horse sexually." Under the influence of amyl nitrite, alcohol and marijuana, the nervous horse kicked an actor in the head. When he didn't respond, two other actors pounded his head against a cement floor. Ronnie and Gerard had to rush onto the set to break up the brawl.

Henry Geldzahler: I think the movies are non-commercial and *really* have to be raw material in Andy's thinking.

Andy Warhol: Really?

Louis Waldon: Art was *dead*. We were making movies! We said it over and over, "If Andy offers a painting, take the hundred dollars. Don't take his art." That's what we would keep saying, trying to keep Andy away from art, to keep him making movies, because that was the big movement going on. But they had a back room in the Factory. So Andy had several young kids from college come down. He was silk-screening over and over. Then they kind of put it on hold.

Interviewer CBS News: Andy, why are you doing these movies?

Andy Warhol: Um, it's just easier to do. It's easier to do than painting. Because the camera has a motor and you just turn it on and you just walk away. It just ticks all by itself.

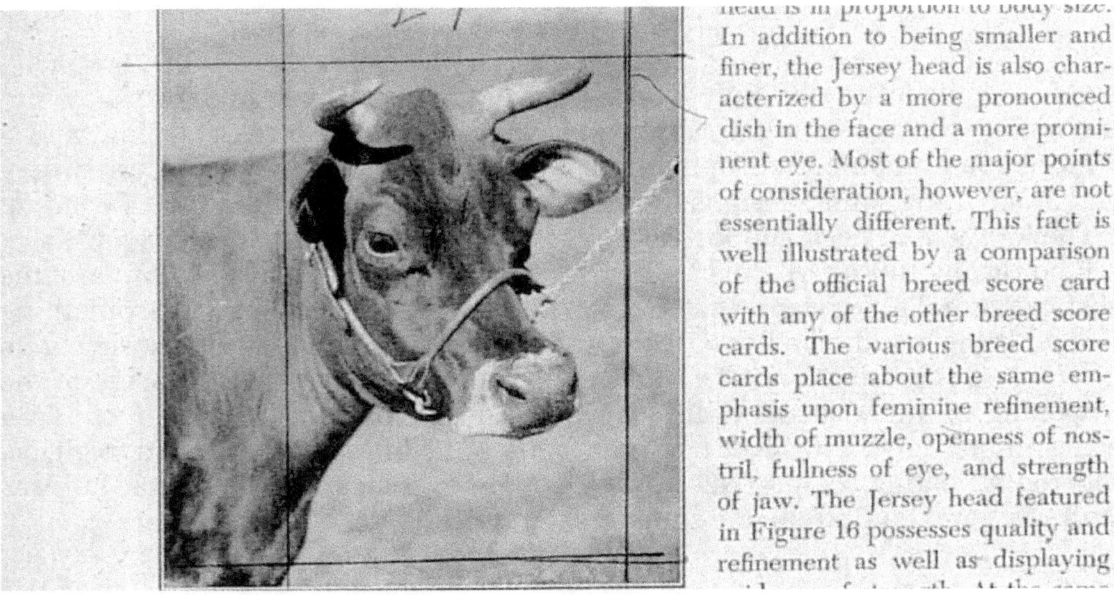

head is in proportion to body size. In addition to being smaller and finer, the Jersey head is also characterized by a more pronounced dish in the face and a more prominent eye. Most of the major points of consideration, however, are not essentially different. This fact is well illustrated by a comparison of the official breed score card with any of the other breed score cards. The various breed score cards place about the same emphasis upon feminine refinement, width of muzzle, openness of nostril, fullness of eye, and strength of jaw. The Jersey head featured in Figure 16 possesses quality and refinement as well as displaying

The inspiration for the Cow wallpaper, culled from an agricultural magazine.

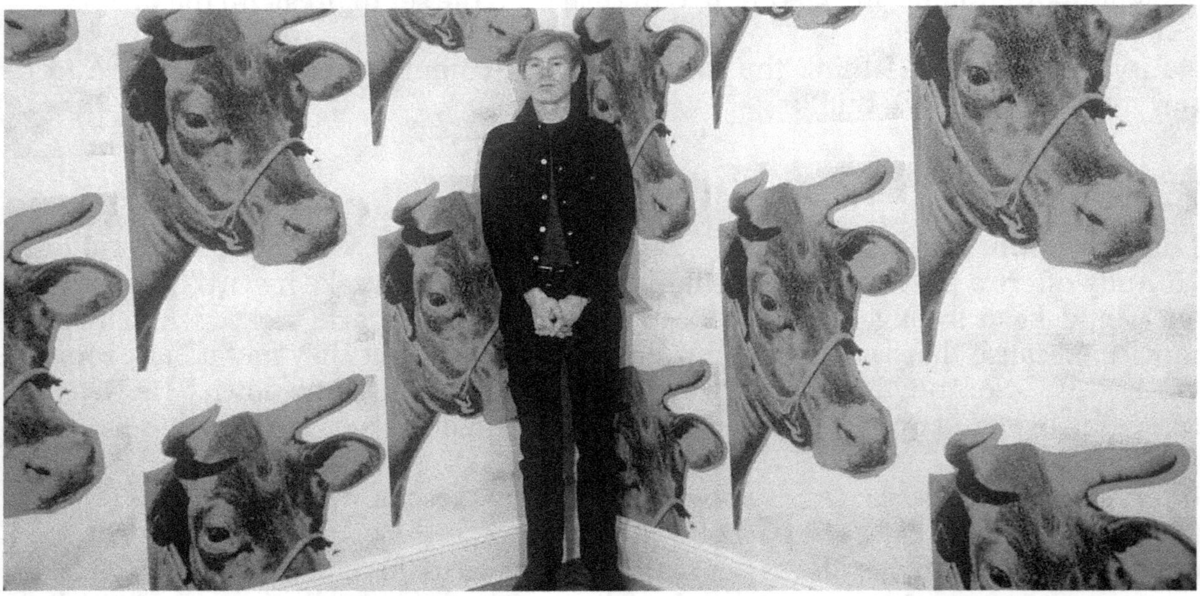

"Don't take his art." Andy has a quiet moment with his 'Cows' before the crowds arrive. (Photo: Steve Schapiro)

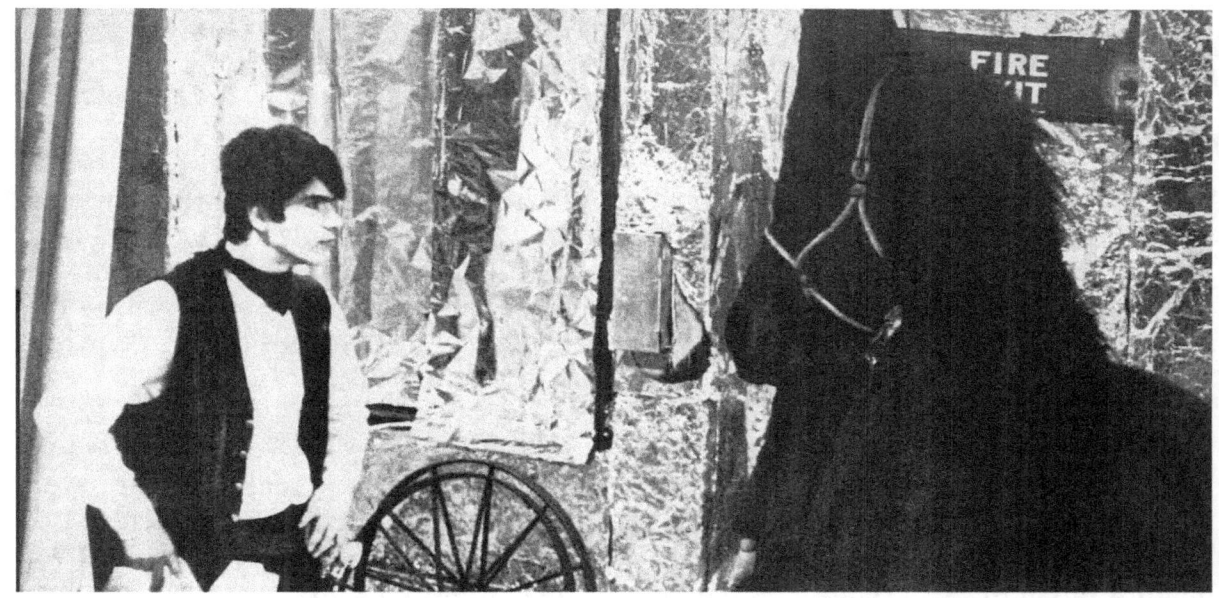

At the Factory ranch filming 'Horse', cowpoke Larry Letreille (Henry Geldzahler's then boyfriend) prepares to mount his uneasy horse.

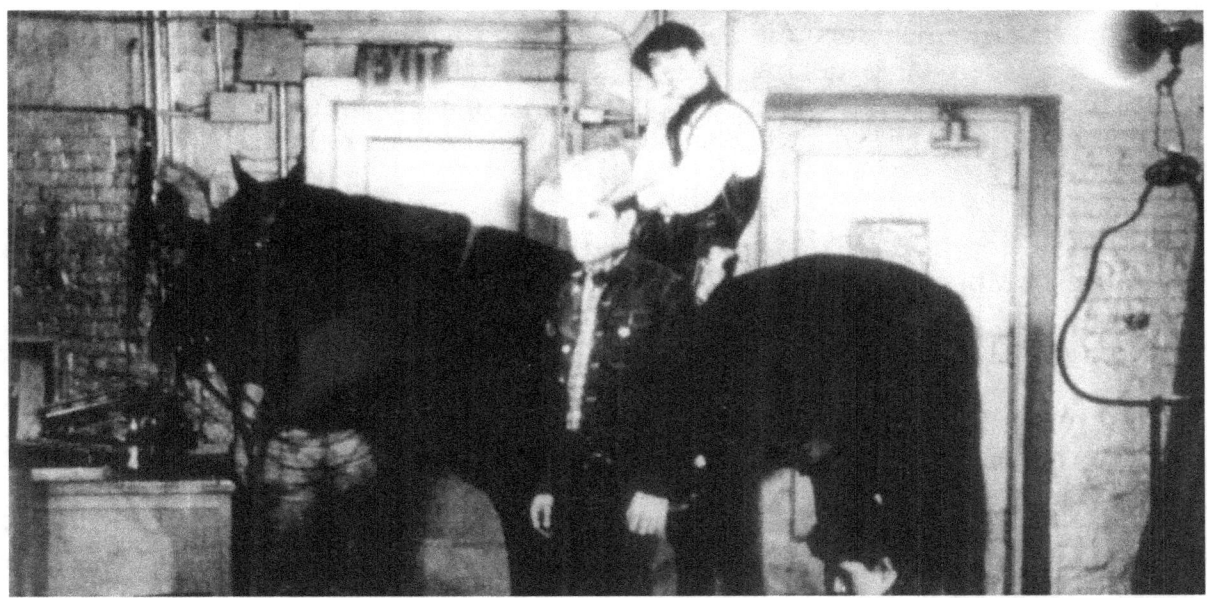

The horse and hapless actors, before all hell broke loose. (Photos: Billy Name)

Interviewer CBS News: Is there anything special you're trying to say?

Andy Warhol: No... (loooong silence)

This CBS interview took place around '65. Warhol sits at a table with the newsman and Chuck Wein. Above them floats a Tiffany chandelier, so it was probably at Serendipity III. 'Drella' speaks in his usual deadpan monotone, while the unwary newsman slides into the trap. Struggling to get a foothold, he is met with stony silence, the horror of every interviewer. The giveaway of Warhol's cruel intent is at the end, when Chuck Wein has to bow his head to hide a grin.

Victor Bockris: The '65/66 period is the period in which he's making a film every two weeks. These films were scripted, sort of. From the time he would turn to Ron Tavel and say, "I want a film—white, I want it to be white." Ronny would say, "You mean a kitchen?" — "Yeah, a *kitchen!" Ronny would go away and write a script that would take two days, and Andy would read it and say, "Great." The film would be arranged for two days later. By the time the film got developed, the whole thing took about two weeks. So, in two weeks they were shooting the next one.

---

*In 'Kitchen', a vehicle for Edie Sedgwick, she, René Ricard and Roger Trudeau, sit around a kitchen table talking, though the soundtrack is mostly inaudible. Edie complained that "I live my part too, only I can't figure out my part in this movie." Perhaps she got the gist of it when she wound up strangled on the table.

Kip 'Bima' Stagg: The Factory was seized by a mass delusion: Edie would be the next Marilyn Monroe and Andy would get a 100-picture deal from the studios. Every time the phone rang, they thought it was Hollywood.

Warhol called 'Kitchen' "Illogical, without motivation, much like real life." Norman Mailer called the film a "horror." Though he couldn't wait to escape the theater, Mailer would later (in 1970) try to emulate Warhol with his own dreadful attempt at moviemaking, 'Maidstone', featuring Ultra Violet as herself. The great novelist may not have been much of a moviemaker, but he was an excellent film critic: "One hundred years from now," he prophesized, "they will look at 'Kitchen', and see the essence of every boring dead day one's ever had in a city." Or in a Warhol film.

Roger Trudeau, w/ Ron Tavel below, holds cue card. (Photo: Billy Name)

Victor Bockris: As soon as he shot a film he forgot about it. He'd say, "Okay, now I want a film about—" whatever. That was the central operating line. Andy had retired from painting. The only paintings he was doing were copies of work he had already done. He did start to do an occasional portrait to make money. Then Edie Sedgwick became the first really famous female Warhol Superstar. There were a couple of female superstars before her, but they weren't famous. Their names are not memorable—Baby Jane Holzer, Naomi Levine,—but Edie was something else.

CBS News Interviewer Dave Dugan (to Edie Sedgwick)
How does your family feel about your being in these movies?

Edie Sedgwick
Agghhhh! They hate it. They're terrified; they think I'm beyond belief. *Out* the window with me! And they've decided I shouldn't have any money.

Andy Warhol: If someone wants to be in movies, you can buy their life, and say: "We are doing two movies of your life for that year."

Gerard Malanga: Edie, when we met her she was already at the end of going through her second trust fund, so she had been put on a side allowance, of like one thousand dollars a month, which probably went a long way in those days. And Andy was financing the movies with the sale of his art and with the advertising jobs he was still getting. I mean, the movies were not making any money, so Andy was not paying anyone to be in them. It was basically volunteer work.

Leee Black Childers: You never knew when the camera would be rolling and it didn't much matter anyway. But, this broken down couch they had up there—if it were around today it would be worth a million bucks! And there were all these people sitting on it, and they began to improvise. Next thing you knew, Ondine was giving Gerard a blow job on screen, and this whole audience of film students is taking notes. I said, "Geraaard, aren't you embarrassed?" He said, "What, what? It's art, it's art!" And they're taking *notes*. What were they writing down?!?

We blew a bundle on that artistic onscreen blow job. Unfortunately, it was censored by Standards and Practices for American television (it's still on the DVD, and in every university, so there). Warhol even got Jack Kerouac to make an appearance, doing an athletic handstand on a footstool, while behind him Ondine and Gerard lay comfortably supine on the filthy couch. They loved it in Europe. "It's art!"

Gerard Malanga: Andy created his own Hollywood, based in part on having been rejected by Hollywood. He wanted to be taken seriously by a Hollywood that shut its doors on him, so Andy kept on making movies anyway. But, like in the artwork, where Andy was kind of imitating the history of art, the same thing happened with making the movies. We had started out with making silent movies with the Bolex and then we graduated to sound movies with the Auricon camera. Then we went from black and white to color. It kind of followed the history of movies, the pattern. Hollywood had its own set up, its own system, its own vocabulary, and Andy's vocabulary was totally incomprehensible to what they were doing.

Billy Name: Well, it's not like there was a selection process—there were no audition type thing. It's not like 'A Chorus Line', where you came when you got the call. No, they would come in through me, or in the poetry world they would come in through Gerard, or they would just come in, or we would go out and find them and *tell* them to come in *(laugh)*. Because the art world was still somewhat insular then in Manhattan, everyone in New York culture knew each other and they weren't known by the rest of the world yet.

About this time a lanky young film technician and aspiring director named Paul Morrissey stepped into the picture, and immediately began making waves on a beach in Fire Island. 'My Hustler' (about an old queen who rents a boy from Dial-A-Hustler), actually had an audible sound track for the first time, thanks to Morrissey, who wasn't a big fan of Warhol's silent films. The bustling style of the newcomer (some would say interloper) showed up everywhere in our sixties beach footage, a farrago of leaping, twirling, and dashing into water, while Warhol stoically huddles behind his trusty Auricon. Morrissey, who was certainly movie star handsome enough to be in front of the cameras, wisely did not take that overbooked ego trip and chose instead to go where his talents would be most needed. Then again, that ocean did look pretty cold. . . When biographer Victor Bockris interviewed him, Paul Morrissey explained why he wound up directing (without credit) those movies. . .

Paul Morrissey (from 'Warhol, the Biography'): Andy wasn't doing experimental photography—he was experimenting with people. From the beginning, I could see that what he was doing was very interesting, because it left the camera on human beings who were characters, and the basis for all dramatic fiction is character. It was simple. Andy wanted films that weren't directed. . . I was able to provide the framework in which a film that was basically undirected had some direction.

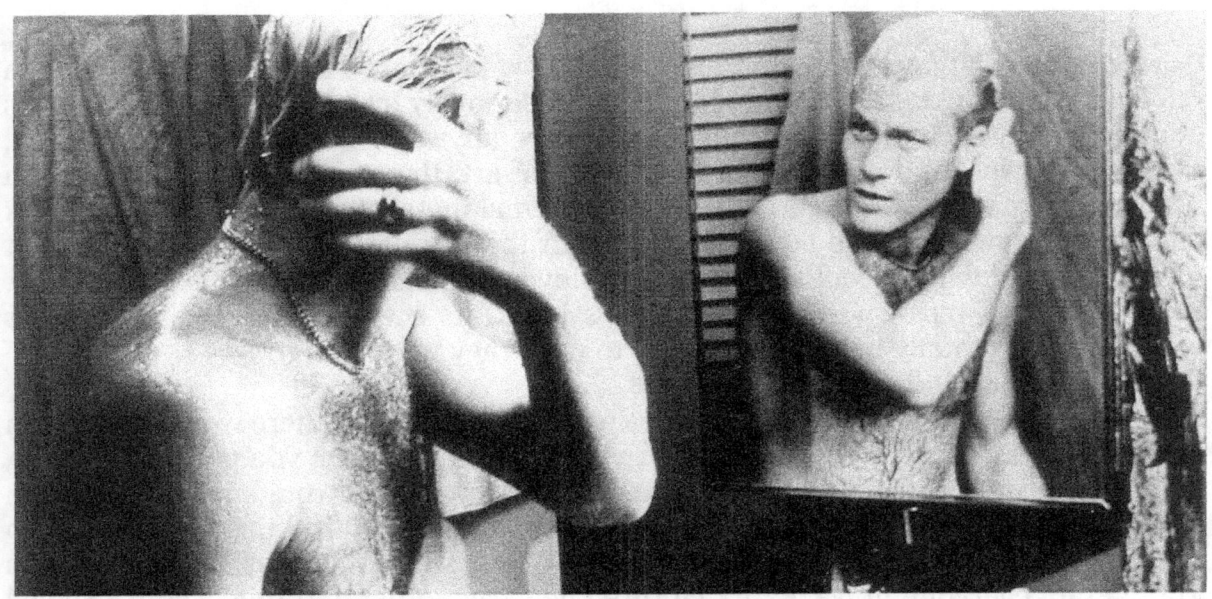

Paul America, star of 'My Hustler', who also filmed a couple of sequels (unreleased), was "the one true love" in the life of my wild, beautiful, cousin, Colette O'Sullivan. Tragically, she 'fell' out a NYC window in her 20s. Paul was killed by a car at the age of 38.

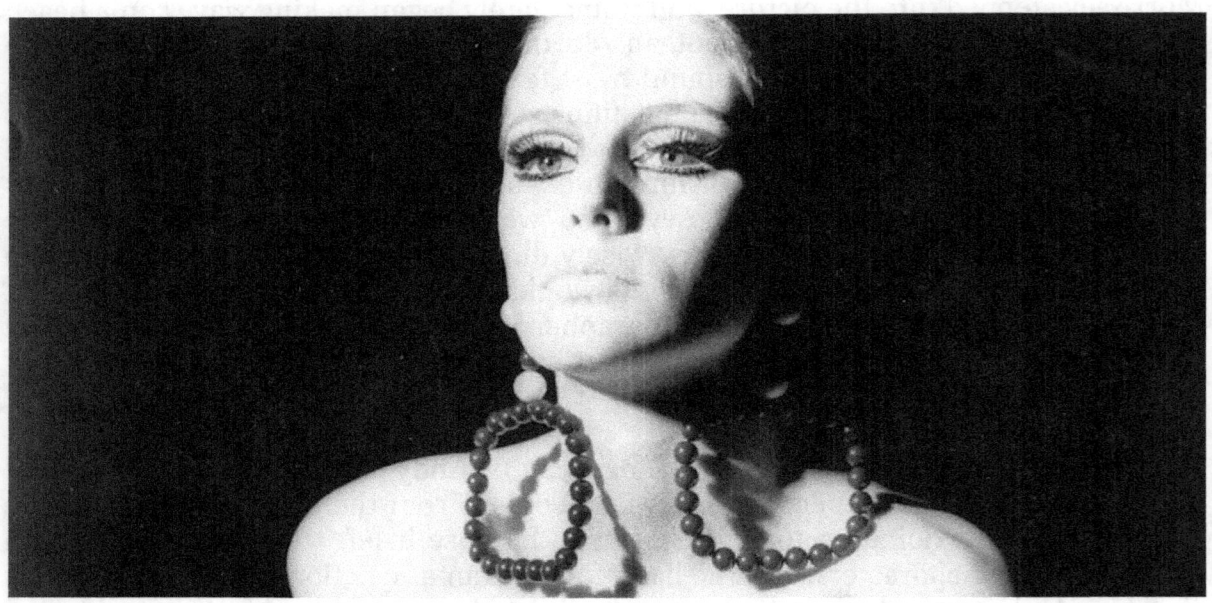

Another pretty new face, who—like all the rest of us—wore Betsey Johnson and Rudi Gernreich from the boutique 'Paraphernelia'. . . Warhol Superstar Susan Bottomly (aka International Velvet) always dressed in full-on '60s fashion mode. (Photos: Billy Name)

Danny Fields: Andy said, (*mimicking*) "Oooh, there are so many people. How am I going to get them all into one frame?" Paul said, "Well, all you do this thing called panning. You slowly move the lens from one side to the other until you get them." And Andy said, "Ooooh, I tried that and it was all jerky, all stops and starts." Paul said, "You must learn to do it gently, so it's smooth and the motion of your muscles does not come out on the screen." From that moment on, Paul was Andy's technical "Let's make real movies" kind of person. And Chuck (Wein) was there at the same time. I can't imagine they loved each other. That's okay. I can't imagine even that they loved anybody, except everybody loved Edie.

Victor Bockris: 'Girl of the Year'. . . The very title kind of set you up for the fall, but on the other hand he probably realized, the kind of thing he was doing, he would need to have a new 'Girl of the Year' because of the pace of pop culture. And because of the fact that he'd be working them to death, and they wouldn't survive for much longer than that anyway. So that's basically what happened. He got Baby Jane, he got Ultra, he got Edie, where for the first time, you saw the rise and fall of the 'Girl of the Year'. He got Nico, then he got International Velvet. Some of them have much shorter spans than others.

Mary Woronov: The next thing was International Velvet, Susan Bottomly. So, Susan, you know, is going to be a model, this is her big thing. This is a woman with ninety-two thousand eyelashes. She could barely open her eyes. She said to Andy, "Listen I'm getting this call, and we'll have to stop filming." We were in a bedroom in the Chelsea Hotel, and were going to have to stop filming, so she can get this call. And I just thought, "Fuck you, bitch!" We're attempting this movie; she doesn't know what she's doing, and I was pissed off. Then the telephone rings and I wouldn't let her answer the phone. She flipped out! When nobody did anything to stop the movie, she left. Then, she came *back!* That sort of heightened and made it this S&M scene. But here they think, "It's not supposed to happen." Hey, it's called Improv.

Oh Mary, you are just so mean. But I can see your point, after watching 'Chelsea Girls' (all six hours). We used the footage of you beating up poor, cowering Ingrid Superstar, and then wading into whiny Susan, though she was quite lovely despite the stratified layers of false eyelashes. But that's what girls did in the sixties. Yikes! You show no mercy. David Croland agrees, because you were slamming around his girlfriend. Ever the gentleman, he did nothing. Then again, you are six feet tall in your fabulous buckled jack boots.

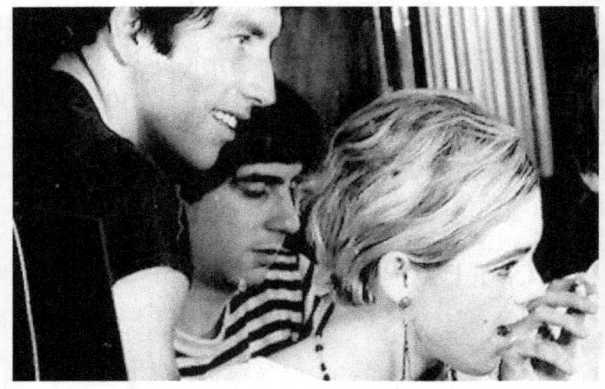

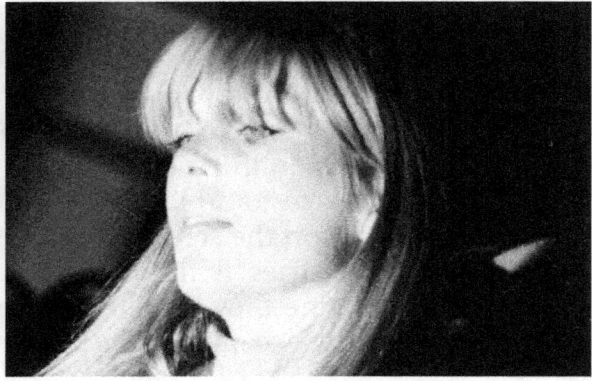

Roger Trudeau and Danny Fields with Edie Sedgwick, reiging 'Girl of the Year' for 1965. (all Photos: Billy Name)

Nico, 'Girl of the Year' for 1966, usurps Edie's crown, and could care less. She "just wants to be a singer."

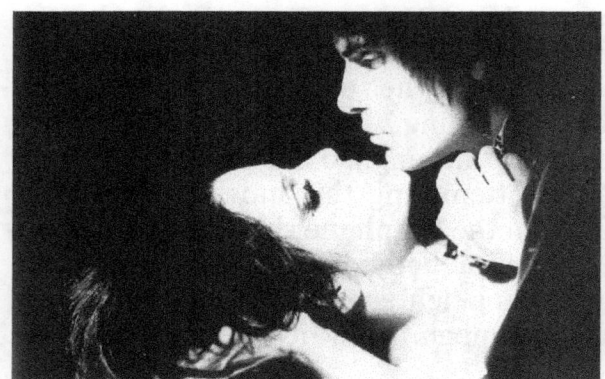

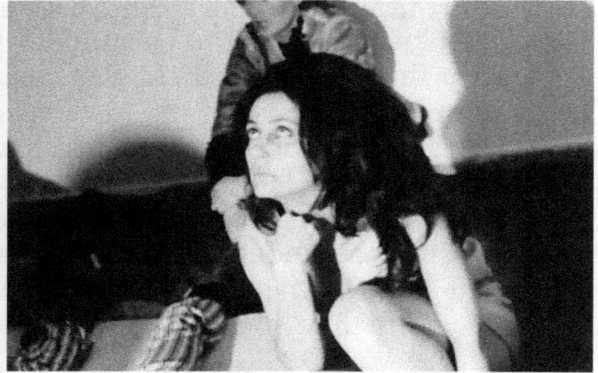

Susan Bottomly rests her eyelashes, while Allen Midgette also does his best to stay awake. This picture would later become a famous poster.

Ultra Violet awaits her cue, on location in her newly acquired, unfurnished (except for the mattresses) U.N. Plaza apartment.

David Croland: The Chelsea Hotel, how did I get here? I was with my girlfriend of three years, Susan Bottomly, and she lived here, and that was convenient for Andy, because he was filming 'Chelsea Girls'. I was in one of the rooms with Mary Woronov, Mary Whips, Mary-Mary *(laugh),* Ingrid Superstar, and Susan—the three girls in the bed. And my reaction was, "Oh, this is way too real!"

The Cheslea Hotel, home to artists and Bohemians from around the world, was also home to many of the Factory's superstars. Warhol would often find himself there, or at the next door Mexican cantina, El Quixote, which is still serving authentic sangria and margaritas. However, since we did our interviews at the Chelsea, it has changed hands. Stanley Bard, its stalwart manager who has been there forever and knew everyone and took care of them all, has been summarily ejected, along with many of the longtime residents, including Victor Bockris. It closed for renovations in 2012, but one hopes there are a few hold-outs hiding under the floorboards to haunt the invaders. We mourn the passing of yet another great New York institution.

David Croland: Stanley! Here's the guy you should be interviewing. You should talk to this prince over here. Look at him, he's the greatest—he is *it*! He knows them all. So cool. Stanley, here's a copy of my magazine (LID, the Warhol issue). Look, all your old friends are in here. The last time I saw Edie was when she lived here.

Stanley Bard: And Nico. And Susan. I knew her father, who was District Attorney of Boston.

The dark-haired Boston debutante with the flapping eyelashess and seductive smile may have reminded Warhol of a young Elizabeth Taylor and her beloved racehorse, but Mary Woronov simply wanted to break her leg and shoot her. No matter, International Velvet was a blue ribbon winner with all the boys. . .

Billy Name: Susan was just so beautiful. I photographed her in a scene from 'Four Stars', the Warhol movie with Allen Midgette. Allen is the one who played Andy on the college tours, impersonated him at Andy's request. But he was actually one of the male stars in more films than any of the others, except maybe Joe Dallesandro, who came later.

Allen Midgette: Here I am, back in a room at the Chelsea Hotel, where I used to live, and where a lot of other people from the Factory— *(laugh)*. Exactly, we're all here. Well, it was almost like a club? Yeah, strange locale. I don't even remember half of what I was doing, but I got back to New York and started working at a place called Arthur discotheque. David Croland used to come in with International Velvet. She told me she was working with Andy Warhol, and I said, "Oh, that's nice." She said, "I think he would really like you," and I said, "That's okay." Then, a week later, Andy came in and he said, "You know, I'd really like you to, well, be in my movie." I said, "Well, you've got a lot of actors already, don't you?" and he said, "Yeah, But we want a *star*." I said, "What about Gerard Malanga?" And he said something about him being too short. I already knew about his movies, and they weren't really what I wanted to do. As an actor, I always want to engage my heart. I don't want that to be separate. And so, I started telling him what *I* wanted. . . Anyway, what was I saying?

Ivy Nicholson: You were a star! That was just great not to having to go through all the Hollywood producers, and banging and having the door close. If Andy chose you, you were an immediate star. He gave us confidence. And he had style. The entire Factory was silver, so, silver goes with stars. Superstars! I loved the way he filmed some women totally nude, and they didn't even have big breasts. They were a bit droopy, but it was so natural. I told him I would not be nude. "I'm going to wear see-through panties, and don't you dare let that guy take his trousers off!" Which he did! He knew I had a fiery character and would go off once in a while. So, after I almost broke the camera, he said, "I did it to provoke you." If provoked in a movie, I look like a great actress.

Allen Midgette: Andy says, "Oh, *Ivy's* going to direct this movie," and I'm thinking, "Oh shit." She gives me a piece of cloth about that big, and I have to wrap that around me with no clothes on. And in the center of the room is this incredible Egyptian lion Sphinx. Andy says, "Okay, let's shoot in front of this." Ultra says, *(mimicking her French accent)* "What should I say, Andy?" He says, "Well, tell me about anything, talk about what you had for breakfast." And she says, "Oh, I like bread, and butter, and marmalade." I'm thinking, you're sitting on a sphinx on LSD and listening to this shit. It's like, unbelievable.

Ultra Violet: I don't know if they were on drugs, because the thing with a Warhol movie, they would *carry* on, and they stopped when the film ran out. It was all improvisation, which I was not quite used to—to be yourself.

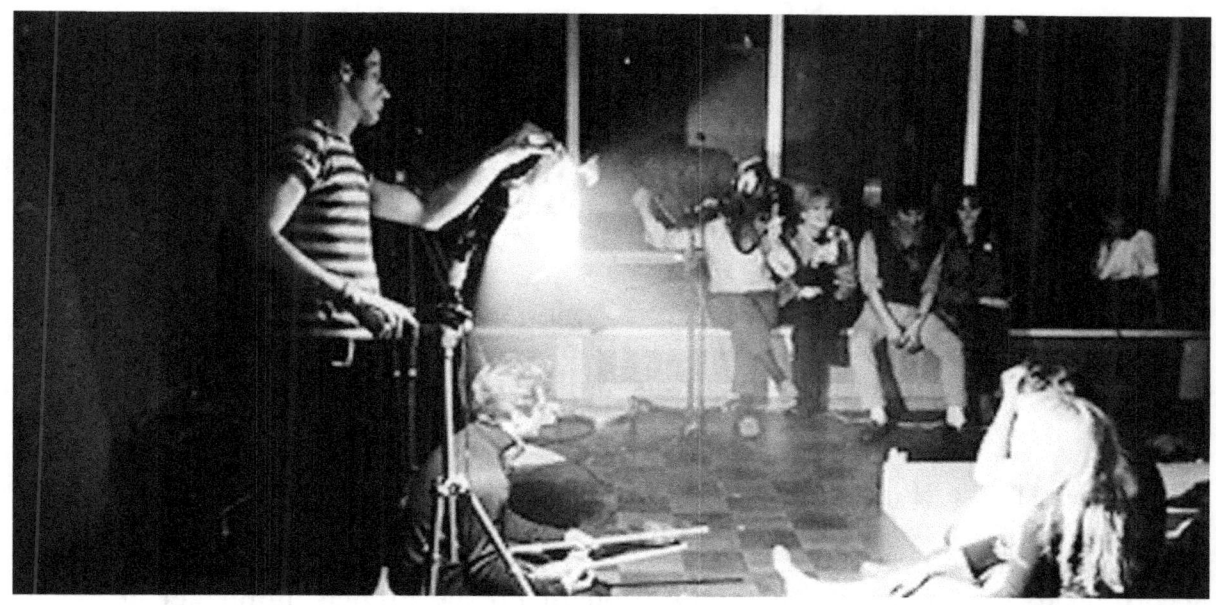

Billy is busy setting up lights in Ultra Violet's apartment, a non-indigenous flower planted in the luxurious United Nation's Plaza skyscraper. (Billy Name Collection)

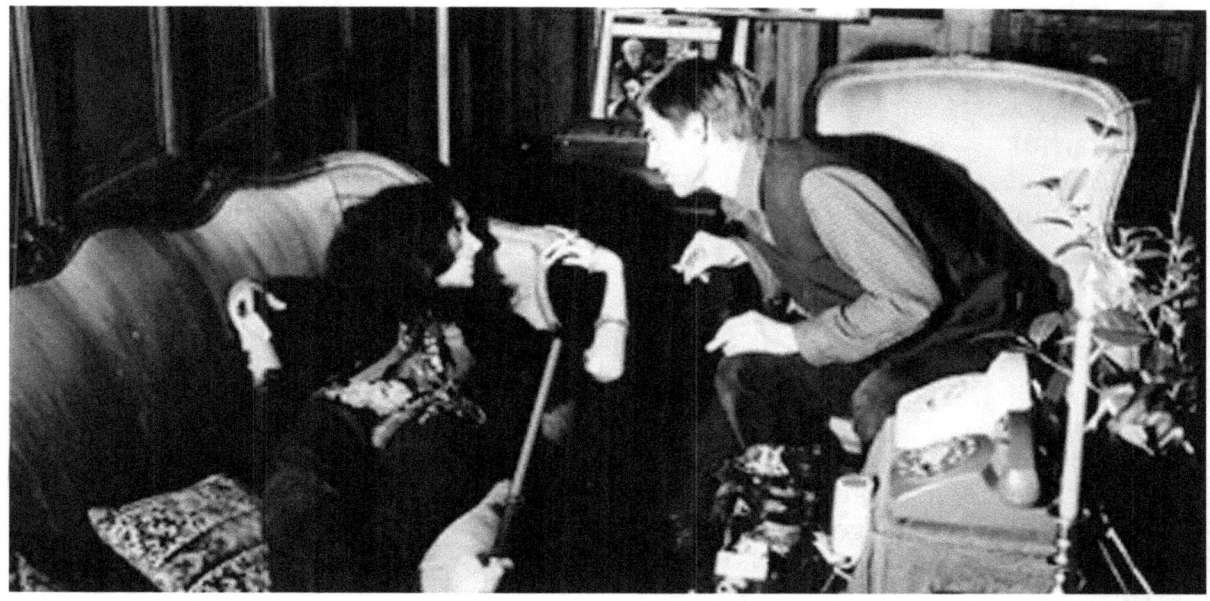

Allen Midgette offers Orion a little puff of homegrown on the film set. (Photo: Billy Name)

Mary Woronov: . . . Well, I do not know about *that*. We were having—I wouldn't call it fun. I mean, most of the time what we did was wait for something, I do not know what. It was like: "Are we going here? I don't know, are we going there? Well, where is Warhol going? Well, I don't know. Well, we will sit around and wait. But, so and so left. Yeah, and so and so didn't. Well, lets make a film about a telephone call." I mean it was nuts! It wasn't fun, no one was having fun. It was really very tedious.

Ultra Violet: So, I think those Warhol films, though they are real sleepers, the concept was extraordinary. I think it was minimalism in film.

Ultra Violet, Bibbe Hansen and Brigid Berlin were among the few women who were privy to Warhol's musings on the filmmakers who had influenced him, as opposed to what he was prone to tell unsuspecting journalists, who wrote it all down as gospel. According to Brigid Berlin, when she brought up the French filmmaker Jean Luc Godard, Warhol replied, "Oh, fuck Godard. And it's not *God*ard. You're putting him up there, in *Heaven*." Godard, still down here in 2014 at the age of 83, is in post-production on his 116th film, a selection for the Cannes Film Festival.

Interviewer Aaron Sloan *(to Warhol)*
Whom do you consider to be most influential on your method of filmmaking?

Andy Warhol
Well, uh, I guess I'm influenced by everybody. But I like the way Godard works, just because I think he's bringing television out to the movies. And I think that's what we're trying to do, too.

Interviewer
When you set the cameras up, do you think that you're going in a certain direction?

Andy Warhol
Uh, I guess we haven't really thought about it. We're doing mostly experimenting right now. We're just learning how to use the camera. I guess we started out in one direction and now we're going in another direction.

Interviewer
What direction do you think you started? . . .

Andy Warhol

. . . Aaaah, just funny pictures. I don't know, they always say that nothing happens in a movie, but we're trying to get something to happen.

Interviewer

Well, should something happen in the spectator's mind, or should it happen in the *mis en scène* of your approach to the character?

Andy Warhol

Uuuhh, I believe, both ways.

Warhol's by-now signature drone was captured with varying degrees of success by nearly everyone in the Factory, especially Allen Midgette, the reluctant thespian who wound up most effectively mimicking him.

Allen Midgette: We were just shooting. There was no name. I mean, there was no *script!* How could there be a name? The names came afterward, and that was really all there was. I never in my life believed that these would be considered films. But, I have been wrong about a lot of things. Which is cool. It doesn't matter; there's no right or wrong anyway. It's all up for grabs.

Ivy Nicholson: I remember in one scene, I wore an orange Bill Blass gown that Andy gave me. He had me talk about my life, my childhood, my parents. I remember going there and falling asleep like everyone else did.

Jonas Mekas: That's when he was permitting people to improvise. Andy never scolded them, never disapproved, they were very free. When the sound period began, they were permitted to improvise, to say whatever they wanted to, to unload themselves. They became like psychoanalysts. . . So, it did not come out of thin air. There was already the background. The passion was there, for cinema

Billy Name: We shot reels, and reels, and reels of film, which most people would say are "nothing or boring or uninteresting," but people who curate his films know about them as art pieces. . . And Jonas Mekas did for Andy's film what Henry Geldzahler did for Andy's paintings. He was the imprimatur who said it was art.

Jonas Mekas: I was invited to introduce an Andy Warhol exhibition at one of the museums in Vienna. . . And, they decided to screen 'Empire'. So I introduced the film, and said, "I wonder how many of you will stay to the end. When we showed it in New York, back in '63, forty people stayed from three hundred." Here, there was about one hundred people. So, the film starts. I go out, meet some friends, have some wine, come back when the film ends. Nobody has left! A woman comes up and says to the audience, "Since all of you stayed, we will have to have a *lottery* for this round trip ticket, New York-Vienna." The newspapers in Vienna had made it into a contest! They said, "An eight hour film, how boring." So they offered a free plane ticket for the one who stayed to the end. But they *all* stayed, so now they will have to have a lottery. I was crushed, of course.

Billy Name: Jonas Mekas wasn't sure about the films, because so many of his film-makers in the Co-op stable, so to speak, were of the avant-garde world, and all these heterosexual guys didn't really find an interest in Warhol's work, and didn't think it was art. Jonas said, "Because these people, serious people are questioning this, I have to sit down and look at all of Warhol's films." So he did. And he decided that it wasn't frivolous, that it wasn't surface culture and it wasn't something to be dismissed. So as Henry Geldzahler proclaimed Warhol and Pop artists were actually art, Jonas Mekas proclaimed, contrary to the avant-garde dismissal of "this frivolous stuff," that Warhol's film work was serious art.

Henry Geldzahler: I think Andy Warhol's imagery and consistency has made him one of the leaders in the Pop art field. . . Whether that's enough, I'm not sure.

In the archival film we used, Geldzahler is nervously watching for Warhol's reaction, and gets one. Warhol forgoes for the camera the usual deadpan expression and looks quite taken aback. Warhol and Geldzahler had a falling out soon after. Geldzahler not only was preoccupied with a new love interest, but he had also lost confidence in Warhol's Pop art, which was losing its cutting edge. According to New Yorker art critic Peter Schjeldahl in the May, 2000 issue: "The original silk-screened paintings now suffer from a worldly condition, that, when new, they brilliantly announced: the takeover of visual culture by reproductions." Warhol must have already known that by 1966. He was now more interested in filming, and becoming more of a personality than an artist. Henry, in his capacity as a curator at the Metropolitan Museum of Art, excluded Warhol from his artists chosen for that year's Venice Biennale, of which he was the American commissioner.

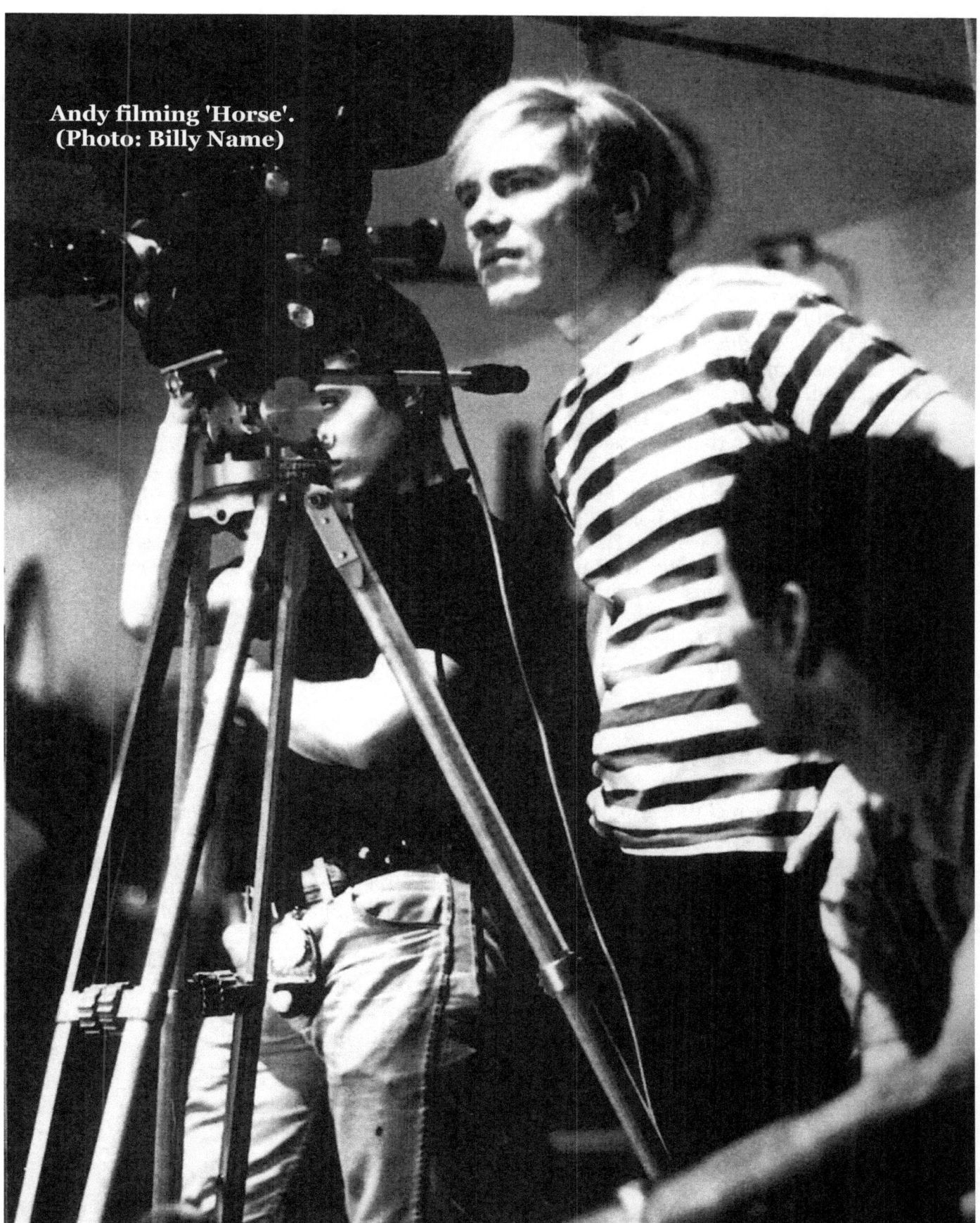

Andy filming 'Horse'.
(Photo: Billy Name)

Henry Geldzahler: I finally understood what Andy was doing with people, and I had to get out of there to save myself. It was so unattractive I walked away. There was a blackboard in the studio and I wrote: *Andy Warhol can't paint anymore, and he can't make films yet.* That's when he was between the two. But he never forgot that.

Vincent Fremont: People claim that Andy always said he didn't know what to do next. He did take ideas from people. He'd ask what he should do, and everybody thought that what *they* said, he would do. . . It was a filtering process. Andy would edit—he was a master at that. But he ultimately made the final decision. Later on, when I used to watch him do portrait sittings, he'd ask a few people around him, "Well, what should I do? What colors?" It was a sounding out. Isn't it better to ask somebody? They get the impression that it comes through them.

Billy Name: Once he became famous as a fine artist, he desired to equal that as a filmmaker. He wanted to portray glamour, because to him glamour was the most powerful thing in the world. He wanted to make stars. So the focus was either Ondine, Edie Sedgwick, Viva, the Lucille Ball of underground movies, Mario Montez, Nico, Allen Midgette—his Superstars.

Interviewer, British Broadcasting
Andy, what do you think it feels like to be a Superstar?

Andy Warhol
. . . Uh, I don't know.

In our sixties newsreel film clip, the cheeky young male interviewer lay stretched out next to Warhol in a large bed in London, while outside in the night, crickets chirped, frogs croaked, and owls hooted, courtesy of my Hollywood sound effects. Warhol's trademark pause was soooo long, that I thought I'd better fill the space. I also larded the following screen tests with music, though this time I doubt Warhol would have approved. The whole idea of the tests, and we watched many, seemed more a test of endurance, the subject squirming and fidgeting in painful silence. As Jonas Mekas told us, "The camera is running, and there is you. Now what do you do?" Well, if you are poet and Factory Prime Minister Gerard Malanga, and you need a good head shot of yourself for promotion purposes, you come up with the whole idea. . .

Gerard Malanga: The screen tests started because I needed a publicity still for all my poetry world adventures, and I thought what a nice idea, to maybe do a photo of me in some movie. So I asked Andy to shoot a three-minute portrait of me, which became one of the subjects for the 'Thirteen Most Beautiful Boys'. And then we just continued doing it—Andy and I kept bringing people to the Factory. I shot some of them; Andy shot some of them. There has been a bit of contention about that, if it was a considered a true collaboration. For me it was film archiving. Andy was doing a living portrait, a living record of that person. Whether they were invited to the Factory or they happened to come by, we would say, "Let's do your screen test." None of these screen tests really amounted to giving those people the opportunity to go on in the underground film world. It was kind of a parody on Hollywood. Hollywood would make a thirty-second screen test, we would do a three-minute one.

Billy Name: But it's not the *star*, it's the final *film* that's Andy's favorite. There are a lot of Edie Sedgwick films where Andy would just say, "Oh, she really didn't do anything." But there are some where she would just be so the divine Edie that it doesn't matter. Her screen test photos were just so beautiful. *She* was just so beautiful! I shot them simultaneous with Andy doing the filmed screen test.

Edie Sedgwick's first film for the Warhol Factory had been 'Vinyl', where she had simply stretched out on Billy Name's silver storage trunk, smoking cigarettes while Gerard was 'sadistically' tortured, writhing in metaphysical agony. Billy told us they'd had an S&M expert on the set, who had probably consulted for free. . . Warhol's decision to drop his new discovery into the film had been resented by the others, especially Gerard, since the project had been 'conceived' without the gentler sex in mind. Yet her silent fleeting presence had jumped off the screen, and she'd immediately been transformed into Warhol's favorite. . .

Gerard Malanga: It *was* against my wishes at first. I was a little upset. I thought, "This is supposed to be an all-boy movie." I mean, what's a girl doing in this? Because Andy threw her in at the last minute. But then it worked out fine. She just sat on the silver trunk doing her nails, and actually she did my hair. Billy has that shot where she was teasing my hair. That was before we just, you know, so it's one of these great moments. . . The opening shot of the movie is a close-up of my head, my face, I think, and then Andy zooms back, and there's Edie.

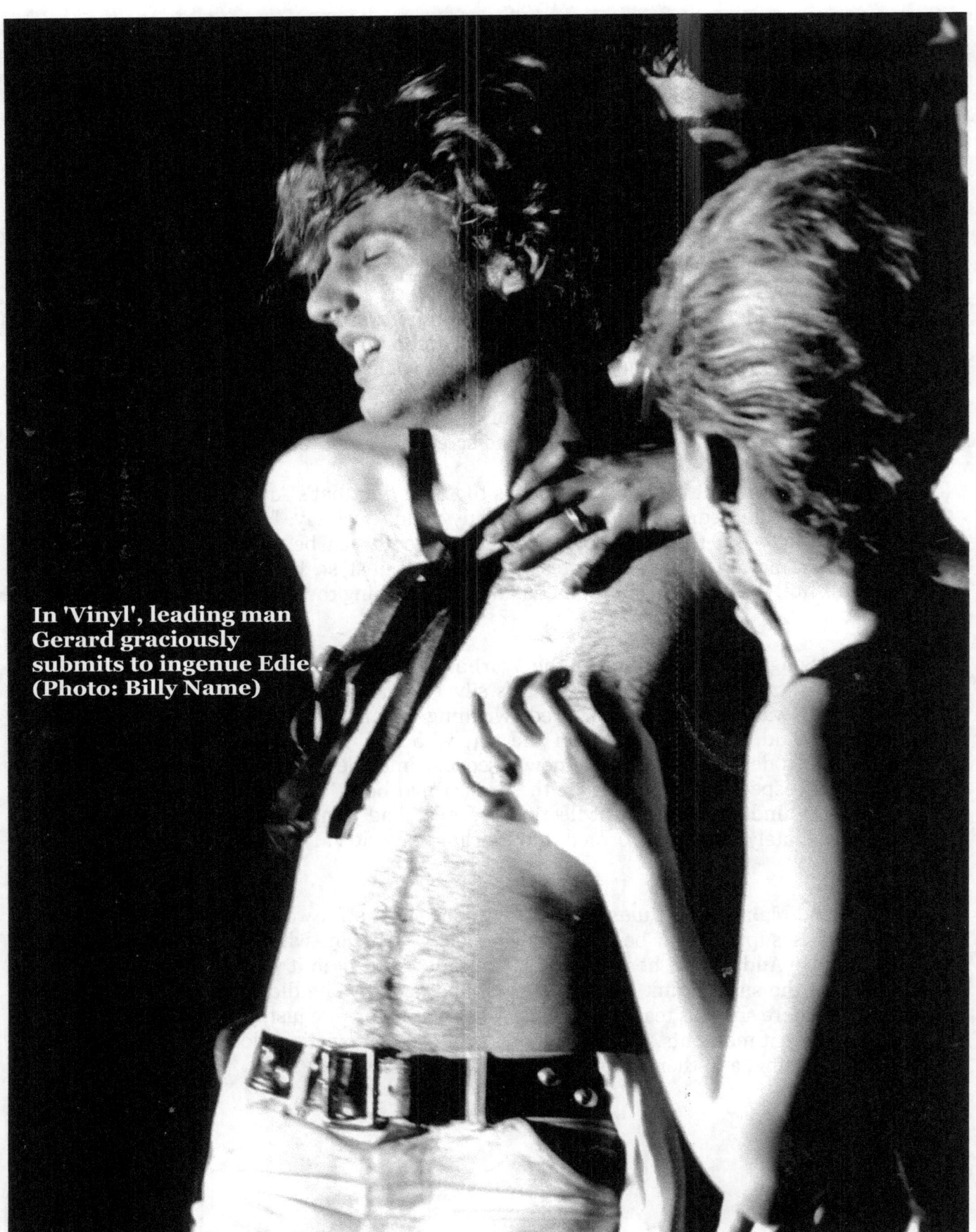

In 'Vinyl', leading man Gerard graciously submits to ingenue Edie. (Photo: Billy Name)

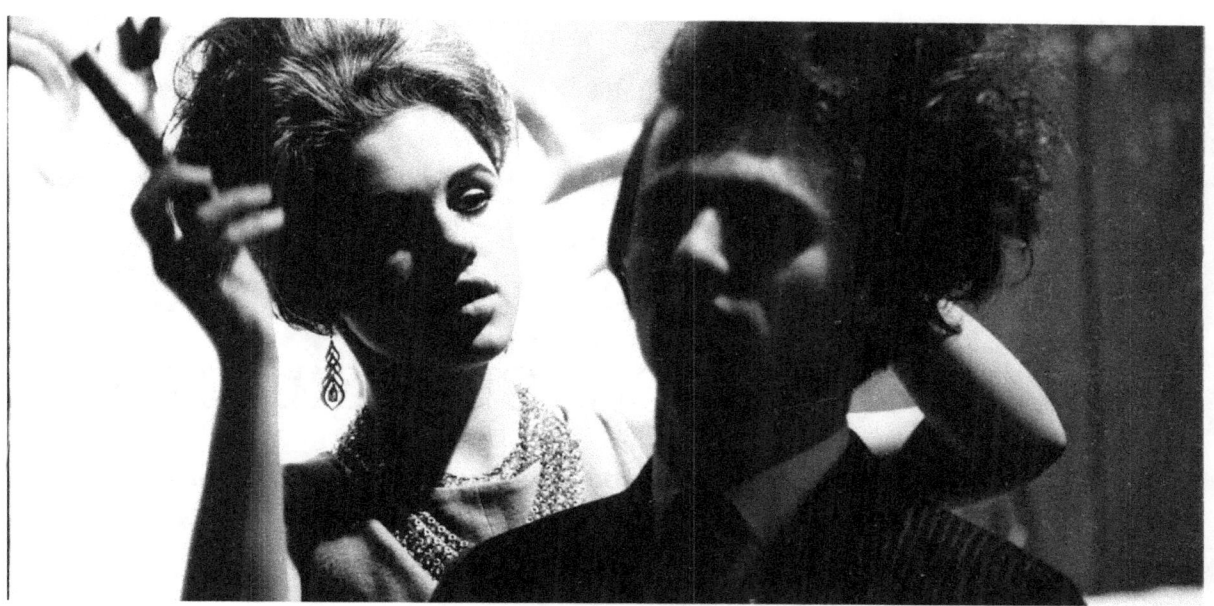

Edie teases Gerard, and his hair during filming of 'Vinyl'.

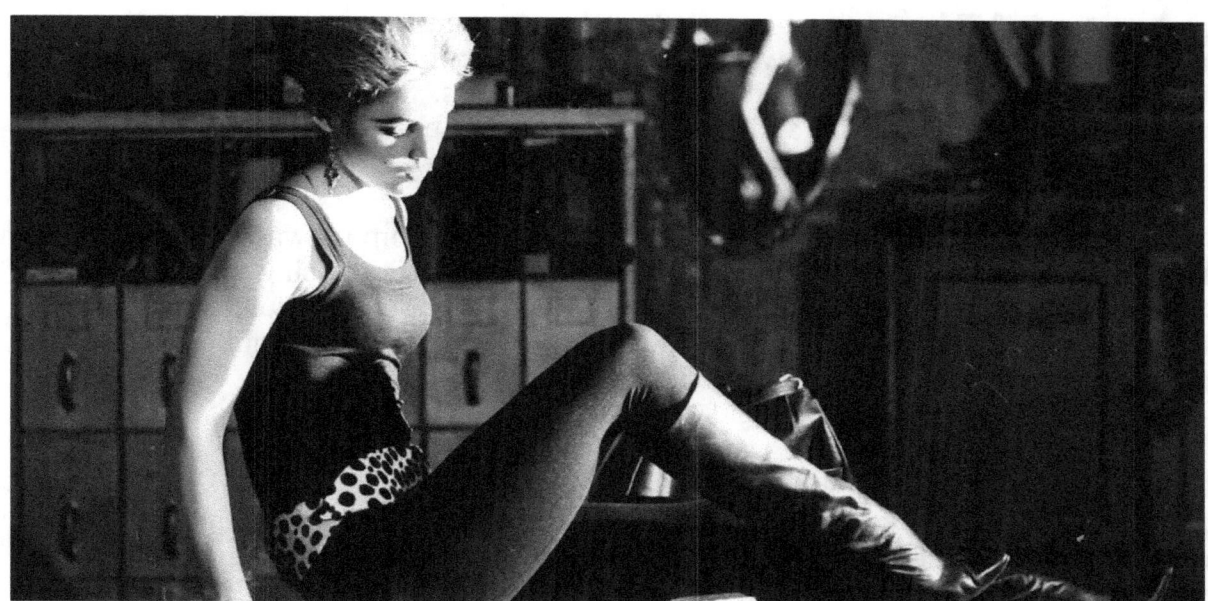

Edie perches on Billy Name's Trunk for 'Vinyl'. (Photos: Billy Name)

EDIE SEDGWICK, SILVER GIRL

Andy Warhol would like to have been a charming, well-borne debutante from Boston, like Edie Sedgwick.
—Truman Capote

Gerard Malanga: Well, first of all, Andy was a real social climber. Right away, he already knew that Edie came from wealth and background, and tradition and good name, good breeding. Andy was impressed of course. "Oh come to the Factory, let's make a movie!" Edie was very open to that, because she had just arrived in New York a few weeks earlier, and she was looking to do something with her life. She did a little bit of painting, but Edie didn't really have a focus. She needed a grounding; she needed an anchor. So this is an ideal situation. It was bees to the honey.

We unearthed extraordinary footage of Edie Sedgwick from the vast archives of CBS news, reported by newscaster Dave Dugan. In it, Edie is dancing at a party in the Silver Factory, and the best part of the sequence is Warhol quietly standing by himself in the background, as usual, watching the frantic activity on a video monitor, a plastic party cup clamped firmly to his mouth.

Dave Dugan, CBS News
Andy Warhol not only uses film, but also videotape. At this party, he just lets his camera observe. The center of his attention is his superstar Edie Sedgwick, who says she left her society background in California to 'find' herself in New York. She has no acting background, but that doesn't matter, because in Warhol films, she just moves and talks as she pleases.

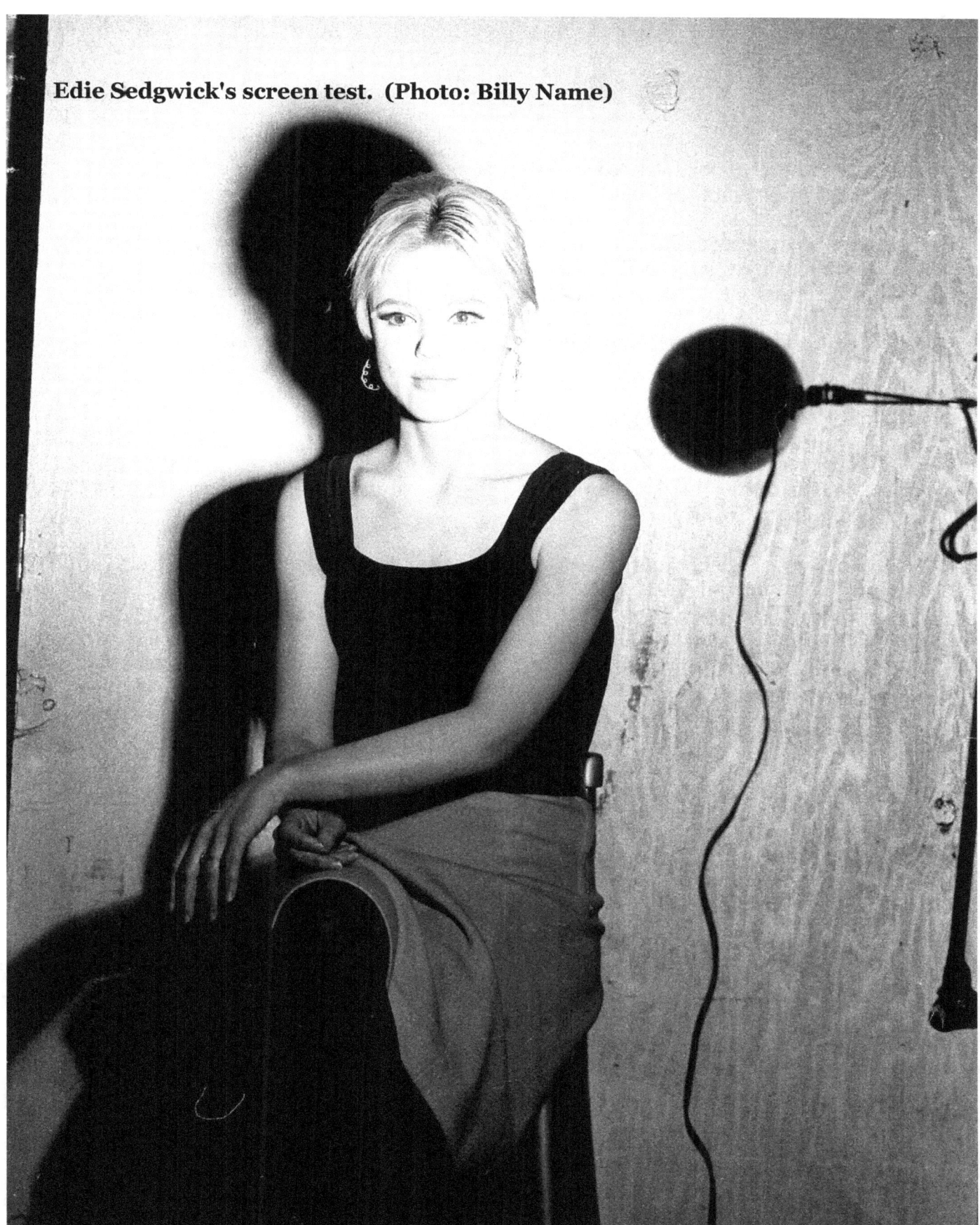

Edie Sedgwick's screen test. (Photo: Billy Name)

Gerard Malanga: 'Poor Little Rich Girl' was made just after we made 'Vinyl', and this is when Andy embraces mistakes. We shot the film, two reels, brought it to the lab, brought it back to the Factory, screened it, and then we discovered that there was an element floating around in the lens, meaning we were out of focus. So we shot the film again a few days later in Edie's apartment, and got it in focus this time. Then Andy decided that we were going to open the film with the first reel that was out of focus, and close it with the second reel that was in focus, so it was an interesting concept. Do you think that Hollywood would accept an out-of-focus movie?

Interviewer, CBS News
How does it feel to act in a Warhol movie?

Edie Sedgwick
Oh, it's so true to life, it's not even acting. It's just so candid, like the camera isn't there at all, like Andy says.

Victor Bockris: Edie became 'it' very quickly. Andy was not a guy who sat around thinking about something. He walked across the room, got hold of it and said, "Let's do this." That, I think, was one of the greatest reasons for his success. He and Edie made eleven films between March and September of 1965. Certainly four or five of them are fairly well known in the canon: 'Beauty #2', 'Poor Little Rich Girl', 'Kitchen', 'Outer and Inner Space' and so on. She was Andy's favorite, because she was the ultimate. He had a goldmine in Edie, and he knew it. "We're going to make Edie the queen of the Factory."

Billy Name: I photographed Andy in the prelude to making an Edie Sedgwick movie called 'Inner and Outer Space'. We had one of the first video cameras from Norelco; Philips gave Andy one for promotional purposes. When Andy made his movies, he just had this dynamic in him, this wonderful something radiating! I would shoot Andy shooting, and people would just pop in, stop by and say "hi," like Eric Anderson the folk singer, with his guitar. Edie's friends. They would just carry on having a wonderful time. For the movie 'Vinyl', with Edie, Gerard Malanga and Ondine, we got an S&M adviser from a leather bar in the Bowery. For 'Girls in Prison', that was when we got the Auricon sound camera, with the expensive tripod for shooting Edie and her girlfriend in 'Prison', Bibbe Hansen.

At the end of Episode I, we used footage of Bibbe and Edie from the original version of 'Prison', though it was shot in early '65, using it to foretell what was coming, much like a movie trailer. So, for the nitpickers out there—sorry! It's sure to happen again. This is a picture book, not a history book. We sold the show anyway, post TV life, to (as I mentioned) hundreds of universities, despite this laxness on our part. They even upon occassion invite us to visit, as Warhol himself once did. Also asked to speak on that college circuit: Bibbe Hansen, who has indelible memories of Edie.

Bibbe Hansen: I felt a strong connection to Edie, much like the older sister I didn't have. She was pretty self-absorbed. but she could be kind. She would spend hours and hours putting on makeup. This could be, and was, quite a pain in the ass. People are waiting; we had reservations, places to be—it just went on and on. . . But when she was done, she looked fabulous! I loved to watch her. I actually learned a lot about makeup and style from her. She had a fabulous style, and she did it all herself.

We licensed footage of Edie from the Warhol Museum, a clip from a movie called 'Restaurant', which was basically Andy filming Edie, Ondine and friends in one of her favorites, *L'Avventura*. Edie is dressed divinely, perfectly made up, chain-smoking, and, as usual, picking up the tab. Suffering from Bulimia before it became a starlet byword, Edie went out every night, ordering two or three main courses which she would then vomit. . . But Warhol kept her busy working on his movies. Earlier that morning, he had filmed 'Poor Little Rich Girl', and in the afternoon he shot Beauty #2, in his same static, black and white 'Godardian' style. . .

Danny Fields: She became 'Girl of the Year' in about six minutes, and everyone wrote about her style and her short hair and giant earrings and her gamine 'Breakfast at Tiffany's' kind of thing in New York, in the midst of all its evil and squalor. She'd take us all out to dinner at the best restaurants. Then, once a month was drug store bill time, and we would go to some restaurant and get a big table, and open up all her bills from about five drug stores. We'd put them in separate piles, and count up how much her make-up bill was for the month: "Why would you have to spend nine hundred dollars on lipstick at Mayfair?" . . . "Oh, they've got a whole new bunch of colors, and I had to try them out." We'd add it up, thousands and thousands of dollars. And she'd say, "Oh, let's just eat," and put them all away in an old shopping bag, and it wouldn't come up until the next month.

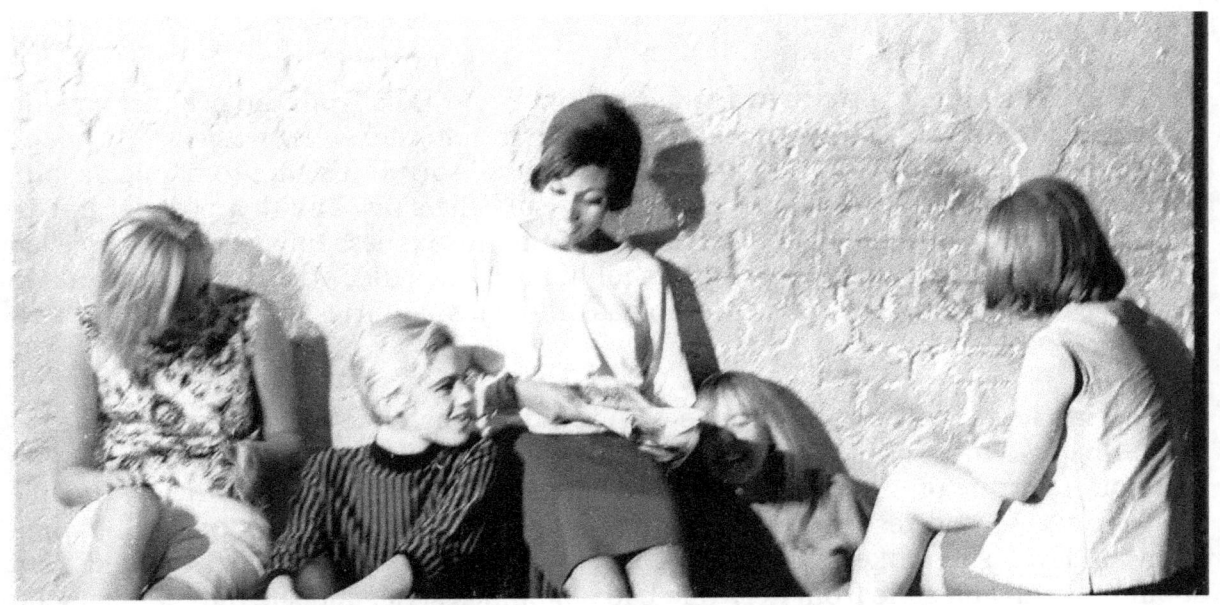

Edie and 'Prison' castmates, including Pat Hartley, center, and Bibbe Hansen, 2nd from right. (Photo: Billy Name)

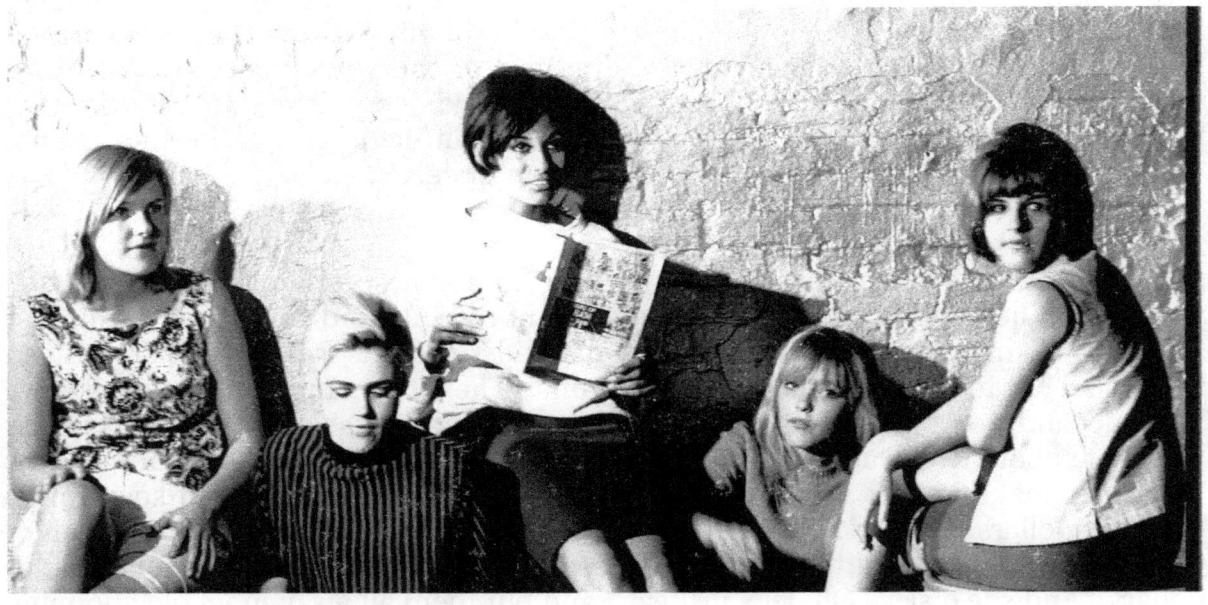

Another still from 'Prison' (Photo: Billy Name)

Edie's legendary spending, eating disorders and substance abuses were obvious attempts to fill a void in her life. For those of us afflicted, no real therapy existed unless one checked in for a prolonged stint at Payne-Whitney. In 1962, Edie, then a patient at the tony Silver Hill in Connecticut, would throw up lunch, then 'escape' into town for a bit of retail therapy—yet another giddy shopping spree. Five years later would come the electroshock treatment. Today, Edie would be invited on 'Celebrity Rehab' or have her very own show on 'E'.

Danny Fields: Everyone gets to the point where the family will try to cut you off. Who could blame them? Why do you need this wild person going around and spending your hard inherited money? It's coming from the trusts. But what are you going to say: "Don't charge it?" She could never *not* say, "Charge it!" So she was the princess amongst queens (*laugh*). Of course, I fell in love with her, though at that point, girls were really not my thing.

Miss Sedgwick sauntered into frame in the film, delicately sat on an arm of the ratty semen-encrusted Factory couch, and crossed her long legs. After licensing bits of Edie from the Warhol Museum at $100 per second (!), we were giddy with the discovery of this rare footage. Clad in her trademark leotard and tee, she does her makeup and perches on a stool for a Warhol screen test as Paul Morrissey checks the lighting. The close-ups of Edie, smiling into a dusty cracked mirror summoned up for us the crash in her life that was just around the corner. I was startled to see the same amazing earrings that she had worn when last I'd seen her, over forty years ago. So was Bibbi Hansen. . .

Bibbe Hansen: Nobody had ever seen anything like them. All the girls wanted earrings like Edie's. I swiped mine from a little shop down on St. Mark's Place. But no one looked as good in them as Edie did, with that wonderful neck and short hair. Edie was actually the second choice to star in 'Prison' with me. The first had been Jane Holzer, but she had made the gossip columns on a couple of Andy scandals, and it had gotten back to her family. So, she was being cautious about any raunchy movie. And of course, there was a secret plan to make the movie salacious. She would be a society girl who had just done some crank, and shows up in youth hall overnight. I would come on to her, a sort of dyke confrontation. Jane was out for that. Chuck (Wein) said, "Edie would be great! Let's get Edie to do it."

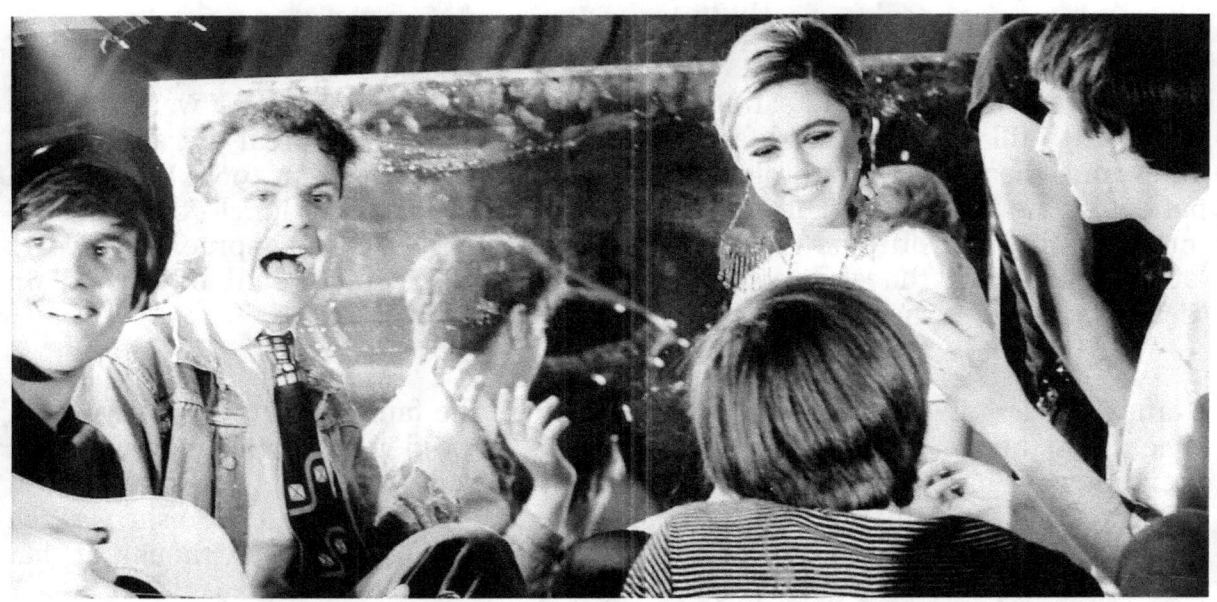

Edie, always the center of attention, being filmed at the Factory with her Cambridge friends. Folksinger Eric Anderson and Donald Lyons at left. (Photo: Billy Name)

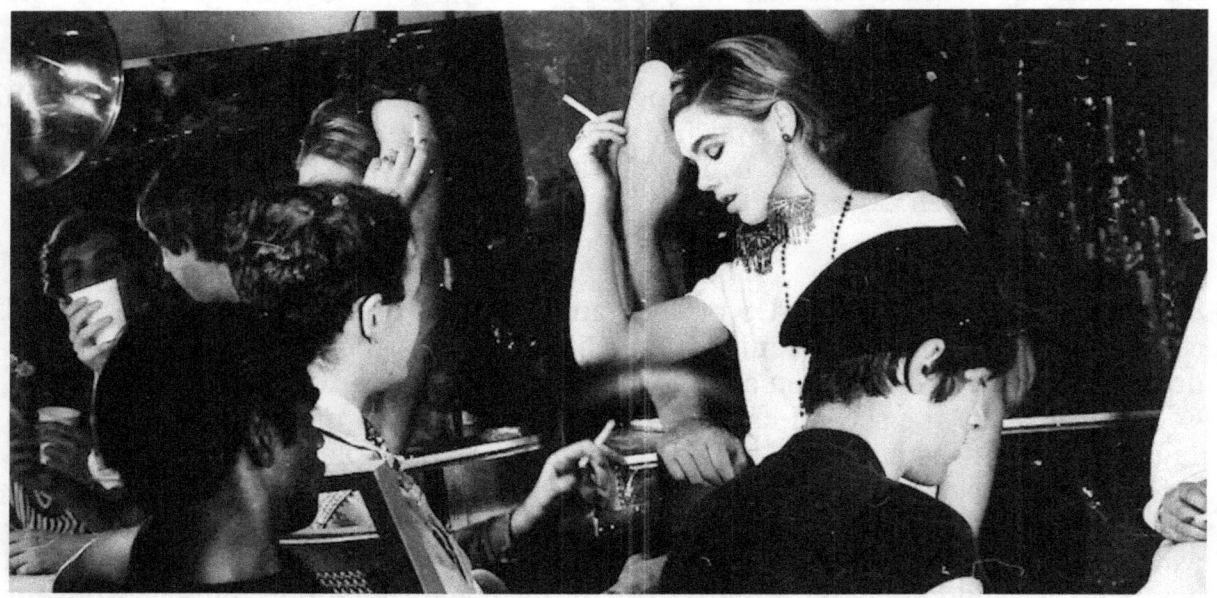

Edie, exhausted and crashing. (Photo: Billy Name)

Gerard Malanga: Edie was Andy's first real discovery, and probably still his greatest discovery in terms of the kind of star personality. . . That was the closest probably Andy would come to Hollywood in a sense, the period when he was making the films with Edie Sedgwick.

Ultra Violet: Edie was an astonishing beauty. She was glamour personified. She danced like nobody else, she had million dollar legs. She could dance all night, and everybody would stare at her when she got on the floor. When I met her she was the Girl of the Year. She had modeled for Vogue and whatever. But she was a child who never really grew up. . . I loved Edie from the beginning, because I could feel she was extremely sensitive and authentic and fragile, and she did prove to be fragile in her life—an extraordinary, meteoric, catastrophe.

Andy Warhol *(from 'POPism')*
. . . A girl always looked more beautiful and fragile when she was about to have a nervous breakdown.

Victor Bockris: One of the things that Andy shows us is that men are often jealous of women because they want to *be* them. And if Andy could have been any of his superstars, he would have been Edie, even though she had the worst life, by a long shot, and was a totally tortured soul. Edie was burning alive. Andy did like to watch that. He did have a fascination with . . . incineration.

By the fall of '65, as Edie was losing her footing at the Factory, her close friend Chuck Wein had come up with an idea for a movie (the aforementioned 'My Hustler'). When Warhol, cast and crew took off for a beach house on Fire Island, Edie was crushed that they took along her French roommate, Genevieve Charbon, as the female lead. Since Wein considered the film his idea (there was no script), he tried to convince Morrissey and Malanga to help him make the movie without Warhol, even going so far as to spike the orange juice with LSD, an oft told tale in Factory lore. This was a bad idea on many levels, although it made for fun photographs, which we used in the series. It did not, however, endear Wein to anyone. He scurried back to New York, to face Edie. Feeling hurt and betrayed by both Warhol and her one-time confidant, Edie continued her descent. When Warhol took her to his first American retrospective at the Institute of Contemporary Art in Philadelphia, they were still considered the 'iconic couple', but they were breaking up, as Edie slid further into a tailspin of drugs.

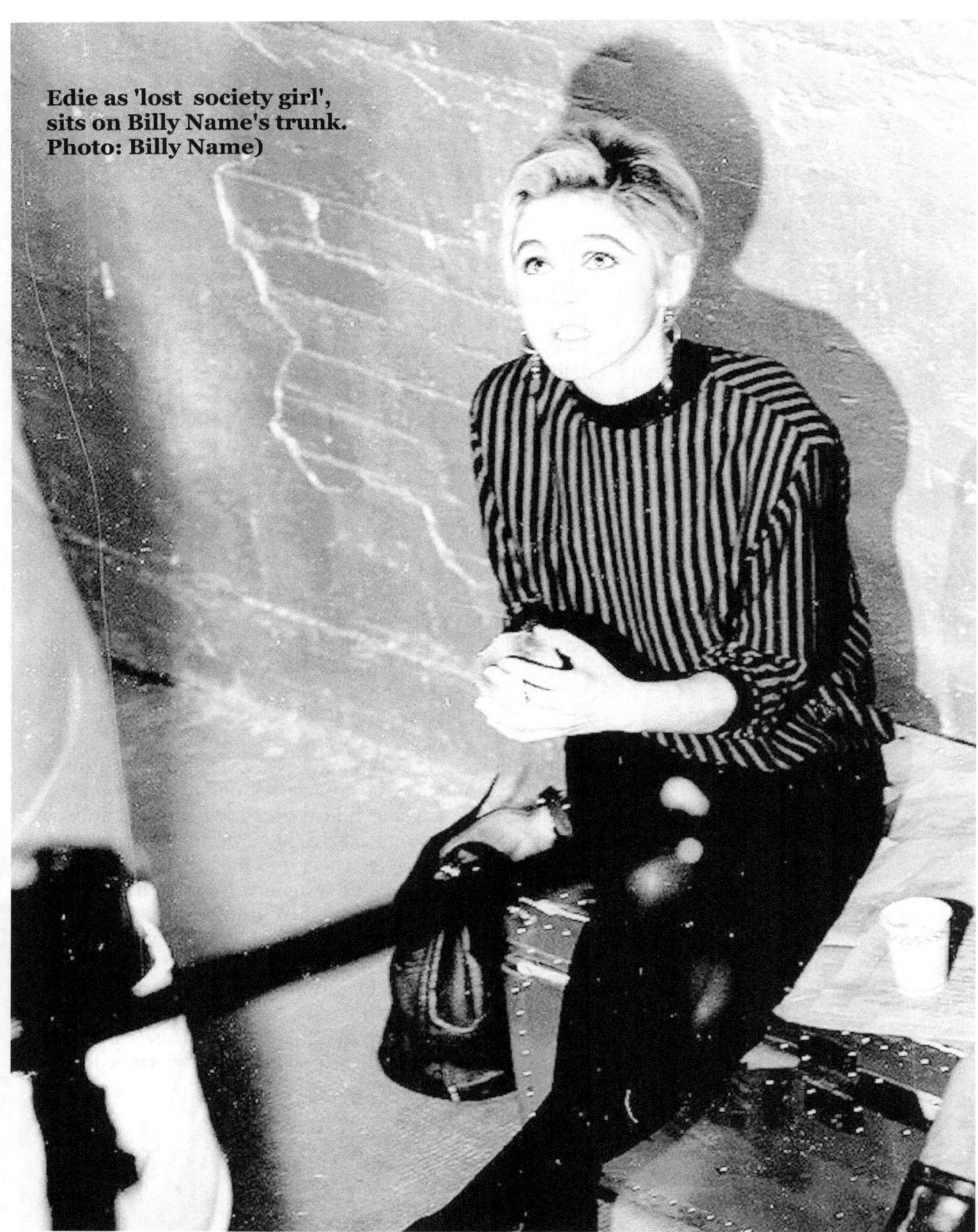

Edie as 'lost society girl', sits on Billy Name's trunk.
Photo: Billy Name)

David Croland: I liked Edie, but she was quiet. She had already become less involved with Andy. She had done her movies; she had done the scene. Edie became more introverted. She was still in New York, but all her iconic pictures had already been published. But Edie Sedgwick was still 'The Girl', and I was a little intimidated by her. She was older than Susan and myself. Not much older, but old enough to have seen exactly what it was like to be with Andy and the scene for two years. And what it did to someone.

Billy Name: Jonas (Mekas) said, "Andy, why don't you do some kind of Warhol exposition or something?" So we decided it would be an Edie Sedgwick 'festival'. And this is the point where Edie had gotten involved with Bob Dylan. Actually, the undercurrent was that she was having this torrid love affair with Bobby Neuwirth, Dylan's best friend, and she was also getting into amphetamines. At her apartment Ondine was being her housemaid, giving her amphetamines. It was like this little French movie. She was having an affair with Neuwirth, but the story was that Dylan was in love with her and wrote all these songs about her and offered to be her manager. She said, "I am tired of making these films with Andy Warhol. I don't like the scripts; I don't want to learn the scripts. He makes me look ridiculous."

Nat Finkelstein: Dylan's crowd felt that some sort of a choice had to be made. It was ridiculous—he would send 'raiders'. That's how he got his hands on Edie Sedgwick, at Panna Grady's place after the shooting of 'Lupe Velez', and Bobbie Neuwirth comes walking in, and says something to Edie. She was with me, so I was an actual witness to this. Bobby said, "He would like to see you, and listen here, I brought for you these two sugar cubes of LSD." And he fed her a little bit of acid. At that point I walked away. I wasn't going to score with her that night (*laugh*). I was not going to be competing with Dylan. . . Now Robert Heide, the guy who produced 'The Bed', tells the story of how he and Edie and Allen Ginsberg were sitting in the Kettle of Fish. . .

Robert Heide: Andy used to come down to the Village and I would meet him. He bought clothes at the Leather Man, and he'd had a black leather suit and a blue suede one made. He said, "Meet me at the Kettle of Fish." I get to the place. Andy's not there, but Edie is, and I sit down and order a beer. Earlier, I'd been wandering around town with her in this limousine, but now tears are coming out of her eyes. I asked her about 'Lupe'. I had, at Andy's request, written a script for Edie, but she couldn't memorize the lines, so it had turned into an improvisation. But anyway, (*mimicking Edie*): "I can't get close to him. I just can't get anywhere, I don't even know who he is!" I thought she was talking about Andy, because she would sometimes ramble on. At that moment, Andy comes in carrying these two bags >

from the Leather Man. "Oh gee, how's everything?" Then a limousine pulls up, and it's Bob Dylan coming out, and I realize oh, that's the limousine we've been riding around in all over town. Bob's wearing dark glasses. It's his 'Blonde on Blonde' period, with the blond curly hair, afro style, pointy shoes. He's kind of wasted. So they sit for a while, and he looks at Edie and says, "Let's split", so they go. Andy is still there. He was very upset by this. She must have told Dylan where we were going. . .

Nat Finkelstein: . . . Dylan grabbed Edie by the hand and said, "Let's go to your hotel." On her way out she turned to Heide and said "I'm his love slave." Well, the end of the story is supposedly Dylan was making her a star, writing songs for her, and why wasn't she getting paid by Warhol? The manipulation worked like that. "Why weren't you getting paid? Look at all this money Andy is making on these films!" Andy wasn't making any money on these films at that point, but it was still planted in her head that Andy was making so much money, and she could be a great star.

In his capacity as advisor and sympathetic ear to Edie, Nat was privy to confidentialities she did not share with most Factory regulars, whose loyalties would naturally remain with Warhol. While Edie was dissembling, Nat suggested she pull herself back from the Warhol machine, but made no attempt steer her in Dylan's direction, since Nat, ever hopeful, thought he might still get lucky. . . Gerard Malanga, who knew better, had his own idea of why Edie finally bolted Andy for what she hoped were greener pastures. . .

Gerard Malanga: I believe Edie was misinformed and also ill-advised by outsiders, who said, "Hey, this Andy Warhol should be paying you!" So the seed was planted. Christmas week of 1965 we were all having dinner at, I forget the name of this restaurant; it was on the West Side near Lincoln Center (The Ginger Man). Paul Morrissey was there, and some from the Velvet Underground. At that point, her allowance had been reduced to five hundred dollars a month, just about enough to pay her rent. She still had her charges covered by her father at certain restaurants; she could just sign the check and send the bill off to Dad. And Andy just held tight. "I do not have any money, I can't pay you, I can't pay you." He was trying to convince Edie. He was getting very nervous, saying, "At some point we are all going to get rich." Edie just could not wait around any longer, and she literally, physically, left the restaurant. She made a phone call, came back and said, "I am leaving." She probably called somebody in the Bob Dylan camp.

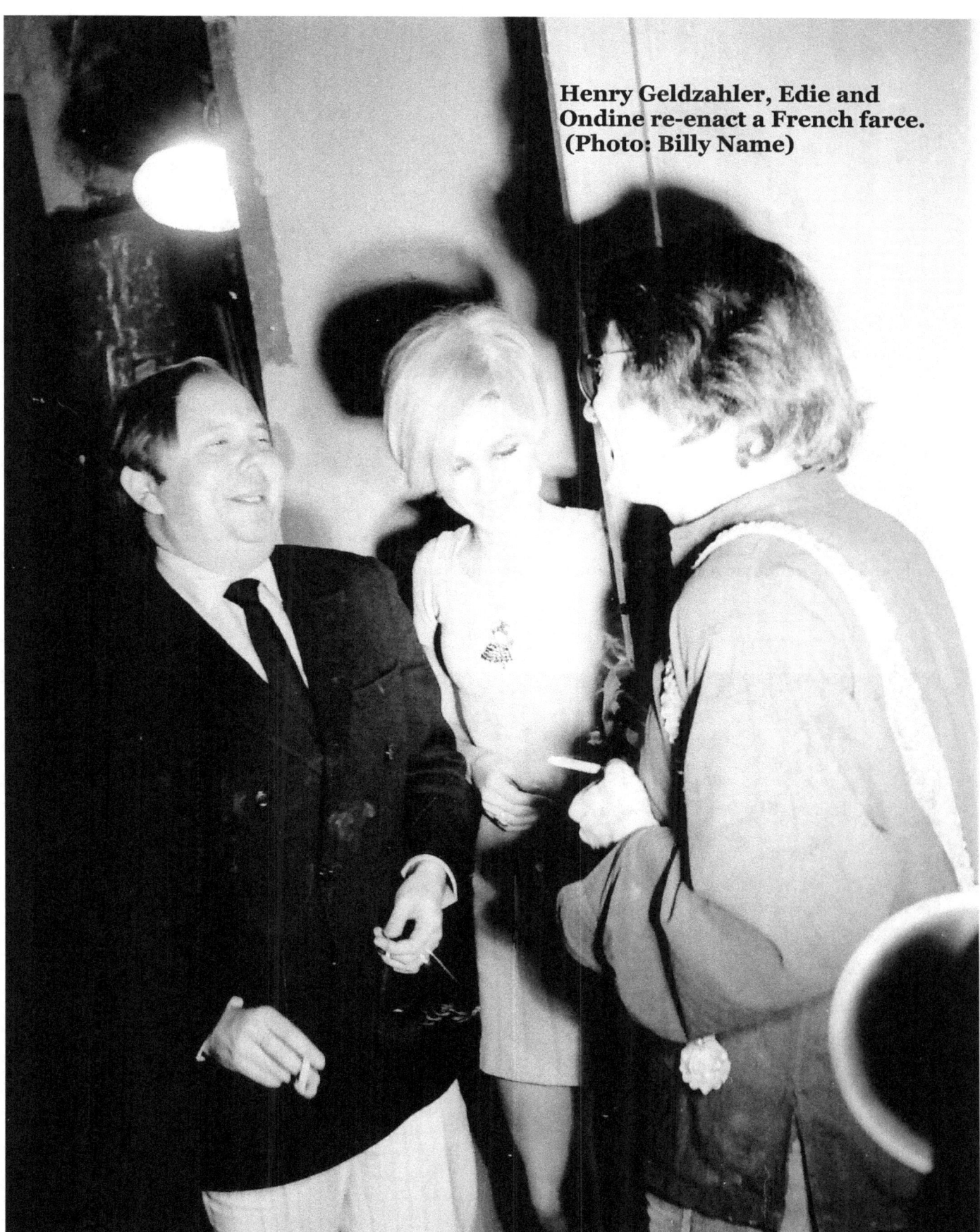

Henry Geldzahler, Edie and Ondine re-enact a French farce. (Photo: Billy Name)

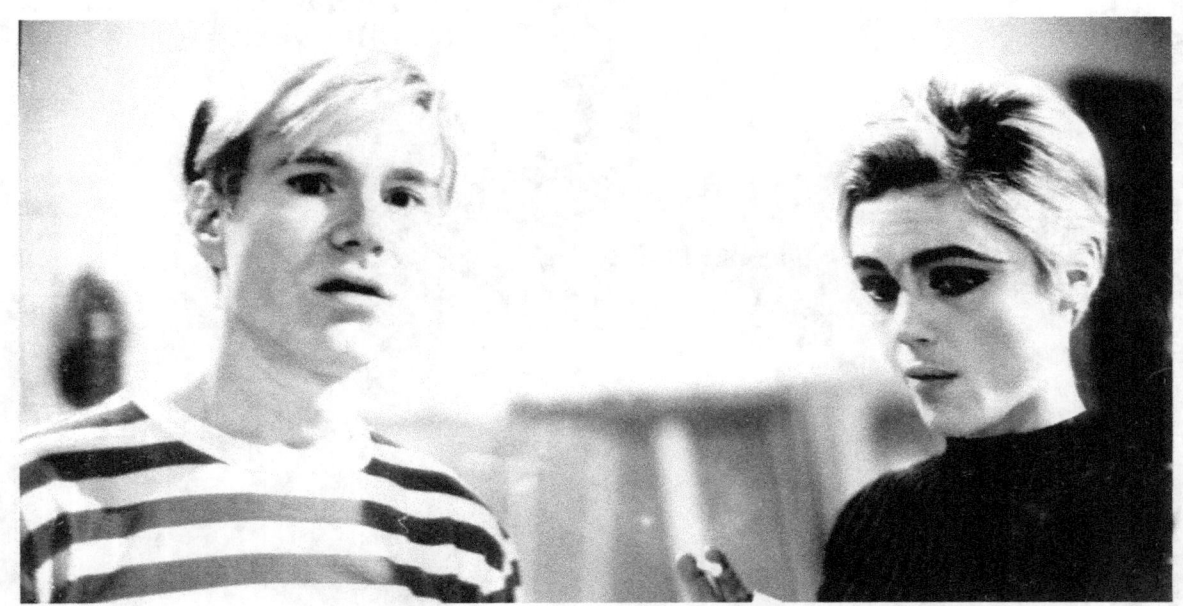

Andy and Edie, caught in a pensive mood. (Photo: Billy Name)

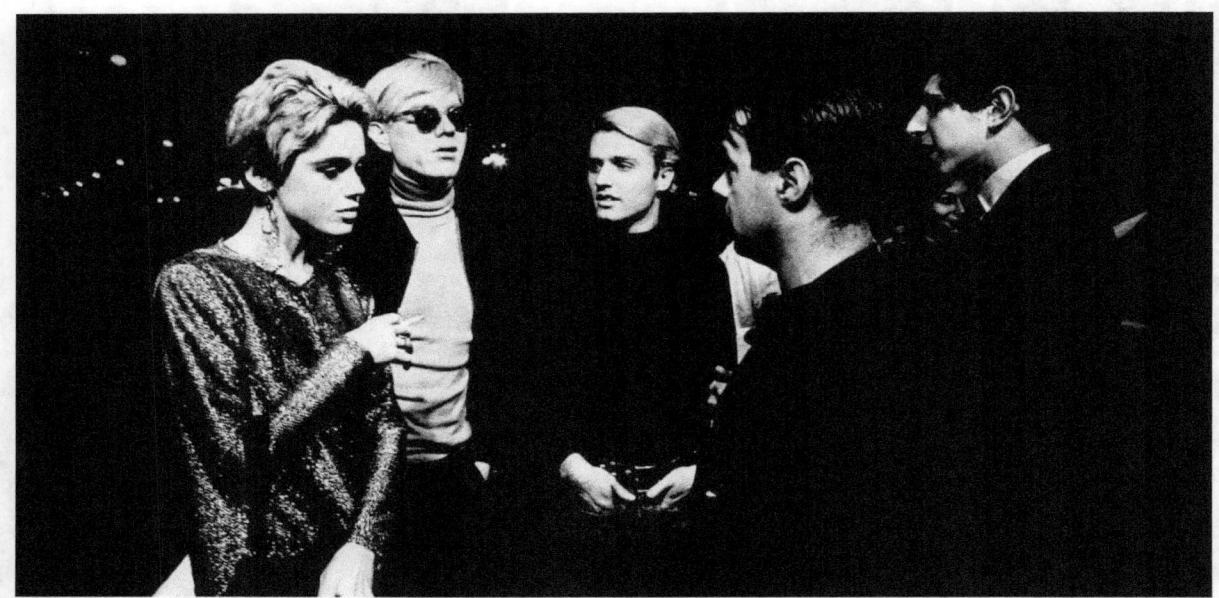

Edie, Andy, Gerard out on the town with friends. (Photo: Nat Finkelstein)

Danny Fields: It was Bob; Bob was in love with her. . . or Bobby was in love with her. Who the fuck knows what those people were thinking? And they hated us, because we were the fags, and they were the heterosexual blues guys. There were two very divided crowds in New York then. I'd been between both. But they were trying to seduce Edie away. Bobby Neuwirth was a Grossman person and he was her lover. He was also Bob's best friend, until you look back, he and Bob sitting there. The Grossmans were saying, "Why don't you get her away from those fags," and "She's a famous beauty. She's certainly got a story. If we could just get her off a few of those drugs she'll be okay." Famous last words: "Do what you can to get her away from those royal fags! They're not doing her any good. They're probably supplying her!" It's ridiculous, you know. A junkie is a junkie is a junkie.

Mary Woronov: Edie. She was the golden girl when I went there. I saw her demise, or her self-ejection from the Factory which is not something Warhol wanted. . . Edie to me was this very beautiful girl who understood that her role, just like I understood mine, because I don't think she was stupid. But she understood that her role was being attractive—that's any girl's role. Only her attraction was: fabulous, rich, beautiful, about to go out the window and *defenestrate*.* That was her attraction and she played it to the hilt. I don't know why she never understood what was really going on, and make the most of it for herself. She seemed to self-destruct all the time, so I have to think that was part of her attraction, and she embraced it. Ondine did much the same thing, only I don't think he thought of it as his attraction, he was attracted *to* it! So Edie for me was something not to go near. I was interested in survival, not in vying with Edie for 'Miss Self-Destruct Mode'.

---

*Mary's use of the French word '*defenestrate*' may have been for our benefit, our coming from Paris and all, but I'm assuming that most people don't know that it means 'to throw one's self out a window', which a number of Warhol's Factory people actually did. Even Edie refers to her strained relationship with her family as "out the window with me." In the sixties, some of us dropped acid and romanticized about leaping from New York buildings. I ran into a few other failed 'dry divers', as the doctors called it, in the D Ward of Bellevue Hospital. Weren't we the lucky ones. Edie wasn't consciously suicidal either, though the self-destruct gene was certainly in her DNA—her two older brothers had mental problems. One committed suicide in a psychiatric hospital; the other died in a motorcycle accident. Like many of Warhol's women, she was a spoiled, stoned, trust-funded sweetheart of a girl, who became frustrated to discover that she lacked any talent other than being beautiful. . .

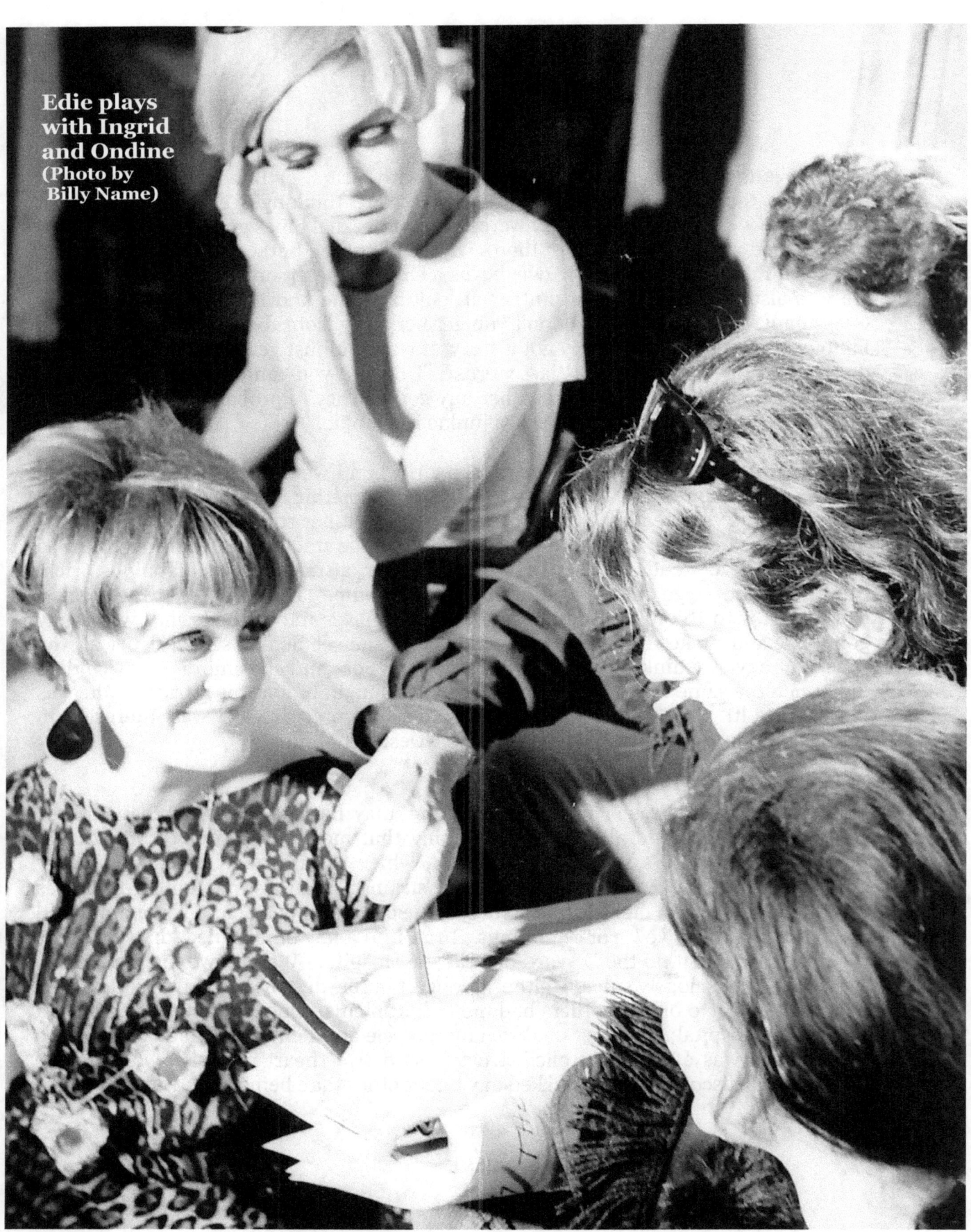

Edie plays
with Ingrid
and Ondine
(Photo by
Billy Name)

Gerard Malanga: Edie was under the impression that her ticket to success now lay with Bob Dylan. But Edie did not have innate talents. She hadn't studied acting, she had a terrible singing voice, and she thought that she was going to be singing duets with Dylan. Ultimately, she ended up not doing anything with him; that just did not happen. When we were just starting to work with the Velvet Underground, Edie was my first dancing partner, but Edie did not want to be a go-go dancer. That was not her image of herself. We were hired to play at this psychiatrist convention at the Delmonico Hotel in New York, with this big ballroom, and there was Jonas Mekas. He's got it documented in his footage. . .

Jonas Mekas: Edie Sedgwick was a very sweet person. I introduced the first public appearance of the Velvet Underground with Edie. We introduced them at the Psychiatrist's Convention. That's where *(laugh)* the first public performance of the Velvet Underground took place, at a psychiatrist's convention.

We licensed that early footage of the Velvet Underground from Jonas Mekas, and it was quite a terrifying performance. The staid black-tie audience was hardly prepared for a song like 'Heroin', accompained by hypodermic needles, syringes, and graphic simulations of S&M. The tense interaction between the Velvets, Edie (who was now having an affair with John Cale) and Gerard Malanga is also revealing. One could read a lot into the body language if one were a psychiatrist. But the shrinks were much too busy fending off the energetic filmmakers Jonas Mekas and Barbara Rubin.

Gerard Malanga: You have Edie and me on stage dancing, and the Velvets behind us performing, and Barbara Rubin doing a total assault on the psychiatrists by pointing a Bolex camera right up into the faces of these people. Andy thought that we could do something with Edie and the Velvet Underground, but there was really no place for Edie; there was just nothing for her to do. Jonas Mekas had approached Andy about doing a retrospective at the Cinematheque, so Andy got the idea of an Edie Sedgwick retrospective, and I think this really was the beginning of the end of Andy's relationship with Edie. Because, what happened was the dynamic changed, and now Andy was thinking, wouldn't it be nice to have the Velvets performing in front of the Edie Sedgwick movies. Well, Edie was not having *any* of this! I mean, she was really upset. It certainly would have been a distraction to what she was doing on the screen. . . Edie, in her naïve way, saw Andy as being her ticket to Hollywood, but she didn't really understand what was going on.

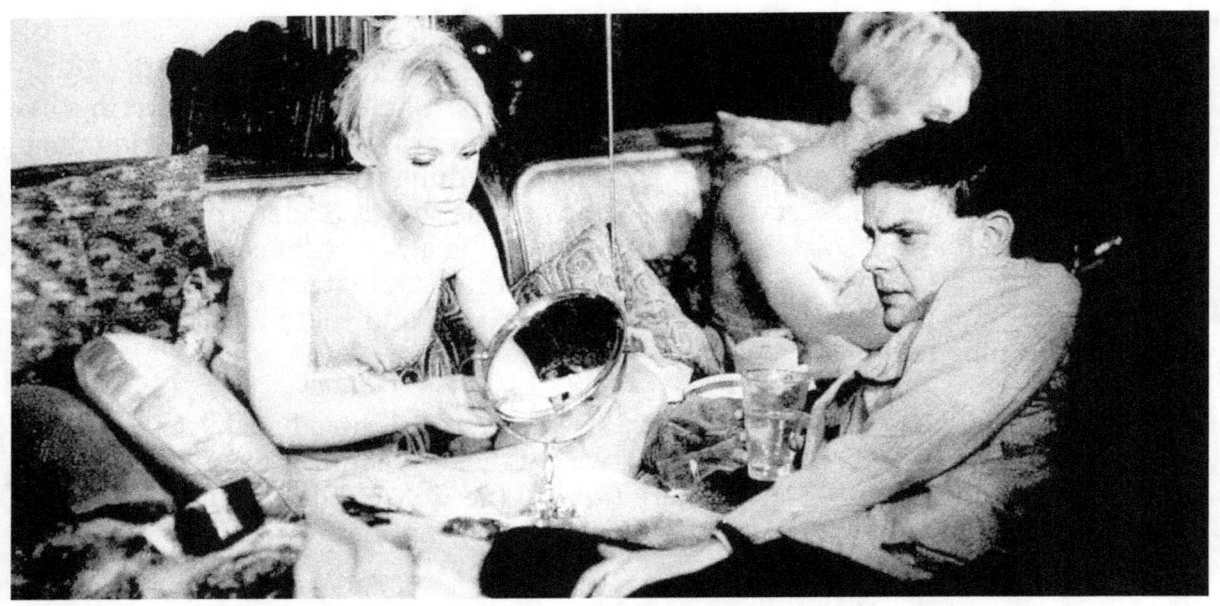

Edie Sedgwick, with worried friend Donald Lyons, preps for her last Warhol film: 'The Death of Lupe Velez', in December. 1965.

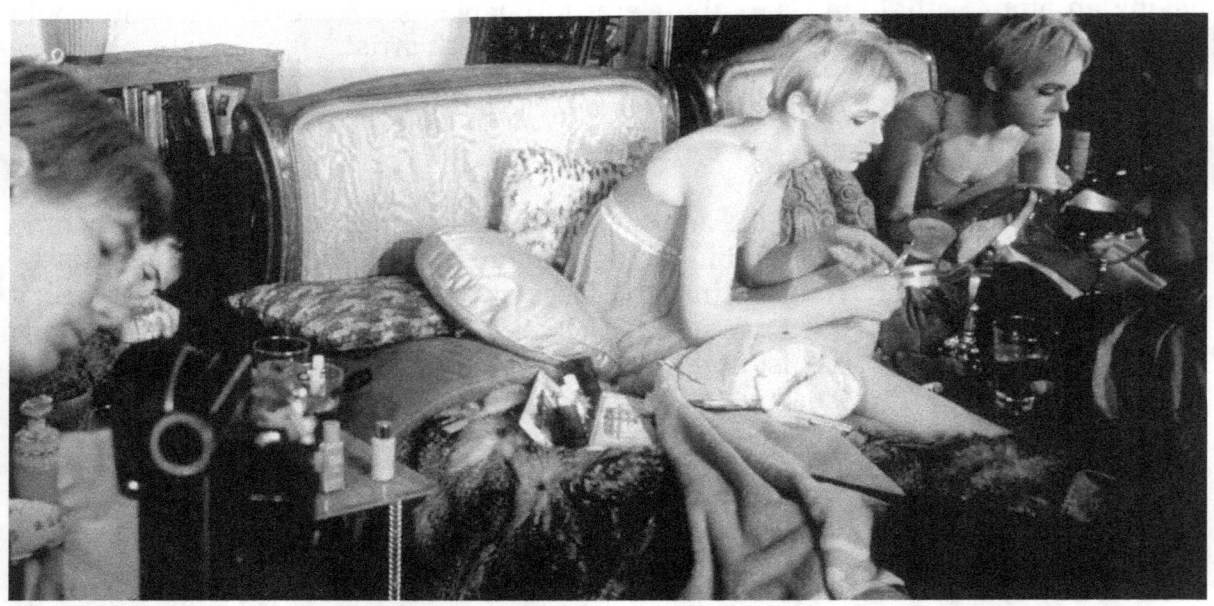

Andy gets camera ready for 'Lupe', which co-starred Edie with Billy Name.
(Photos: Nat Finkelstein)

Andy Warhol: During the 1960s, I think people forgot what emotions were supposed to be.   And I don't think they've ever remembered.

Gerard Malanga: At some point Edie failed Andy and Andy failed Edie.   It was a sad situation.   But we were involved with The Velvet Underground at that point, so Andy had something to fall back on.

Victor Bockris: Edie had been fighting with a lot of people at the Factory, espcially Andy and Ron Tavel, who was hurt that Edie considered his screenplays "perverse." She'd been ripping up scripts like a diva.   At the moment Edie, literally, does her last film* with Warhol, in which she ends up vomiting in a toilet, dying, he brings in the Velvet Underground.   Gerard found them and brought them in.   So the whole year (1966) is taken up with The Velvet Underground.

---

*Edie Sedgwick's last film was called 'The Death of Lupe Velez', based on a script, written on liquid amphertamines, by Robert Heide, who'd been told by Warhol that "Edie has to kill herself at the end."   Based on the last night in the life of Mexican movie star Lupe Velez, the film was difficult to watch.   Edie stumbles about socialite Panna Grady's lavish apartment completely out of it, drinking wine and chain-smoking.   For the 'romantic' suicide scene, she lies on a huge bed surrounded by flickering candles, taking barbiturates.   Unfortunately, the pills made her nauseous, so she winds up with her head in a toilet bowl full of her own vomit (I think that that's how Lupe Velez really died).   Anyway, end of movie.   But Nat Finkelstein took some beautiful 'before' shots of Edie putting on lipstick, which we also used with the museum footage. . .

Andy Warhol
People need to be made more aware of the need to work at learning how to live, because life is so quick and sometimes it goes away too quickly.

At this point, Edie still had her hopes of working with The Velvet Underground.   She did not realize that Warhol had already met his new 'Girl of the Year', who was the antithesis of the all-American, outgoing, heart-on-her-sleeve Edie.   The ghostly 'Napoleon in rags' was now enthralled with a mysterious, pale-featured, non-communicative beauty just in from Paris, by way of Berlin. . .

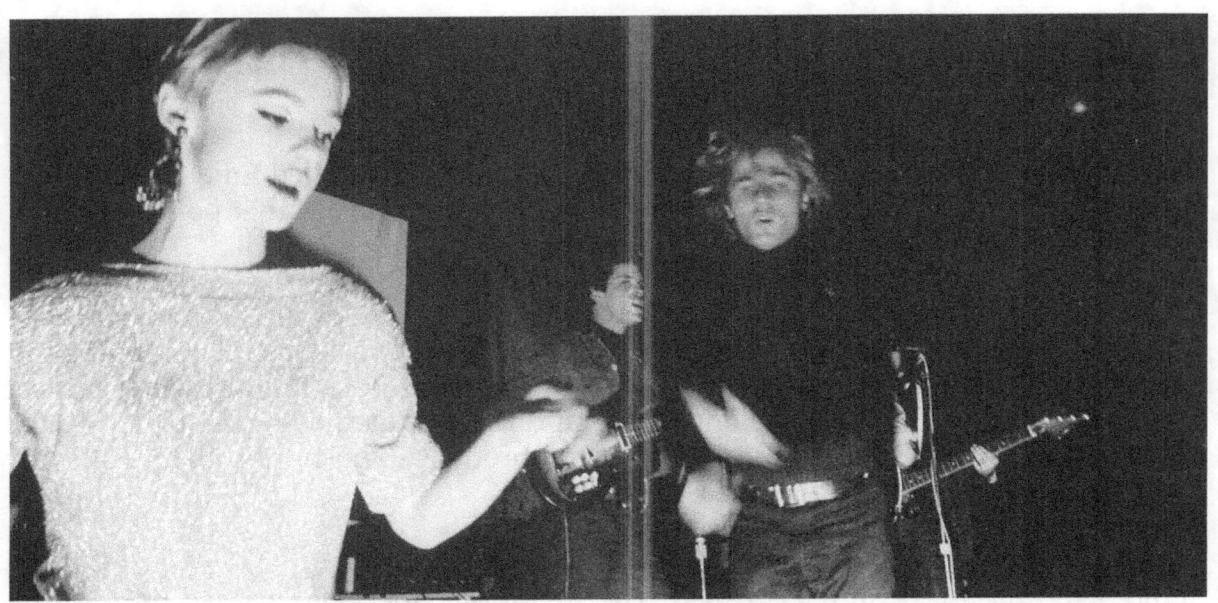

Edie Sedgwick danced with Gerard Malanga and the Velvet Underground before Mary Woronov joined them.

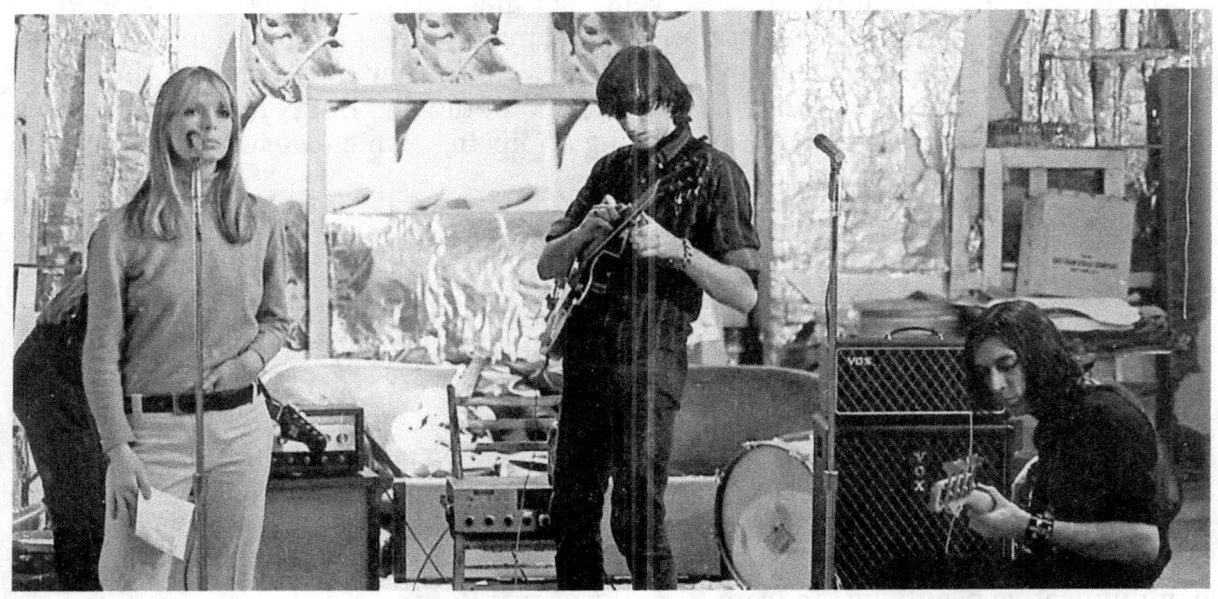

Nico in ice goddess mode, with the Velvet Underground's Sterling Morrison and John Cale, rehearsing at the Factory for the first time. (Photos: Nat Finkelstein))

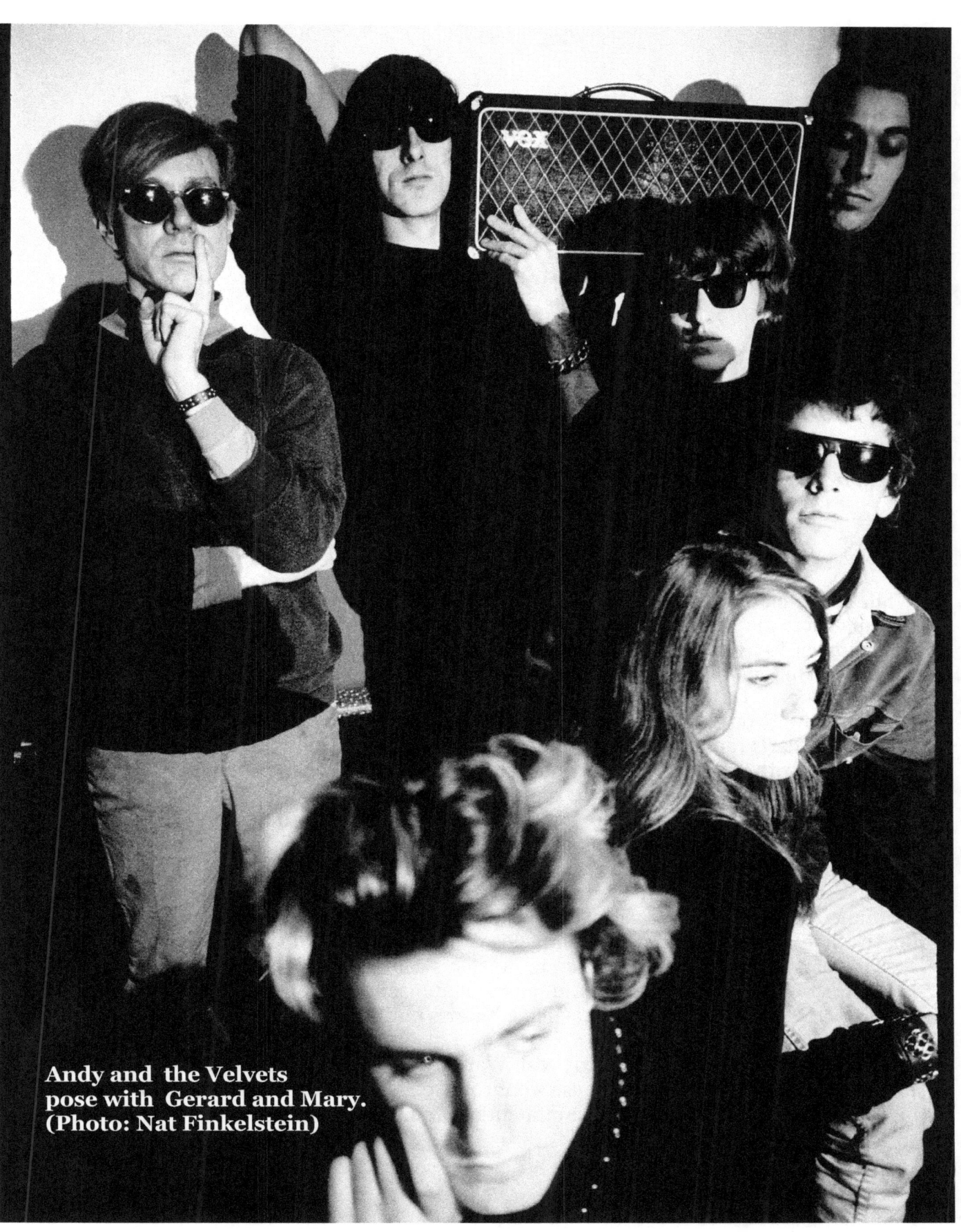

Andy and the Velvets pose with Gerard and Mary. (Photo: Nat Finkelstein)

THE VELVET UNDERGROUND AND NICO

Warhol is conducting with personalities more than with instruments.
—Jonas Mekas

While finishing our series, we attended Lou Reed's sold-out show in Paris, the dark and mesmerizing 'Berlin'. It would be the last time we saw him. We lost the great rock pioneer to liver disease on October 27, 2013 at the age of 71. His decades-long solo career after the Velvet Underground had its ups and downs (of which more about in Book III), but his body of work, and his classics from that sixties Warhol period—'I'll Be Your Mirror', 'Perfect Day', and 'All Tomorrow's Parties'—endure, and play on my Paris radio station into the wee hours. . . Lou Reed founded the Velvets, teaming up with classically-trained musician John Cale who had been working with the avant-garde composer Lamont Young. Lou and John lived together for a time, did a cornucopia of drugs, and created some amazing music. Joining them on guitar was Sterling Morrison, whom Lou had befriended when both were students at Syracuse University. There, Lou had fallen under the tutelage of the innovative poet Delmore Schwartz (then an English Lit. professor), and became inspired to write. Drummer Maureen (Mo) Tucker, the sister of another classmate, was brought on board when Fluxus/occultist Angus MacLise departed. According to fellow spiritual seeker Allen Midgette, Angus wanted to "keep his calm center," having spent time in Nepal with Buddhist Monks. Tai Chi master and masterly songwriter/musician Lou Reed always kept a calm center, practicing his arts until the day he died.

'The Velvet Underground and Nico', with Warhol's peel-off banana on the cover and the transcendental Nico singing those wondrous songs is considered by Rolling Stone Magazine to be "one of the ten most influential albums ever recorded."

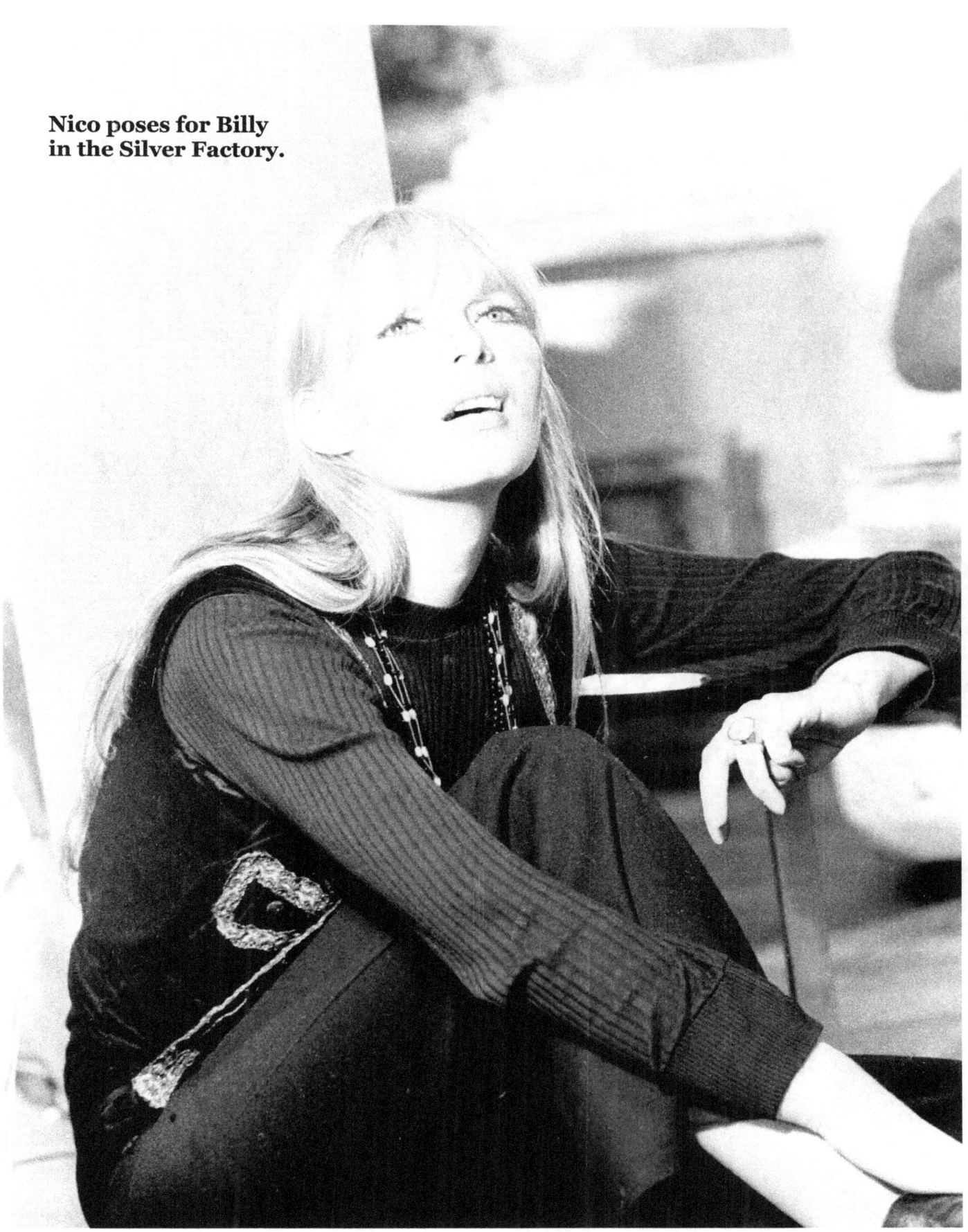

Nico poses for Billy in the Silver Factory.

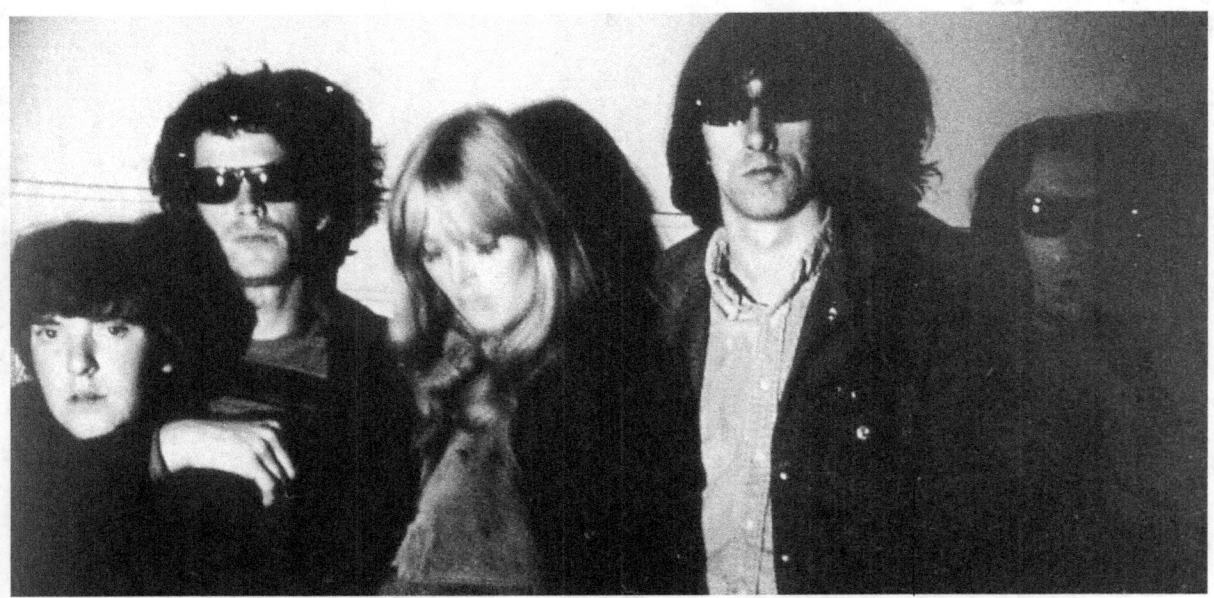

The Velvet Underground, ensconced in the Silver Factory.

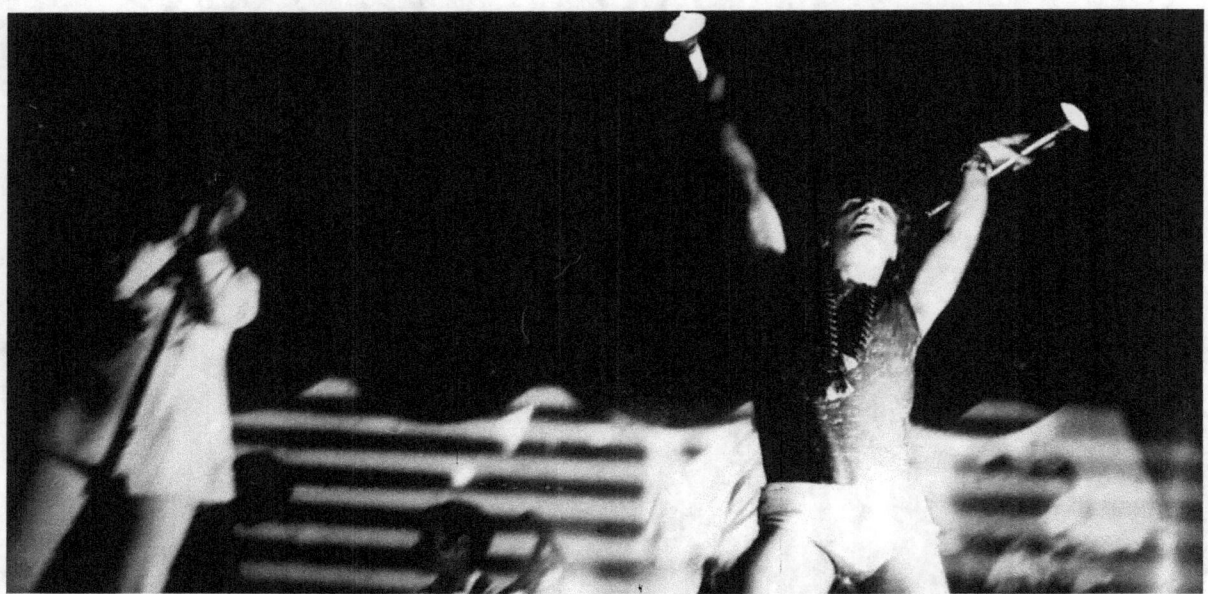

Nico sings while Gerard dances, at the 'Dom' on St. Mark's Place in the East Village. (Photos: Billy Name)

Gerard Malanga: Towards the end of '65, Barbara said to me one day, "There's this group playing in Greenwich Village called the Velvet Underground." So I went down with her. I happened to own a whip at that time, basically as a fashion accoutrement. I didn't even know what S&M was in those days. I had it tied to my belt. So we went down to hear this group performing at this coffee house (Café Bizarre). No one was dancing while they were playing, so I got up and started dancing with the whip, like doing a whip dance. A couple of nights later, Barbara and I brought Andy down, and Andy invited them to come up to the Factory to use the space for rehearsals. So that is how the Velvets were introduced to the Factory.

Jonas Mekas: Barbara did drugs, and had a situation with delinquency. When the parents wanted her out, the police said that if somebody would give her a little job and supervise her, they would let her go. So her parents asked me if I would do that. I said, "Okay, sure, let her come." She befriended all the filmmakers and the poets, and before you knew it, everybody. So, it was *she* who brought the Velvet Underground to me, to the Cinematheque. They began to practice there, before she took Lou Reed to Andy and Andy said, "Oh, let's do something." She was the catalyst that brought many of the superstars to the Factory, through she appears herself only briefly. Barbara did not want to be herself.

Barbara Rubin, one of the most industrious "squirrels" in the Silver Factory, was a tireless collector of downtown characters, some famous, others soon to be. Jonas Mekas filmed her in action, in his signature staccato style, as she brought together a vivid assortment of "geniuses" to attempt a meeting of the minds at local Village coffee houses like the Figaro. What the fuck was she thinking, throwing all these self-centered egomaniacs together? I applaud her. It turned out for the most part to be a thankless task, but the footage was historic. Rubin's film 'Christmas on Earth' (1963) was made on a 16mm camera lent by her mentor, Jonas Mekas. It was not meant to be your family holiday favorite. Overflowing with a panapoly of flesh cavorting in a New York apartment, the film is considered to be "one of the first sexually explicit works in the American post avant-garde." Barbara Rubin's heavy drug use would eventually undermine her. She began to grate on certain Factory members, and when 'the pack' attacked she left the scene entirely, and found another life in France, where she married, had children, and died at the age of 34.

Warhol biographer Victor Bockris, who also did a book about the Velvet Underground with Gerard Malanga, had an insight on the women who wandered into Warhol's world, and figured it out—or imploded. . .

Victor Bockris: Andy's favorite song on the Velvet Underground's album was 'All Tomorrow's Parties'. . . "What shall the young girl wear, for all tomorrow's parties?" Riches and shrouds, female images of the sixties. One of the important things we're missing here is the female contribution. This is not an all-male world, although it's a hardcore gay one. But there are women in it who are important within the operatic mythology of what is going on. Jonas Mekas said it beautifully in the Village Voice, describing a performance of 'The Exploding Plastic Inevitable', the multimedia show Andy created around the Velvet Underground. Mekas said, "Warhol is conducting with *personalities* more than with instruments." And that gets to the core of what Warhol is doing. He's always the conductor of the personalities in the situations.

During the sixties, Jonas Mekas was already considered 'the father of underground cinema'. Now in his eighties, still working, he made a place for us in his packed schedule (which may have included an angry wife and a young French girlfirend), then rushed off to Paris and Japan. Whew! In the early CBS News archive footage we excavated, Jonas looks remarkably the same as he does today, minus the liver spots. CBS showcased a wonderfully mad filmmaker, the boyishly handsome Piero Helizer, as he shoots 'Venus in Furs' (then called 'Dirt'). At this time, the Velvet Underground was still far underground. The rare footage shows them all dressed up in sad and ridiculous Halloween costumes, desultorily doing a gig while a fat lecher in the background tries to molest a nurse. The Velvets are good, but, oh, the film. . . It's bad.

Jonas Mekas (*as an intense young filmmaker*)
Like any art, cinema has the narrative aspect and the poetic aspect , and so-called underground filmmakers are exploring the poetic aspect of cinema.

Dave Dugan, CBS
Jonas Mekas is the founder of a Filmmaker's Cooperative in New York that distributes underground films. And this is one of the filmmakers at work, Piero Helizer. He's shooting a film entitled 'Dirt', in 8mm color, with the help of a musical group called The Velvet Underground.

'Leee' Black Childers: Everything that came out was psychedelic, so I didn't know at first just what the Velvet Underground were. I liked that they sang about bondage and forbidden subjects like heroin. Andy should get a lot of credit, because he had nothing to lose, and they had nothing to lose, and Nico had already lost whatever she had, meaning her brain. He just said, "There are no rules, write about whatever you want." 'All Tomorrow's Parties' is brilliant stuff that we weren't hearing at all. That >

whip dance with Gerard waving that whip around? No one knew what that was, including Gerard. I didn't know at first what 'Waiting for the Man' was about. I'd thought it was something vaguely homosexual.

Lou Reed: This is not nuclear physics, this is three chords. *(He sings)* "I'm waiting for my man, twenty-six dollars in my hand."

Lou Reed played his guitar in a little British doc called 'Transformer'. Dave Stewart interviewed him about his life with the Velvets and he was quite open and actually charming. Lots of wonderful back-story and guest rock stars and music. I had to keep getting copies of the DVD because editors and music people would drop by and lift them, and if that isn't a four-star review I don't know what. The French are simply gaga over Lou. A lot of them also love heroin, so bobo-chic (*Bourgeois-bohemian*).

Victor Bockris: Lou was a good example of somebody whose life which was changed by about one hundred percent, by meeting Andy. Bob Heide was at the Café Bizarre when Andy first saw the Velvets, and he said to Andy, "Gee, do you think we should buy them?" And within forty-eight hours after they met, and Lou came to the Factory, they immediately offered him the deal. The first move Andy makes with them, "You gotta get a new lead singer, and it has got to be this woman." Now, to say to Lou Reed, "You have to get out of the center of the stage; you've got to get someone else. . ." And actually, it's a stand-in for Andy, because Nico is this blonde Nordic goddess with the high cheek bones and the pale skin, *just* like Andy!

Lou Reed: Andy wanted us to use Nico and we went along with it at the time. We didn't really feel we needed a chanteuse. But Andy asked me to write a song about Edie Sedgwick, so I did and called it 'Femme Fatale', and we gave it to Nico because she could sing the high chorus. . . Andy wanted her, so he got her.

We found archive footage of Nico from an obscure collection called 'Nico, Heroine' filmed at a concert in Manchester England. The sound quality was dreadful, and Nico looked ravaged by life, yet traces of her haunting beauty remained. She liked Manchester, which reminded her of growing up in war-torn Berlin. Like vintage Deitrich, Nico chain-smoked and spoke in her deep throaty 'Gotterdammerung' monotone, just like she sang. I can still see her stark eyes, her ruined, bitter smile. . .

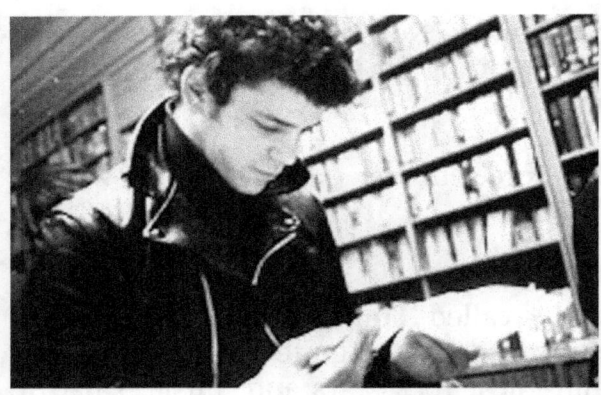

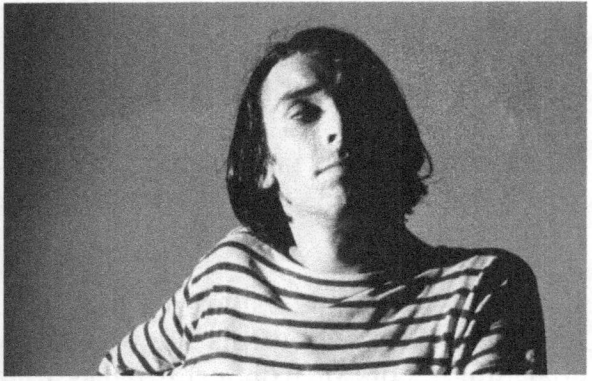

Lou Reed in leather, reading in Bennet Cerf's library at publisher Random House.
(all Photos: Billy Name)

John Cale, *'promenade en mer'*, preening. . . For an earlier period of time, the French nautical boatneck became the 'de rigeur' Factory uniform, but was later traded in for head-to-toe black and lots of leather.

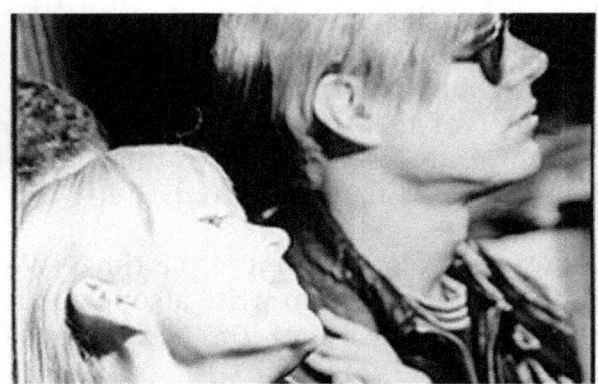

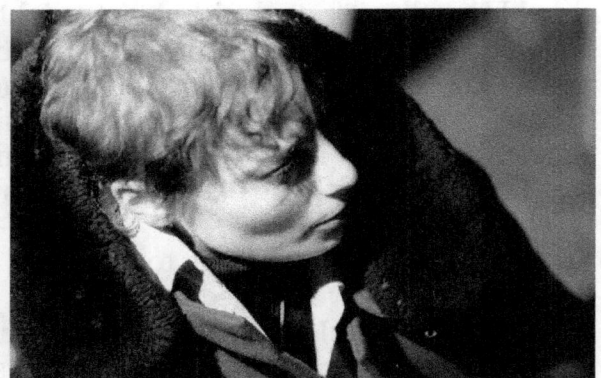

"Just like Andy." Nico inspired the haunting Velvet song 'I'll Be Your Mirror' and 'All Tommorrow's Parties', written by Lou Reed.

If it weren't for Barbara Rubin, Lou and the Velvets wuld never have met Warhol, who called her "one of the first people to get Multimedia interest going around New YorK."

Interviewer *(to Nico)*
How big a part in the Velvet Underground was Andy Warhol ?

Nico
He was in the shadow, standing in the shadow, always behind the camera.

Mary Woronov: Nico was so gorgeous that people would just drop dead. As far as her personality, she was nuts! She was vicious. No, she wasn't vicious, but very dog-like about her bone. Like, she wanted to be a chanteuse. Eileen Ford (then the top model agency) is *dying* for her to just stand still for one second so that she can get a Polaroid of her, and sell it for a million dollars. "No! I want to be a singer." Oh, she was just moronic in this way. Also, she was extremely—she wasn't self destructive, she was *destructive*! But everybody forgave everything because she was *gorgeous!*

Nat Finkelstein Basically, Nico and I had a rapport, and I became her friend. She would call me up at two in the morning and say, "Oh please, please I need you. You must come, you must come. So I would jump out of bed and say, "Tonight's the night!" I'd grab some hash, go down to Jane Street. We would get high, we would talk and she would then tell me that she had a crush on Peter Fonda. I was . . . crushed.

Surrounded as he was by beautiful women, poor old Nat never gave up trying. The problem was, the men were also beautiful. The feisty photojournalist seemed to be in unconscious competition with handsome Gerard Malanga, who was hardly aware of it, since he was running around on filming errands for Andy, and had a nightly gig with the Velvet Underground and its fledgling groupies.

Gerard Malanga: What became known as The Exploding Plastic Inevitable started developing into a full-fledged multimedia show. Andy was going to include films behind the Velvets including 'Vinyl', so it was an integrated affair. Andy was pretty much into dimensions and layering, and this is just another dimension to what he was doing with his art. Now he had live art! Maybe Andy saw himself as a music promoter. Maybe this was another way of gaining the attention of Hollywood.

Andy Warhol: Every song has a memory. Every song has the ability to make or break your heart, shut down the heart and open the eyes. But I'm afraid if you look at a thing long enough, it loses all of its meaning.

Nico, Andy, and Mary. (Contact sheet: Nat Finkelstein)

Lou Reed: Andy said *(mimicking)* "Oh, what are we going to do, I don't know what to do. We gotta have something that's fun. Oh, why don't you play and I'll show the movies and we'll have lights and—" And there you go. We were wearing sunglasses so we weren't blinded by the whole thing.

According to Lou Reed, Warhol literally created multimedia in New York: "The whole complexion of the city changed, probably of the country. Nothing remained the same after that." Lou was prescient—that show was a truly mind-boggling extravaganza, even by today's standards. But I guess if you were working the room with your whips, like Mary or Gerard, you remembered it somewhat differently...

Mary Woronov: We went to Philadelphia and played somewhere, then Andy said, "Now there's a party, you'll all go." The Velvets would dress in black with their black goggles on, and I would dress in black with my black goggles, and we would arrive at these people's houses looking like the death crew! They would be completely rich, and they would say, "Oh fabulous, look at them, they are freaks, oh wow!" I would of course eat myself sick because I was always hungry. The whole thing was just stupid.

Mary Woronhov had spent her college summer of '65 like a lot of us, in Provincetown, that gay-centric art community at the tip of Cape Cod. Back then she was fiercely arty-looking, wild as a horse on acid, mane flying about when she danced. While I and my classic Martin guitar were getting booed off the tiny stage at the Blues Bag, Mary was prancing the nights away on her endless legs, sheathed in tight black jeans and cowboy boots. The following year Warhol and the Velvets would arrive in P-Town dressed like Mary, "looking like the death crew," and the next trend would be born... Mary's pal Billy Name, who started a few fashion trends himself, recalls the 'Velvet Revolution'...

Billy Name: It was first called 'Andy Warhol Uptight'. We projected the film of the Velvet Underground on Gerard and Mary while they were performing and projected various screen tests of all the favorite people. So, you are using film, painting, audio and video, music. "Let's do a production, let's be the big entrepreneur!" It didn't work because you need capital to have that happen, and Andy was so far out there that investors were fearful. So Andy's impresario guy was never able to develop, because he could never raise capital...

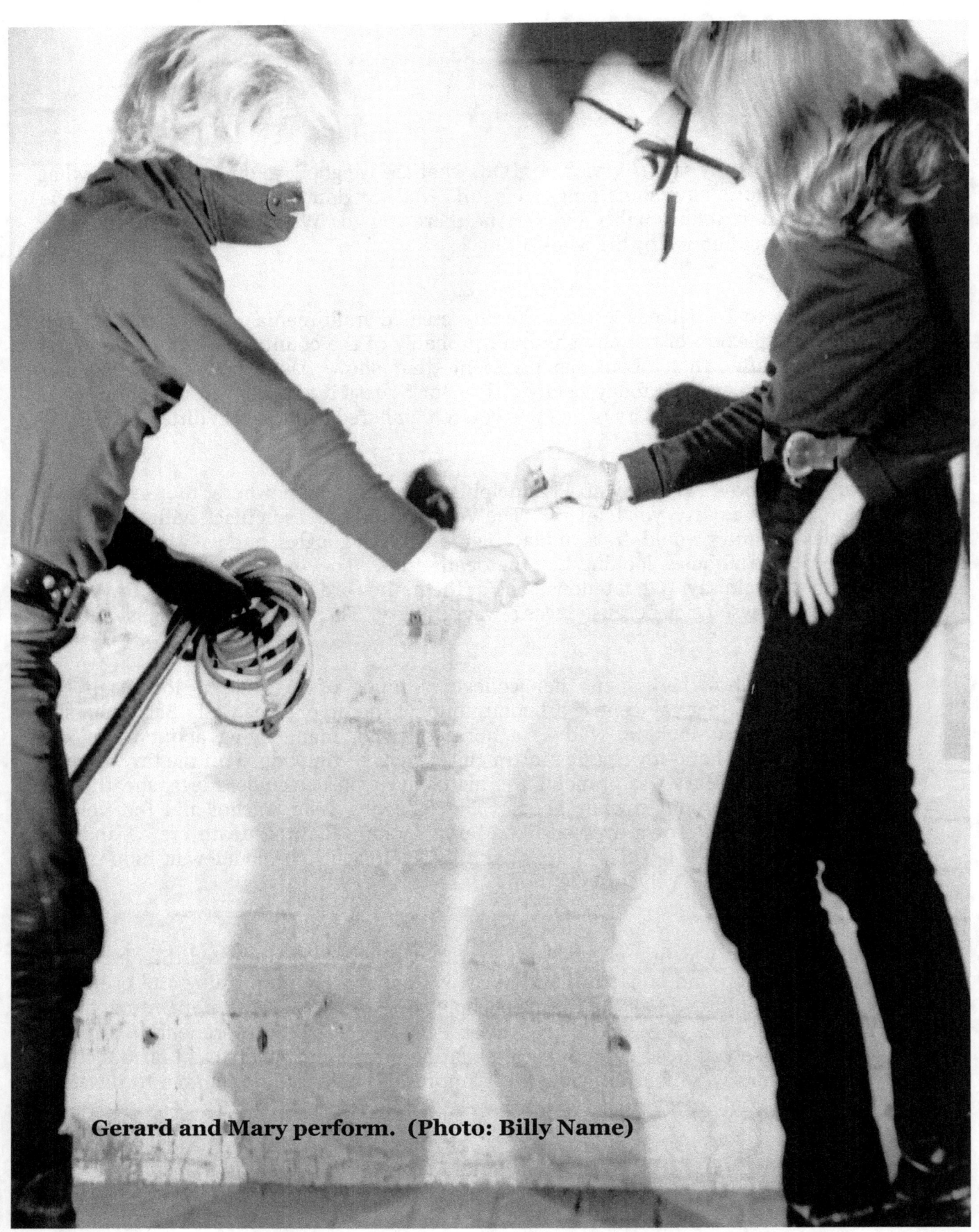

Gerard and Mary perform. (Photo: Billy Name)

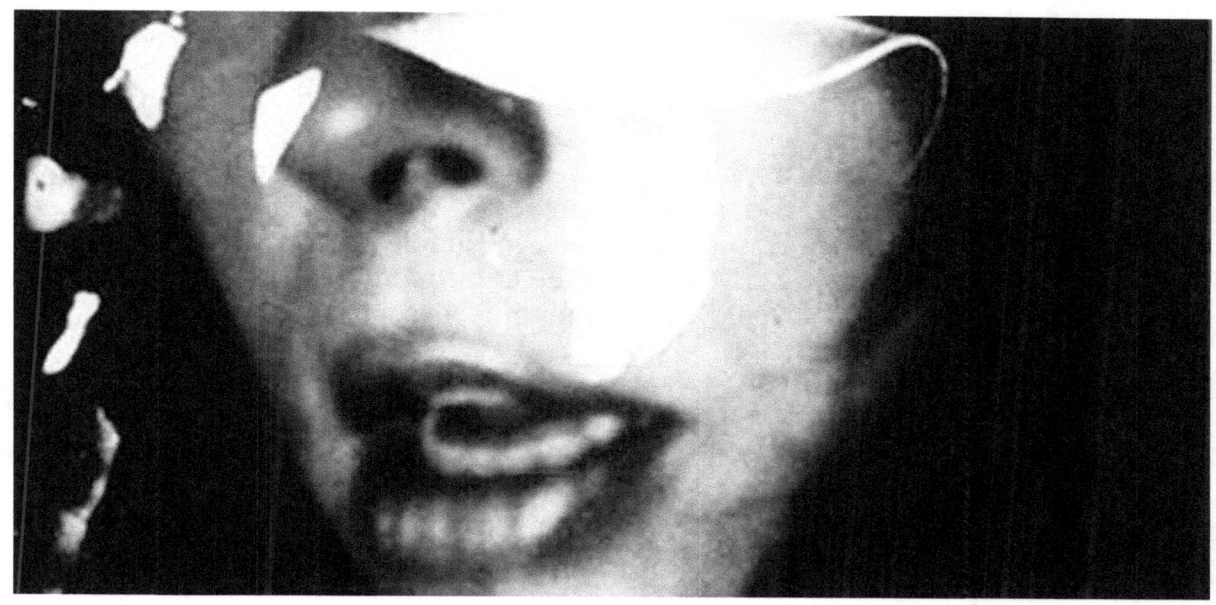

'Andy Warhol Uptight' featured Ultra Violet and Ondine double-projected during a performance. (Photo: Billy Name)

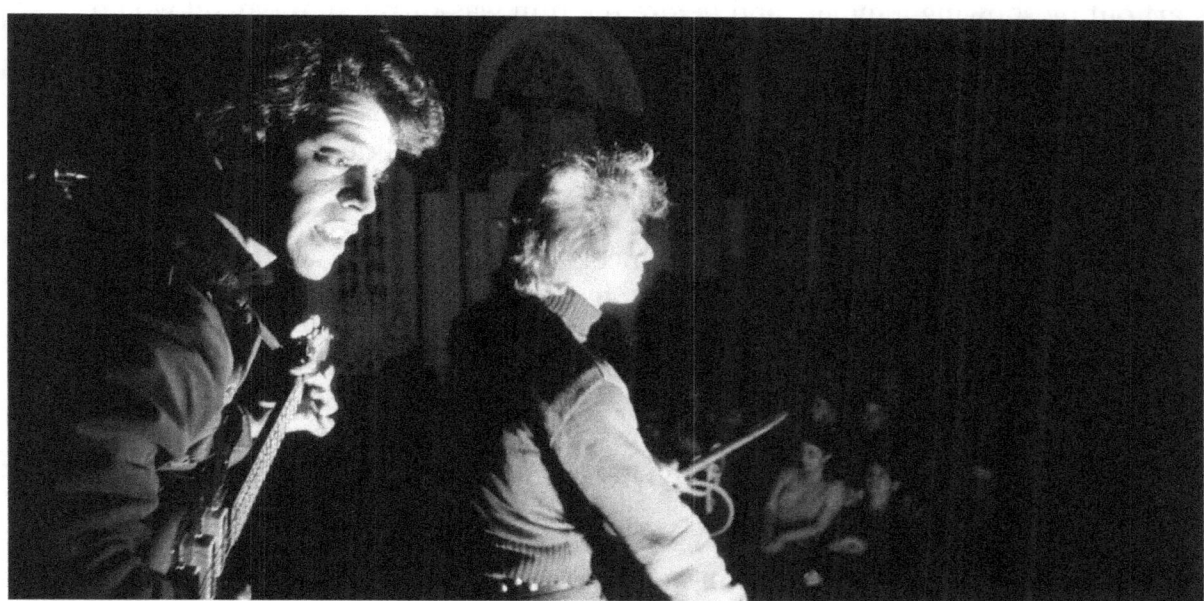

Lou Reed shows his mastery on the guitar, while Gerard manipulates his whip, and the women. Note semi-nude fan in the front row. (Photo: Nat Finkelstein)

According to Billy Name, the title of the early production, 'Andy Warhol Up-tight', not only alluded to the show making people uptight, it also referred to the provocative meth-heads that populated his nether New York world. So, for Andy's nihilistic band of heroin warriors, the warm fuzzy West Coast welcome did not happen. Of their multimedia 'Exploding Plastic Inevitable', one critic labeled it "The Ever Imploding Lead Balloon." Even Cher, who admitted to being afraid of Warhol, weighed in, claiming the EPI would "replace nothing, except maybe suicide."

Mary Woronov: Andy went to L.A. They turned him down! They turned the band down too! L. A. is the capital of bands, not New York. And when we went there, they *hated* us, saying, "The Underground should go underground and remain there, never be dug up." And we hated *them* because it was like a big dichotomy. In New York you were intelligent. iIn L.A., they knew three words: "Wow, wow, and wow."

Andy Warhol: I love Los Angeles. I love Hollywood. They're beautiful. Everybody's plastic, but I love plastic. I want to be plastic.

Gerard Malanga: We got hired to do a gig at 'The Trip' in Los Angeles, We would start out by showing a movie, and before the film was finished, the band would start playing. I would come on with Mary and go through my routines—I was very energetic in those days. The group was not visually oriented. They all wore drab-looking clothes except for John Cale. And Nico, of course, wore white pantsuits. *She* looked good. It was very visual. You had the films and slide projections, so it was a multi-layered experience. Even in its primitive state, it had a sophisticated look.

Nat Finkelstein As far as Gerard is concerned—I have my own thing with Gerard. Gerard was a thief. I say this knowing that there are laws about libel, laws about slander, so I say it publicly: Gerard stole negatives from me. Gerard was working as the intermediary between Andy, myself and Black Star (Agency). I entrusted him with some negatives, some rolls of film to bring back to Black Star. They never appeared, they disappeared, but they reappeared a number of years later, those photographs of the Velvet Underground at the Castle in L. A. . . . .

Nat's fulminations did not earn him points with Warhol, who hated conflict, and this seems to be a case of 'he said, he said'. Other photographers were also there, like Lisa Law and Steve Schapiro, whose pictures we licensed for the series. . .

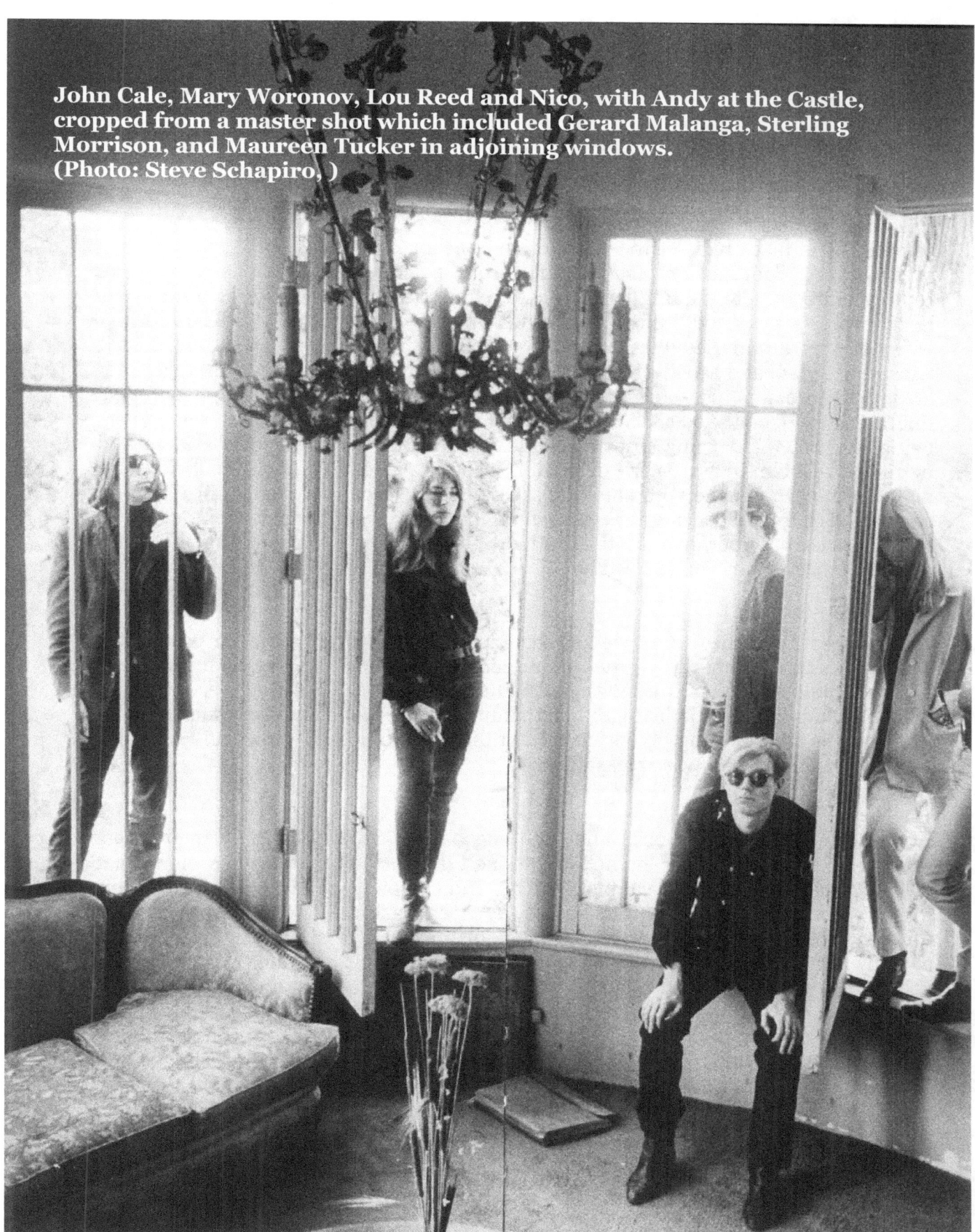

John Cale, Mary Woronov, Lou Reed and Nico, with Andy at the Castle, cropped from a master shot which included Gerard Malanga, Sterling Morrison, and Maureen Tucker in adjoining windows.
(Photo: Steve Schapiro,)

The Castle, a gloomy shambling wreck planted in a shabby part of the Hollywood Hills, was rented by Paul Morrissey to house Warhol and the Velvets for their L.A. sojourn. The place had set the scene for more than a few bad acid trips and drug overdoses. . . Tom Law and his beautiful brother, actor John Philip Law, owned it, renting out rooms to passing writers, actors and musicians, famous or soon to be. For previous articles, I'd licensed photos taken by my friend Lisa Law, Tom's former wife, of the luminaries who'd passed through their portals, including Leary, Ginsberg, Dylan, and David Crosby. The highly respected documentary photographer Steve Schapiro was also on hand—at Warhol's request—busily taking phenomenal fine art shots (published in 'Schapiro's Heroes'). Everyone else just remembers being bored by the dancing hippies, who became hostile when ignored. . . Dispirited by the overwhelmingly negative reception in Los Angeles, the band left before the mob stormed the Castle with smoking sage bundles. (One could rationalize that an endoresment from Cher might have been fatal anyway.) Their subsequent arrival in San Francisco to perform at the Fillmore, noted hippie haven, was met with patchouli incense, and more hostility.

Billy Name: With the 'Dom'* we had the East Coast version of what the West Coast was doing at the Fillmore. We really started stuff like the 'Dom', the first pre-disco, experimental happening, live music dance thing going on. . . But they were all peace and love, and we were all death and methamphetamine, conceptual art and "kill me" *(laugh)*, this kind of thing. We were the antithesis of all of that. Now San Francisco, it was even softer. L.A. was at least hard.

---

*The Dom was a Polish Social and Wedding hall on St. Mark's Place in the East Village. Dom is Polish for 'home', and though the place was basically a dump that reeked of cabbage soup and cat piss, Warhol and company, still in L.A., missed their former playing venue. Demoralized, they escaped back to New York, back to the Chelsea Hotel, and finally, real fame and fortune, with a six-hour film that was actually a number of short films strung together and run in a (then) revolutionary split-screen format, because Warhol was worried—for once—that his audience might get restless with simply watching, say, Nico brush her hair. So, he might put in Ingrid Superstar as the girl next door giving a blow job, or Brigid Berlin screaming obscenities at the camera while rummaging through her drug paraphernalia, or Eric Emerson stripping down to basics. With a split-screen format, Warhol was thrilled that he could compress twelve hours of film into a mere six hours. And so were we. .
.

'CHELSEA GIRLS'
... AND BOYS

This is why I don't go around the Factory—
Andy's paranoia about me and my drugs.
—Brigid Berlin, from 'Chelsea Girls'

Victor Bockris: Andy could never have made 'Chelsea Girls' without Paul Morrissey. But it was totally Andy's idea. . . So collaboration is the core of the Warhol work esthetic, or the work ethic. It's based upon getting people to work with you, but it's as much for the comfort of human contact, and people not being isolated. It's trying to change the image of the artist as a person who sits alone in a garret to somebody who's basically running a Factory. The only thing that went astray to some extent, with Andy's playful encouragement, was it led some people to believe that he didn't really *do* his own work, that other people did it for him, and that certainly is just not true.

Paul Morrissey: We all thought he was crazy, we kept telling him not to do it. We didn't understand what he was doing. *He* didn't know what he was doing, either.

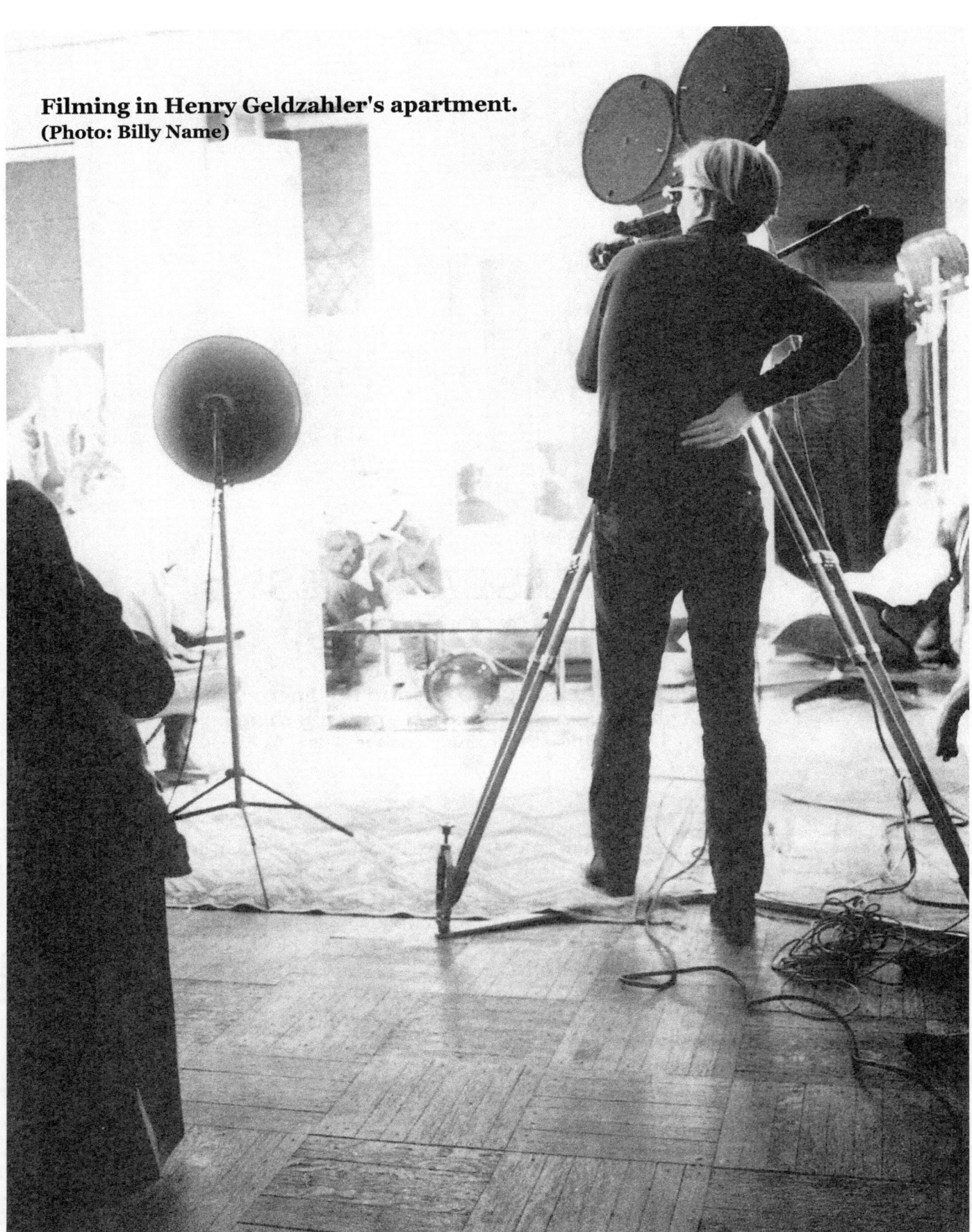

Filming in Henry Geldzahler's apartment.
(Photo: Billy Name)

According to Victor Bockris, Warhol never let his failures hold him back. Rather than bemoan the lack of success of his 'Exploding Plastic Inevitable', he decided to take his growing stable of stars and pit them against each other, in a series of films that would be the antithesis of West Coast hippie-dippy free-love banality. Warhol shot his one and two-reelers in friends' apartments and rooms at the Chelsea Hotel, where many of his stars resided. The resultant crazy quilt of conflict and torture, which I had the pleasure of sifting through for days, panning for those few 'nuggets', as Billy Name called them, is a harrowing montage of what Warhol's world had become by 1966. Among the segments of film I chose for our series were Ondine as an unforgiving pontiff attacking sinner Ingrid Superstar, Mary as 'Hanoi Hannah' attacking Ingrid and International Velvet, Eric Emerson tripping and stripping, and a wonderful bit of the hilarious plus-sized Brigid Berlin 'poking' herself in the ass with a vial of her special amphetamine cocktail, and promising us that, "This is gonna be an O.D."

Brigid Berlin: On drugs! On speed! On *amphetamine*! . . . When 'Chelsea Girls' happened, it would just be outrageous. Oh, you'd do anything, thinking that it would never come out.

Vincent Fremont: Brigid Berlin is a dear friend of mine, and I've known her since I first came to New York. She's famous for being in Andy's 'Chelsea Girls', which embarrassed her Conservative Republican family. Her father ran the Hearst Empire. So, to have a daughter who was in 'Chelsea Girls', an underground film, was quite shocking to the Park Avenue, Fifth Avenue sets that her parents frequented. J. Edgar Hoover was her father's best friend. You are talking about a very conservative background.

Robert Heide: Andy spliced some of my play 'The Bed' into 'Chelsea Girls'. Richard Bernstein had a loft in the Bowery and that's where we filmed it, and Andy actually got up on a ladder with the camera. Danny Williams was his boyfriend. Both of them wore these striped boat-necks that were in style at the time. Edie also wore those. And we filmed it there, on a big bed in a loft. 'Chelsea Girls' was to be Andy's first split screen film, and 'The Bed' has been in the segments. . . So I think it did influence the style of 'Chelsea Girls', those rooms at the Chelsea.

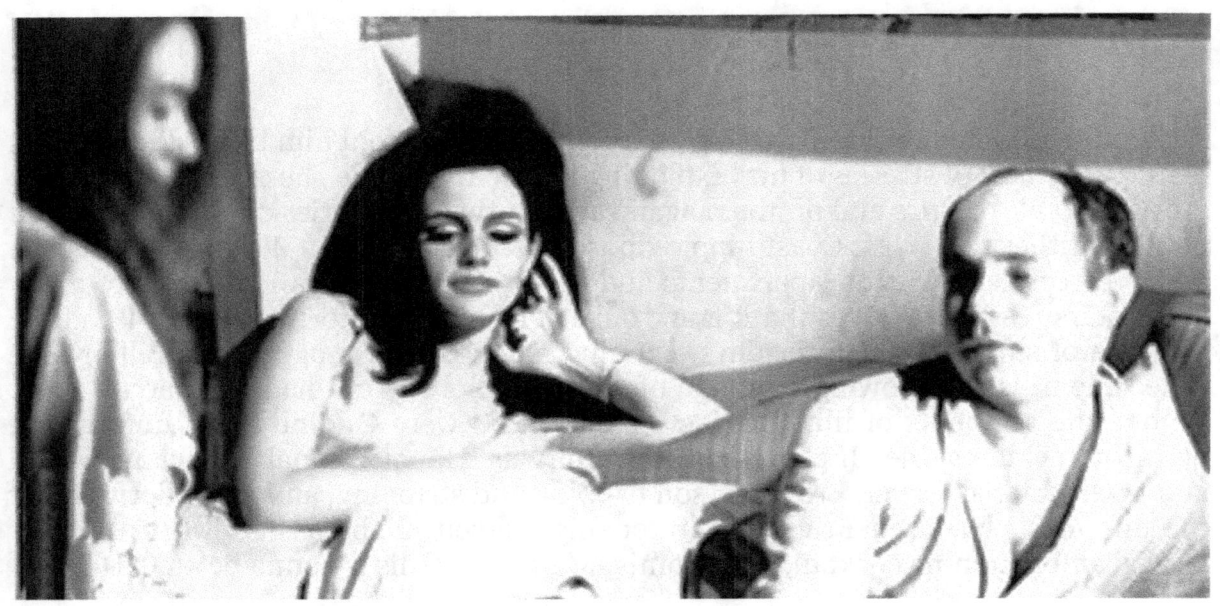

Mary Woronov, Susan Bottomly and Ed Hood filming 'Chelsea Girls'.

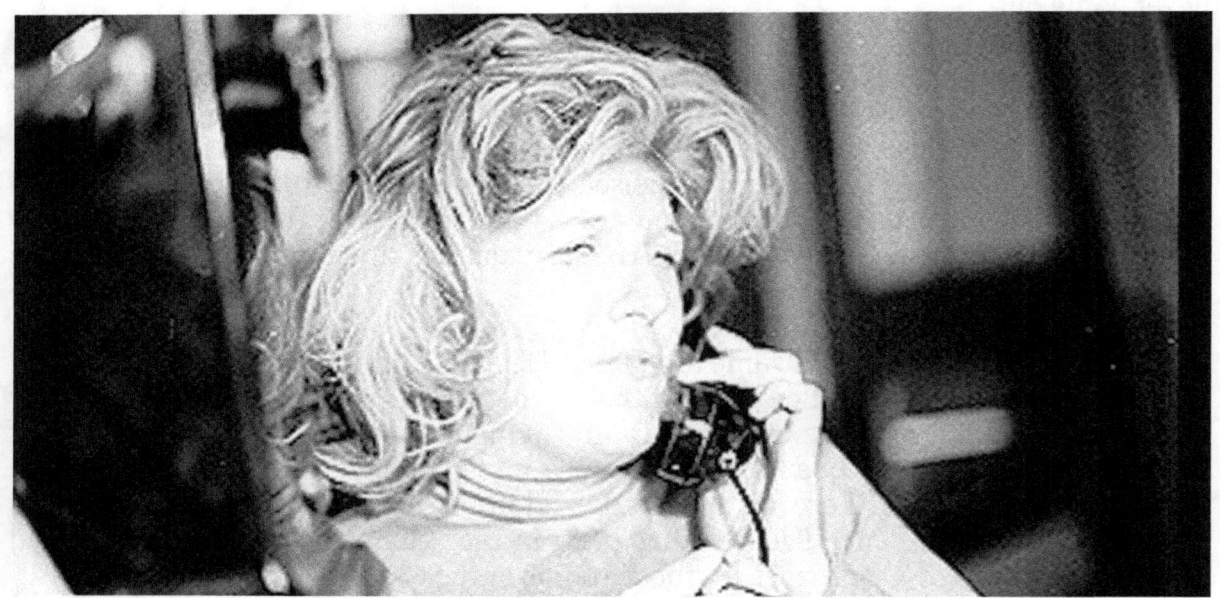

Brigid (Polk) Berlin, on the phone as usual, with a cigarette, as usual. (Photos: Billy Name)

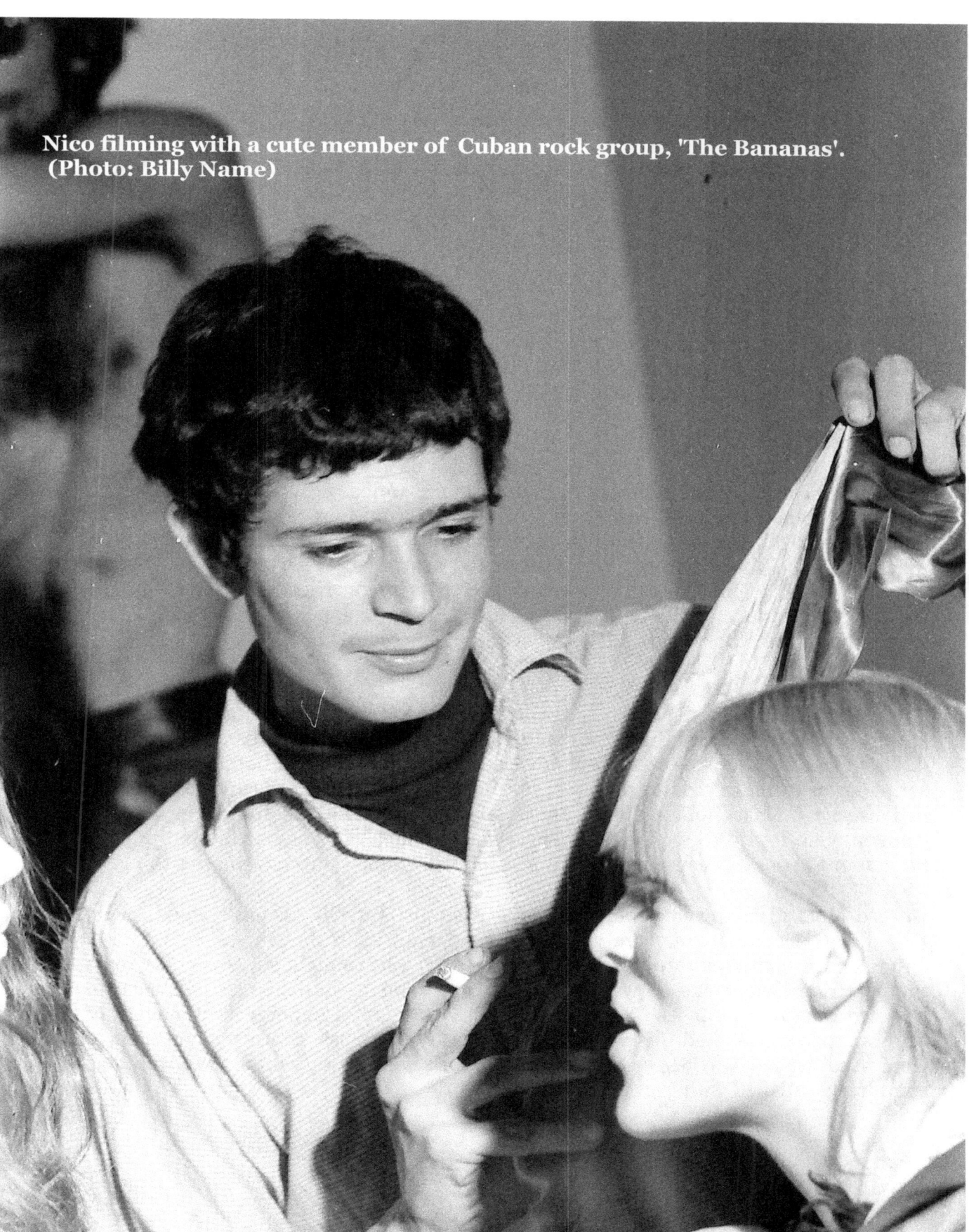

Nico filming with a cute member of Cuban rock group, 'The Bananas'.
(Photo: Billy Name)

Billy Name: 'Chelsea Girls' was an art film by Andy Warhol that finally went beyond the appreciation of the art world. When we finally released 'Chelsea Girls' in the first run theaters, the headline on Variety was 'Chelsea Girls'! Boffo 20k Warhol Success!' In those days, it was a big deal, twenty thousand dollars.

Victor Bockris: 'Chelsea Girls' really was the single work which changed everything at the Factory. . . It made, relatively speaking, a lot of money. Andy got fifty percent of that. And the distributor got fifty percent. He really made bad distributorships. Most of these deals were terrible, his business deals. But, it made him about a hundred times more famous. . . It didn't make *them* any more famous.

According to Victor Bockris, "Warhol had always been able to plead poverty," with some justification. His entourage lived like church mice. Billy Name managed on about ten dollars a week, Ondine was always broke, and Gerard Malanga never had an apartment of his own. The much publicized success of 'Chelsea Girls' didn't have much effect on their finances, or those of the actors who energetically screamed, stripped, freaked and fucked their way across the screen. Nico, ever the enigmatic ice maiden, simply brushed her long hair and gently spoke to son Ari. Mary Woronov, on the other hand, had her own hair-raising ideas. . .

Mary Woronov: 'Chelsea Girls' . . . I was feeling good by then. I knew my place. I knew I was wanted, and I did what I wanted because there was no structure. Warhol did not direct. I knew the script, nobody else knew it. They didn't bother reading the script. I mean these girls were so stupid. But I knew it backwards and forwards. I had a sense of what should happen, and I was pretty strong at making it happen. But someone like Ingrid (Superstar). . . There was the idea of tying her up and putting her under the desk, because she was unreliable and stupid. But that was her thing.

Gerard Malanga: Ingrid Superstar was a sweet girl, terribly misunderstood, made fun of, joked at, but a sincere good-hearted person, who thought of herself as a Superstar. Chuck Wein brought her to the Factory. She thought she was going to be the next Edie Sedgwick—no way could that ever happen—but she was still great in her own way in the movies. She was like the Eve Arden of underground movies, of Andy's movies. She had this wonderful kind of dippy, dipsy, character that kind of victimised her in a way, especially in 'Chelsea Girls'. But I don't think that Andy was completely satisfied with Ingrid.

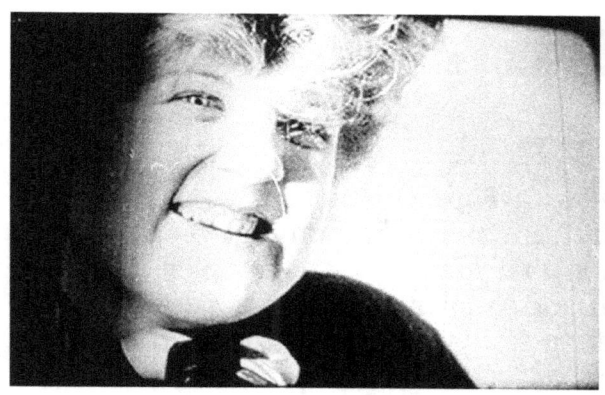

'Chelsea Girls'. Brigid 'Polk' Berlin, the tough girl who took no shit from the boys.

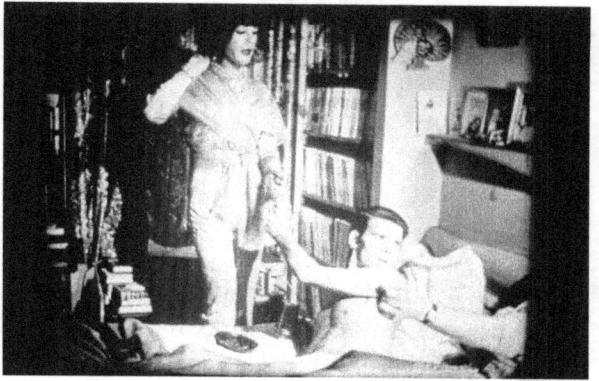

'Chelsea Girls'. Mario Montez attemps to seduce Patrick Fleming and Ed Hood.

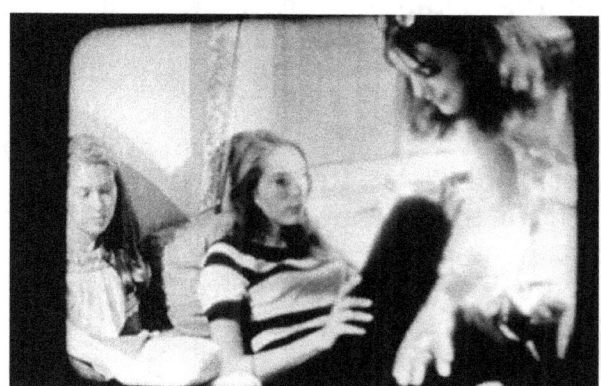

'Chelsea Girls'. . . Mary Woronov, aka 'Hanoi Hannah', no slouch in the mean department, attempts to ignore Susan Bottomly.

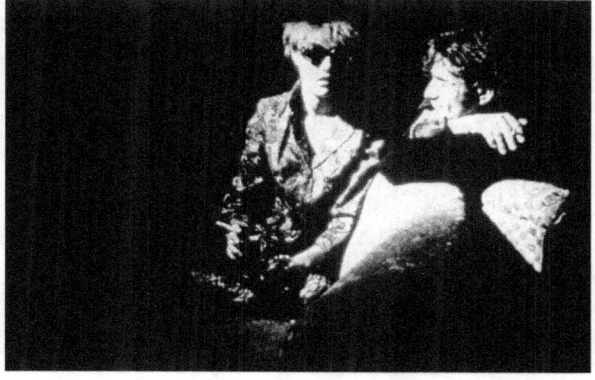

"I'm not a lesbian!" In 'Chelsea Girls', Ingrid Superstar confesses to 'Pope' Ondine,.

(All Photos: Billy Name)

Ondine (as 'the Pope'): You're a lesbian! Admit it, admit it!

Ingrid Superstar: I'm not! I'm not!

Billy Name: 'Chelsea Girls', that one reel with Pope Ondine. It's so stark in that black and white chiaroscuro, and there's this scratch on the film that keeps running through the whole thing. It's like a creation that Man Ray would never be able to think of. And that one with Eric Emerson and Pepper Davis is very dramatic too, with her head back. So glamorous! It's like a Hollywood still, with an avant-garde perspective.

Billy bandied about the avant-garde word with such merry abandon that we soon began to think with a different perspective ourselves. Were we ever a part of that hallowed world? Perhaps. . . Once upon a time, we had sat (and squirmed) through interminable Fluxus 'happenings', ten-hour concerts with one note, and modern interpretive dances in excrutiating slow motion. For an audience of attention-deficited speed freaks, this would be considered true torture, so how come we all did it? If I could remotely remember, I would tell you. According to Billy, Warhol attended many an avant-garde event with him or Gerard or Jonas, and figured his own creation would be greeted with the same reverence at the Cannes Film Festival.

David Croland: 'Chelsea Girls' was asked to be shown at the Cannes Film Festival in 1966. Andy brought it there, and invited me, Ultra Violet, the whole group. They didn't show the film, ha ha—it was too much for them. They said it was *much* too dirty to show. And it was such a long film, six hours, so we had a lot of time on our hands. We drove to St. Tropez with Nico driving. We almost got killed three times. I'm thinking, "Okay, you have to keep your eyes on the road. You're beautiful, but I want to live, I'm only eighteen years old."

Taylor Mead: Henri Langlois *(Founder of Cinémathèque Française)* showed 'Chelsea Girls', and I'm with Jean-Jacques Lebel. *(To camera)* "Hi, Jean-Jacques, what happened? You inherited the biggest fortune in France; where are you?" . . . He was one of the few avant-garde people in Paris working. He came to see 'Chelsea Girls' with me, and some of his friends. They walked out on 'Chelsea Girls'! I said, "What the hell am I doing in Paris?". . . Andy was there, and he said, "Oh, Taylor, we have all these roles for you. Come back to New York."

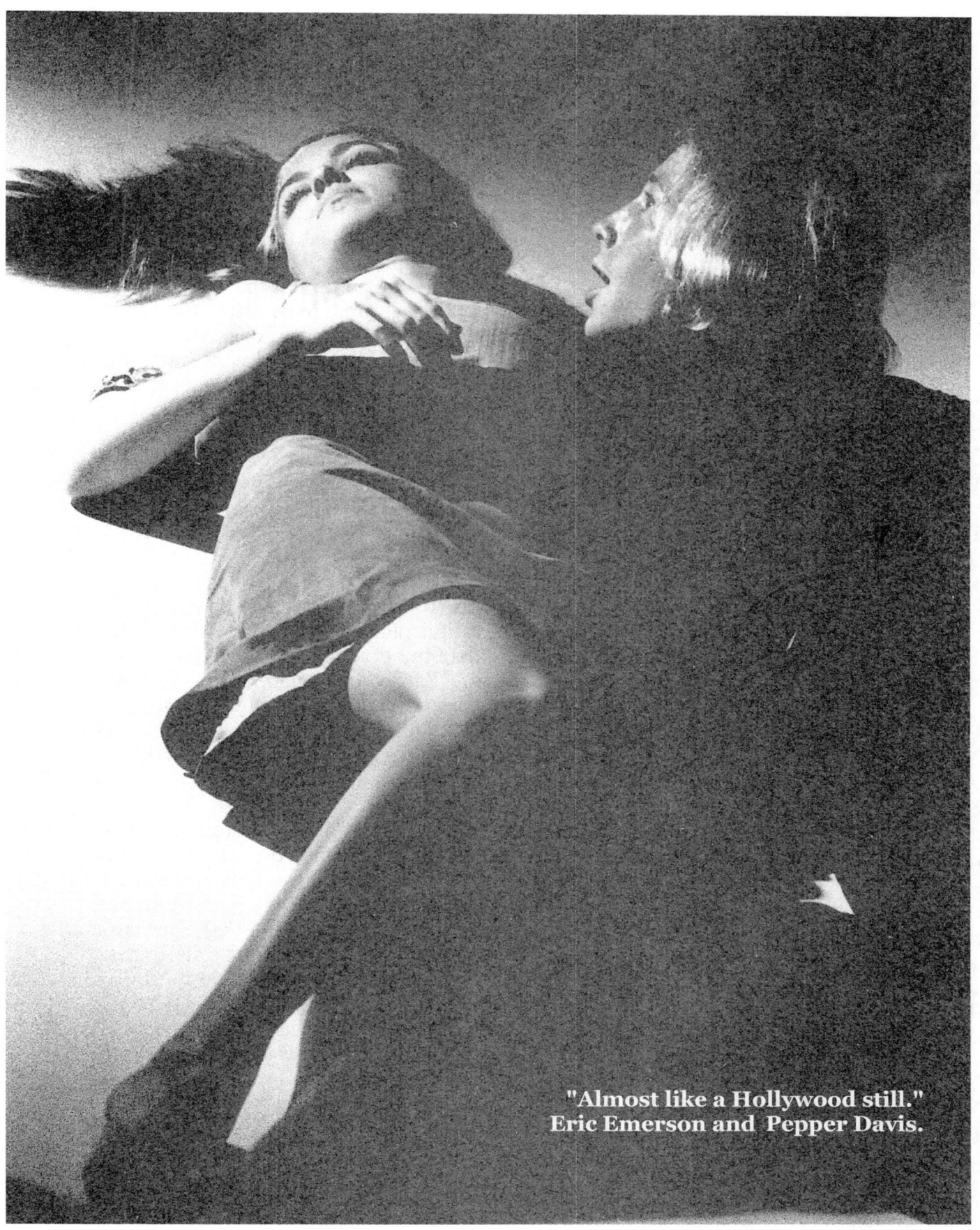

"Almost like a Hollywood still."
Eric Emerson and Pepper Davis.

Revered artist, poet and activist Jean-Jacques Lebel is still alive and well and living in Paris. Watch for him in 'The Beat Hotel' (2011), where he reminisces about the famous residents of 9 Rue Git-le-Coeur, which included Burroughs, Corso, Ginsberg and Orlofsky. . . Taylor Mead, who figured he had been a Beat from the beginning, ended his European exile with that Paris Cinémathèque première of 'Chelsea Girls'. He was ready to return to Warhol and the fold. But as far as the French were concerned, Warhol was now the 'Caligula of the underground movement'. He in turn considered French cinéma, and Godard in particular, 'booooring', though what fun to cite Godard as a "favorite influence." So, no cheek kissing there. Already hurt from the snub by the Film Festival officials, whose disparaging word of mouth had followed him to Paris, Warhol was ready to bring home his straggling troops. . . According to David Croland, Warhol had taken ten people and paid for everything, with little to show but bad reviews in *Réalité* and *Cahiers de Cinéma*, and humungous nightclub bills. The crowd included Nico, Ultra Violet, Gerard Malanga, Paul Morrissey, Eric Emerson, and Warhol's roughneck boyfriend Rod La Rod. David had come with his girlfriend, 'International Velvet'. . .

Dave Croland: I had never been to Europe. I was sophisticated, but not like European sophistication. There was this beautiful blonde girl sitting at the table across from me. Beautiful! I said to Andy after the dinner, "Who was that?" He said, "David, don't you know? That is Brigitte Bardot." Whooo, okay. I'd been talking to her all through dinner just like she was a normal person. We know she was *pas normale,* she was a goddess. How old was Bardot in 1966? Let's just say she was perfect. Then we went dancing. And of course Brigitte caused a sensation wherever we went in France. We were dancing like we did in those days, barefoot.

Billy Name: The International release of 'Chelsea Girls' kind of eclipsed Andy's desire for further commercial success, because it's labelling an artist. . . As for The Velvet Underground, they were not something that Andy could take on as a controlling manager, as he did with 'Chelsea Girls', and say, "I am going to make stars out of them," because John Cale was in the same world as John Cage; he was a classically trained musician. These guys were like Beethoven; they don't want to hear criticism. There is no way you can tell them what to do, because you do not know anything. These are genius musicians, who ended up by making music that has influenced youth and rock groups from the sixties and ever since. There are music magazines that make these annual 'One Hundred Greatest Albums of American Rock and Roll'. Number one is always 'The Velvet Underground and Nico'. All the people in the music world know, that it is the influential root of punk dirty rock and roll.

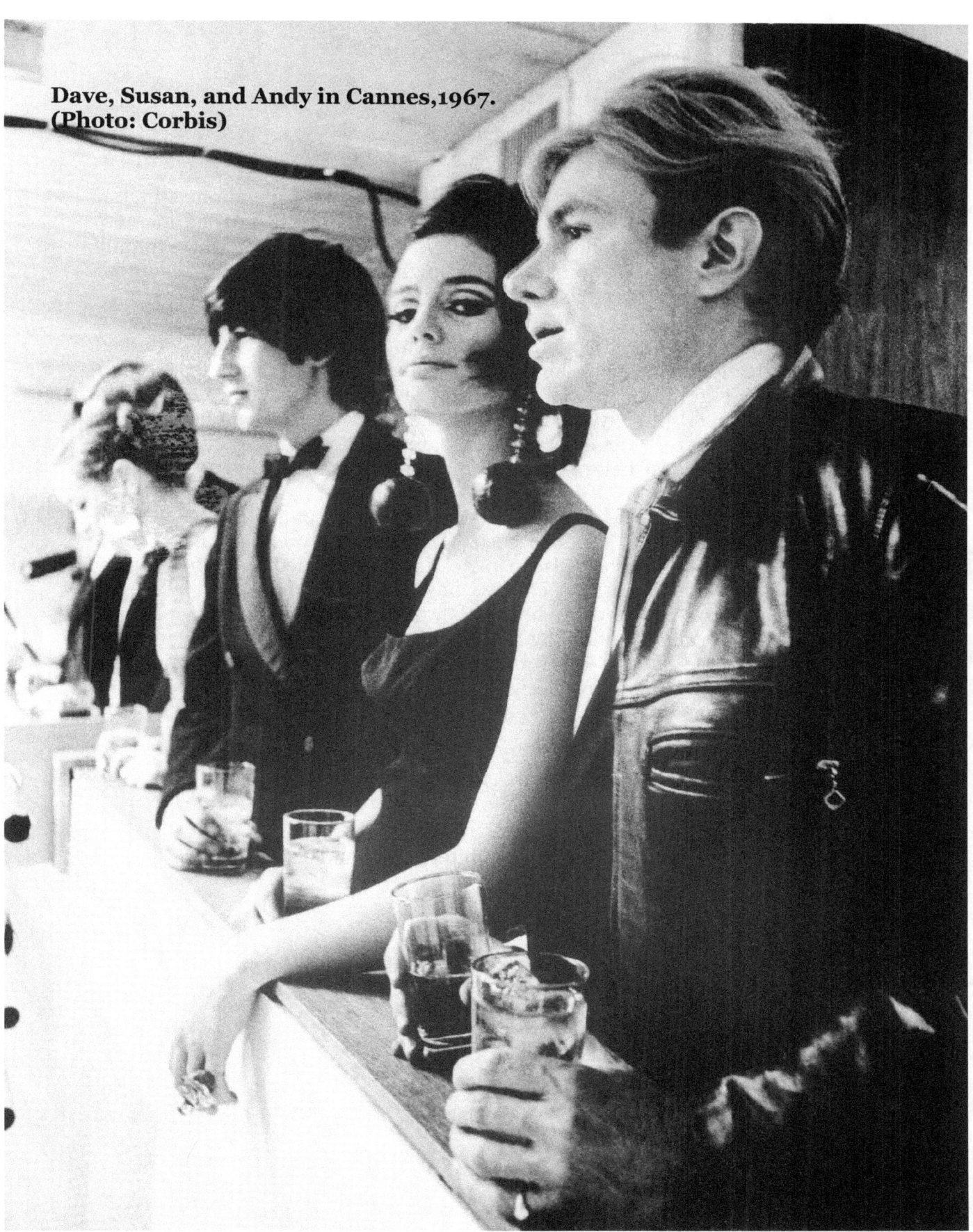

Dave, Susan, and Andy in Cannes, 1967. (Photo: Corbis)

LID Publisher and former "Factory Boy" David Croland had mentioned in our documentary that the non-showing of 'Chelsea Girls' in Cannes happened in 1966, when, in fact, they all went the following year. This is understandable, since filming with any Warhol project could go on and on—it might even become part of another film—and we obviously didn't care about time frames, either.

After their French sojourn in 1967, Warhol made a stop in London to meet with Paul McCartney and Beatles' manager Brian Epstein, to discuss backing for a British tour by the Velvet Underground, just as everyone's favorite free-loving acid-headed album, 'Sargeant Pepper's Lonely Heart's Club Band', was about to be released. The discussions went nowhere. McCartney was apparently more interested in getting Nico to move out of his house before future wife Linda Eastman showed up.

By the time Warhol and his jet-lagged Superstars returned from Europe, Lou Reed had hired a new manager, and dropped Nico. The break-up was quite bitter, with recriminations all around. Warhol, disconsolate, had also decided to tearfully dump (by popular request) his obnoxious abusive boyfriend, Rod La Rod. While he appeared to be on top of the world and feverishly working, Warhol was in fact closing himself off physically and emotionally. As the Factory and its ongoing insanity swirled around him, the hangers-on were now clinging to the side of a rudderless ship in a maelstrom, which may have been Captain Andy's only way to abandon it.

Interviewer Aaron Sloan
What is your impression of American youth today?

Andy Warhol
Well, we like it better when boys and girls can intermingle and change.

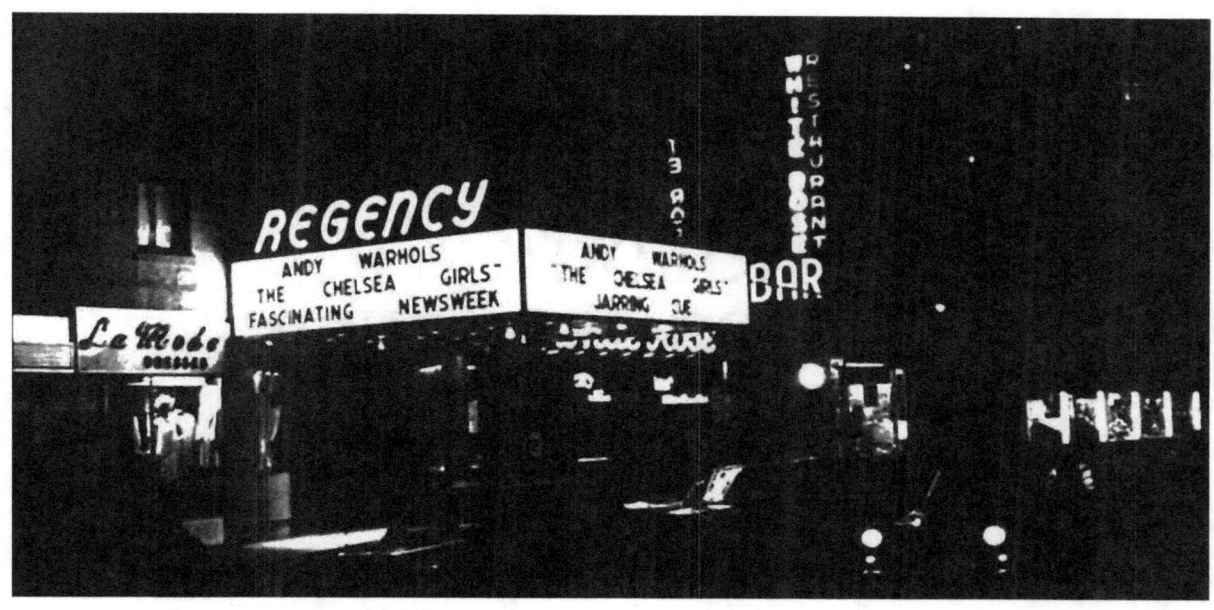

"Boffo 20K Warhol success!" The ground-breaking 'Chelea Girls' rocks the Regency, and Warhol's world.

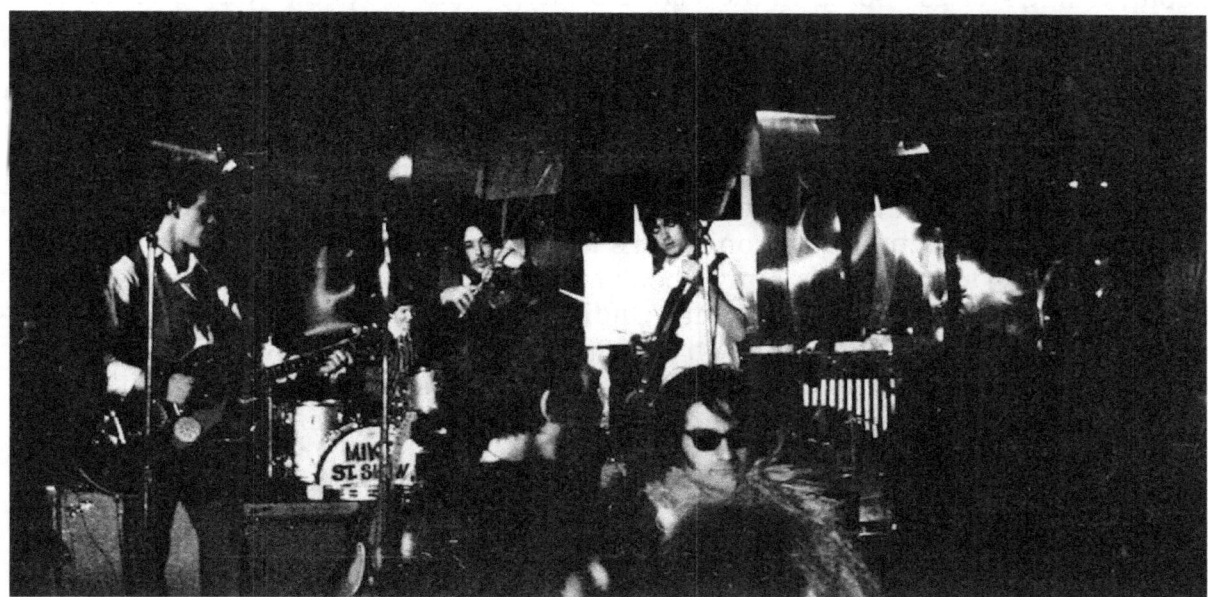

Ondine enjoys a night out with the Velvet Underground, shot in the signature black and white high contrast of Factory photographer Billy Name.

TRILOGY...
FILMS! BOOKS! MUSIC!

Work for no meaning.
—Andy Warhol

Victor Bockris: In the year of '66, Andy records The Velvet Underground, the first record—'The Velvet Underground by Andy Warhol'. He shoots 'Chelsea Girls', which made him a famous director. He was looked at as an American Godard. He's also writing his first book, 'a', the novel, which is a trilogy of works, because they're all made by the same base-group of people, ten to twelve people sitting around talking about, telling stories. Songs in the Velvet Underground are about this. The 'Chelsea Girls' are people doing what the others are talking about. And 'a' is people talking about what people are doing in these two things. . . People rejected it completely. But 'a' is one of the top ten books of the sixties. If you are making a list of books that kind of *are* the sixties—'Naked Lunch' would be one for example, and 'a' would be one. The 'Essential Lenny Bruce' would be one. These people stepped out and laid down their rap, and it became recognized as a Bible of that time. You could make a list, and 'a' would definitely be on it. It's an extraordinary book, and I don't know why people don't read it. It's Andy's book about the Factory. It's just driving around in cabs and sitting in apartments with Ondine and a few other people central to the scene. They talk about Edie, about all these people—Gerard, Mary, Ultra, Ingrid—and they put them down. They examine them, joke about them. . . In a sense, it's really a book about Andy. The core of the book is Andy actually being honest about his emotions. A cab driver asked him in the middle of the book, "Are you happy?" And he says, "No." And everyone goes, "No?! Why are you not happy?" Basically, it's because he hasn't a boyfriend. He hasn't anyone who is in love with him.

Andy Warhol
I don't really believe in love.

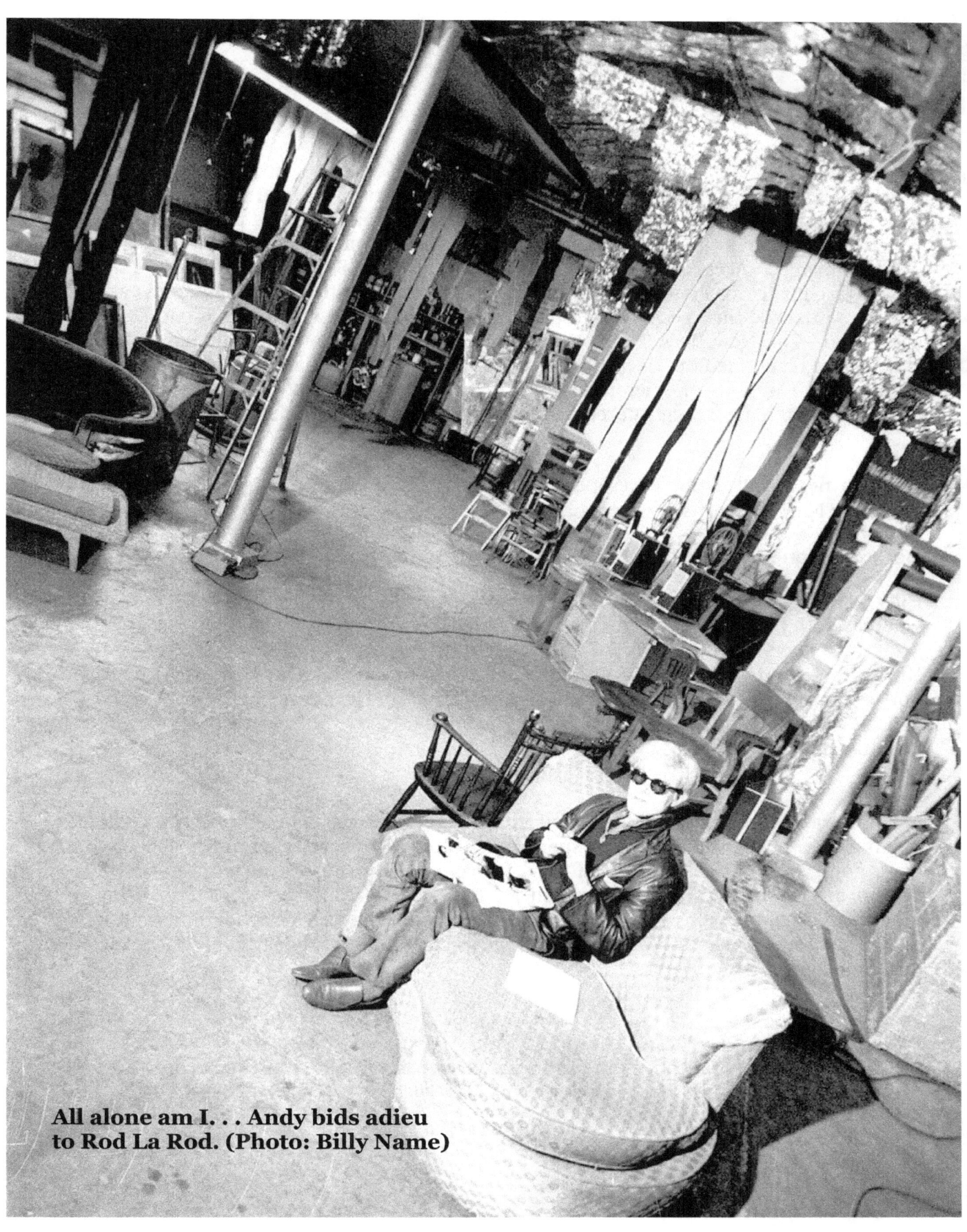

**All alone am I. . . Andy bids adieu
to Rod La Rod. (Photo: Billy Name)**

Warhol worked on 'a', a compilation of twenty-four hours of his tape recordings from 1965 to 1967, but did not publish it until 1968. He originally wanted to call it 'Cock', which might have been lost to posterity in the porn wilderness. Luckily, the wiser 'A-heads' prevailed. According to biographer Victor Bockris, "Billy Name supervised the typesetting for Grove Press, making sure it was presented with every spelling mistake and typo intact so that Andy's intention to make a 'bad' book would be fulfilled." He succeeded—The New York Times Review of Books called it a "Bacchanalian coffee klatch" and bemoaned its "degredations of sex, values. . . the death knell of American literature." I agree with Victor that it's probably required reading if one has any curiosity or even a prurient interest in the Silver Factory and the sixties.

Billy Name: Well, I think we opened the avant-garde world to him, the so-called authentic New York artist's world, because he—

Gerard Malanga: —He might have missed out on that.

Billy Name: Yeah, he was a little too shy, too awkward to find his way into it, whereas both Gerard and I were pretty gregarious *(laugh)*.

Ultra Violet: If you talked to Andy, he never had anything to say. He was a doer, not a speaker. He was the General Motors of Art. He never called back some defective motors, though *(laugh)*. Maybe he should have. But in art, there's never any mistake. Anything goes.

Warhol may not have said much, and there were some who thought he didn't do much either, but anyone who had spent time in the factory attested to the constant work going on amid the clutter of past projects. According to those interviewed, Warhol's reticence was a smoke screen for the press, because he was bored being asked the same questions. David Dugan of CBS News, a favored Warhol interviewer, had fun with him where others failed because Dugan kept tongue firmly in cheek, especially on camera. . .

David Dugan: Andy Warhol tries to say nothing, and succeeds. Other filmmakers try to say a great deal, but some uninitiated viewers might find them confusing. Either way, it's a long way from Hollywood. . . Dave Dugan, CBS News, New York.

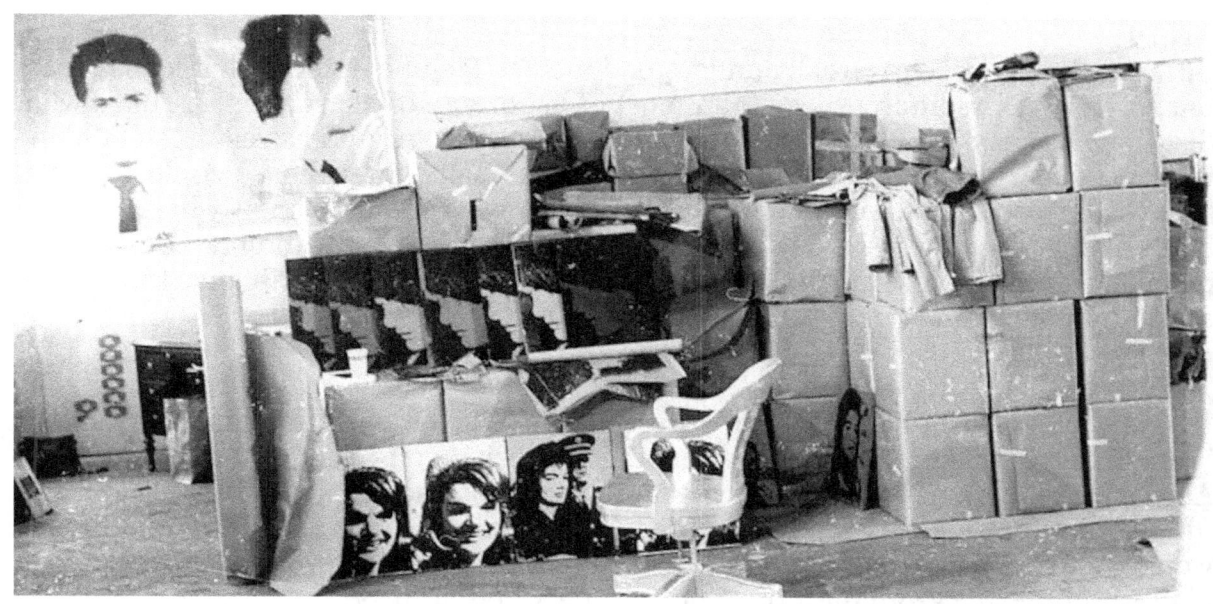

Art amid the clutter, . . The Silver Factory worked at full throttle in the sixties. Upper left: mug shot from 'Thirteen Most Wanted Men', and portraits of Jackie Kennedy.

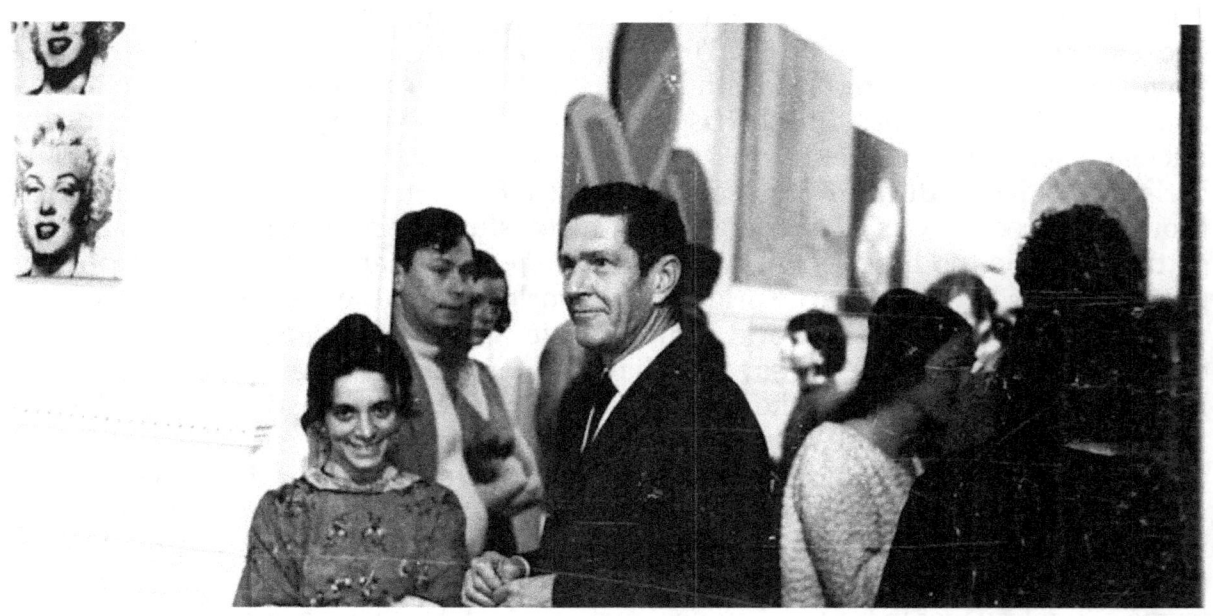

"Anything goes!" Warhol's Marilyns enjoy a sixties gallery opening. (Photos: Billy Name)

Vincent Fremont: Andy really understood media. He understood what icons mean, but he saw it in a different way than most of us, or any of us, saw it. . . That's what distinguishes any artist who's talented and has a vision. Andy was very good at being with people who were not quite thinking in the same way most people thought, because he also thought in an entirely different way. You never knew what he would be thinking or saying next. People said they did, but they really didn't. Lots of crazy people will always talk, talk, talk, and in that talk there is some brilliance that comes and shimmers in and out of it. But it can be dangerous.

I doubt that Warhol could have foreseen the danger awaiting him in his own immediate future, or, for that matter, the pervasive culture of violence in today's America, but he correctly predicted the brutal all-out scramble for those narcisstic fifteen minutes of fame and the ensuing media circus. He sort of started it. Still, one wonders today what he would make of an society with the attention span of a twitter—not fertile ground for the 6 hours long 'Chelsea Girls'.

Victor Bockris: The Factory world started to spin out of control after the success of 'Chelsea Girls'. It was like a brush fire. It started off with a few reviews in places like The Voice that were extreme, but they were underground, essentially. Then, it became this lead story in the New York Times, where the critic, using almost a quote from Henry II demanding the death of Thomas Becket, called upon someone to "put a spoke in Mr. Warhol's wheel. His attack on heterosexuality and the basis of the nuclear family is no longer funny." They meant it, because the success of 'Chelsea Girls' coincided with the release of 'The Velvet Underground and Nico.' And even though the record was not spectacularly successful by any means, it was actually getting into the top hundred. The point is, the powers that be saw that Warhol was going not only beyond the art world into the world of film, the sacred American form; *now* he was going into the world of pop music, which "went into the bedrooms of our children!" They began to say, "We have to stop this guy." And I think that Andy himself became confused by the enormous power he suddenly had. . . If you look at the world's image of Andy Warhol in 1965 as opposed to 1967, with the subsequent change in the culture, he really has gone from being a sort of Jean Luc Godard underground guy in a striped Tee shirt to some pop star on the cover of a big magazine. The Rolling Stones, the Beatles or Dylan weren't putting out the kind of material that Warhol was putting out. There's just no comparison. I don't mean in terms of quality, just in terms of *subject* matter. And it was not acceptable *(laugh)* to put it mildly. It was not acceptable what he did.

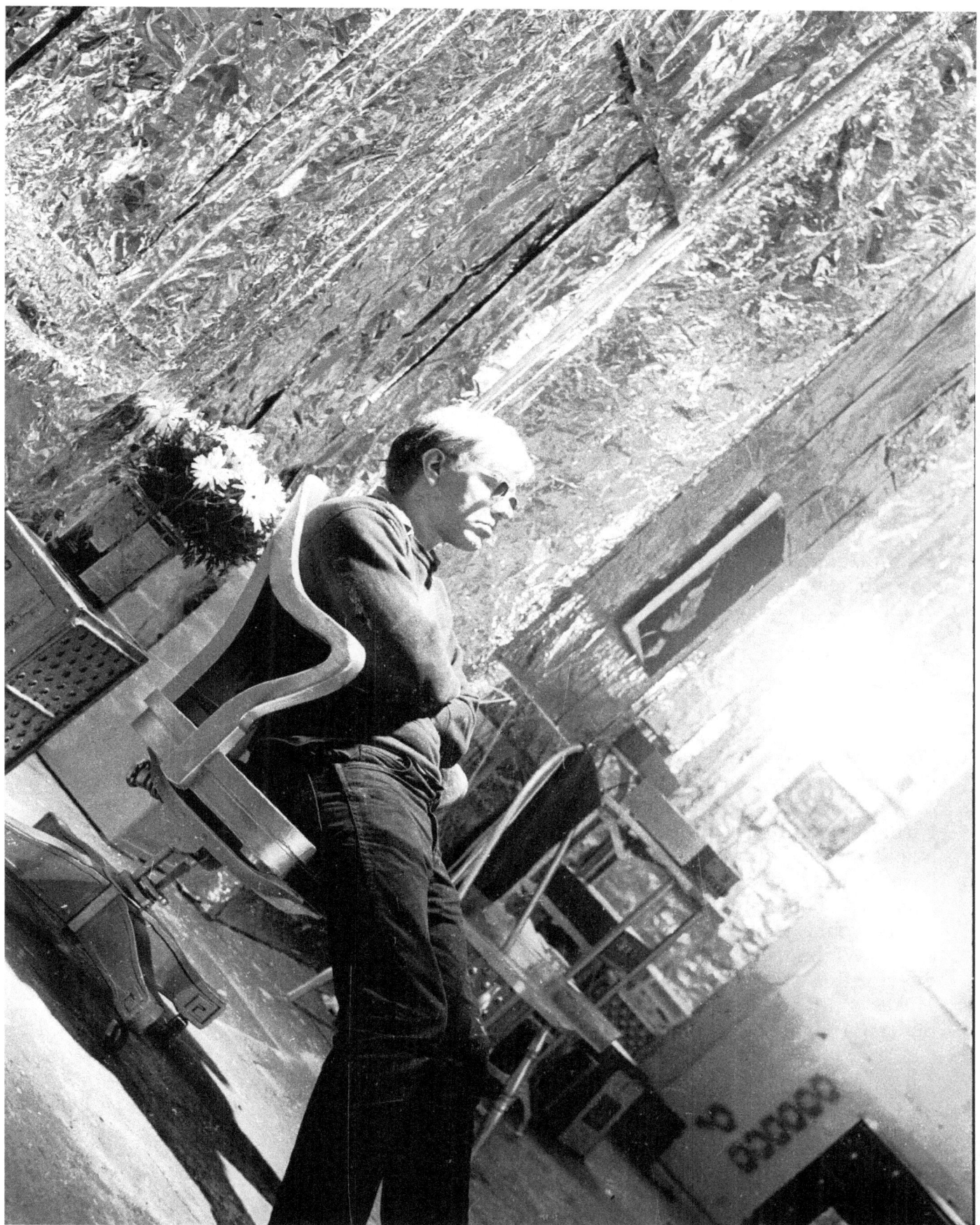

Jonas Mekas: With Andy, before what one could maybe call the 'Hollywood period', some producers approached him. And they thought, "Hmm, with all your fame, and the success that Chelsea Girls had, you should try to make something that could, that would play across the country." So that's where he made two or three or four films that were semi-based on scripts, bigger productions. . . But they *failed!* They didn't work. They were like a mixture. They were not really Warhol and they were not really (Paul) Morrissey, and they were neither this nor that.

Billy Name: Andy was making a film with Paul at Henry Geldzahler's apartment called 'The Loves of Ondine', Andy on the camera and Paul with the microphone, with Ondine in Henry's Eames chair. And in Henry's apartment you could see a John Chamberlain sculpture, one of those bronze chrome-like ones, a Frank Stella painting, and of course, there were Warhols in there, and Duchamps and Jasper Johns. Henry had all these paintings because artists would give him their work, because he promoted the young American artists of the period.

Henry Geldzahler
The problem is to bring the content in, in a way that's not stylistically stale or boring or repetitive. And it's almost impossible to do

Andy Warhol
Really?

Warhol and Morrissey began working on 'Loves of Ondine' in early '67. It was to be eight hours long. Then would come 'Imitation of Christ', with Ondine, Brigid Berlin and Taylor Mead, also clocking in at eight hours. The third, 'Vibrations' with Ivy Nicholson and René Ricard, was planned to run for, get ready, *twenty-four* hours on a split screen. All were to be filmed in the 'Chelsea Girls' mode of confrontational 'love' situations, according to Ivy, who clearly relished her role, insulting and smacking about her co-star. By the next year, Warhol, Morrissey and a contingent of actors would head out to L.A. to make a movie eventually to be called 'San Diego Surf'. While on location, Aaron Sloan, Warhol's West Coast film distributor, and director Robert Emmet Smith made their own home movie on 16mm, entitled 'Andy Makes a Movie', interviewing Warhol, Morrissey and 1967's 'Girl of the Year', Superstar Viva. . .

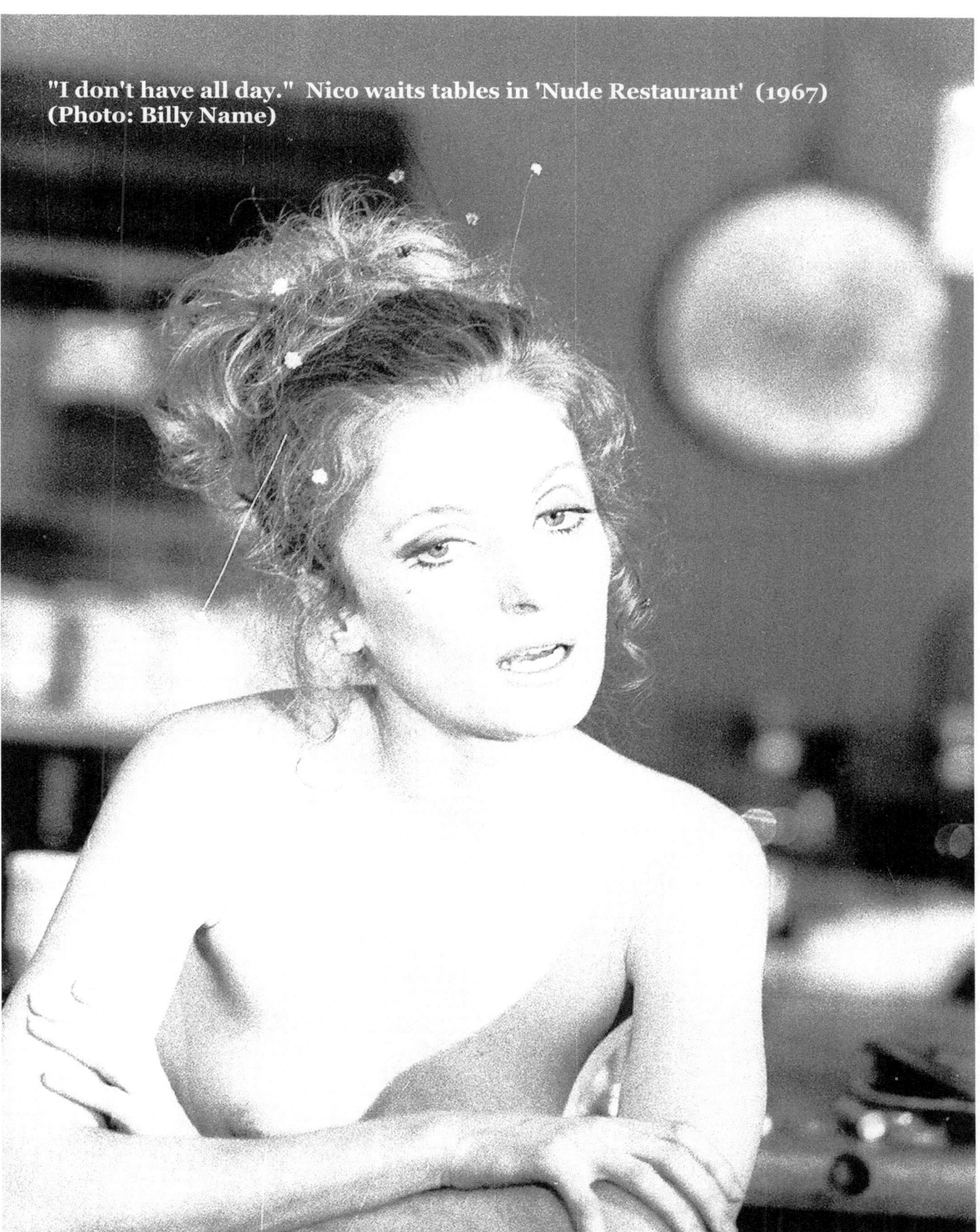

"I don't have all day." Nico waits tables in 'Nude Restaurant' (1967) (Photo: Billy Name)

Interviewer Aaron Sloan
Do you feel at home behind the camera, although you don't like to play with these mechanical things?

Andy Warhol
Uh, yeah.

Interviewer
Do you spend much time in camera shops, as you used to do in art shops?

Andy Warhol
No, I never spend any time in camera shops.

Interviewer
That brings up your relationship with Paul on a technical basis. They say Paul is the one who buys the equipment and tests it out.

Andy Warhol
Uh, yeah I guess. . . I think someone is ringing the door bell.

No one was at the door, but Viva wandered by, and Sloan took up hot pursuit. His elusive prey would also prove to be circumspect, though she professed at the time much affection and admiration for Warhol, whose role, like that of all directors, was "to play God."

Viva: In Andy's movies women are always the strong ones, the beautiful ones, and the ones who control everything. Men turn out to be these empty animals. Maybe the homosexuals are the only ones who haven't really copped out.

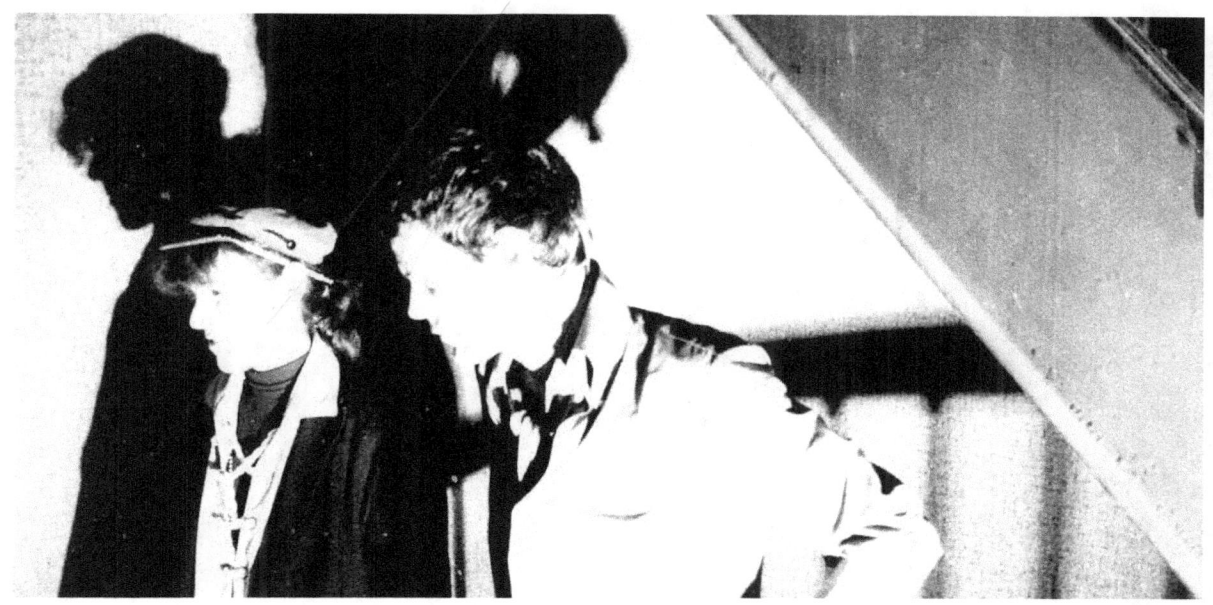

Valerie Solanas and Tom Baker emote in the Factory stairwell. The cast of 'I, A Man' (1967) included Nico, Ultra Violet, Ingrid Superstar and Ivy Nicholson.

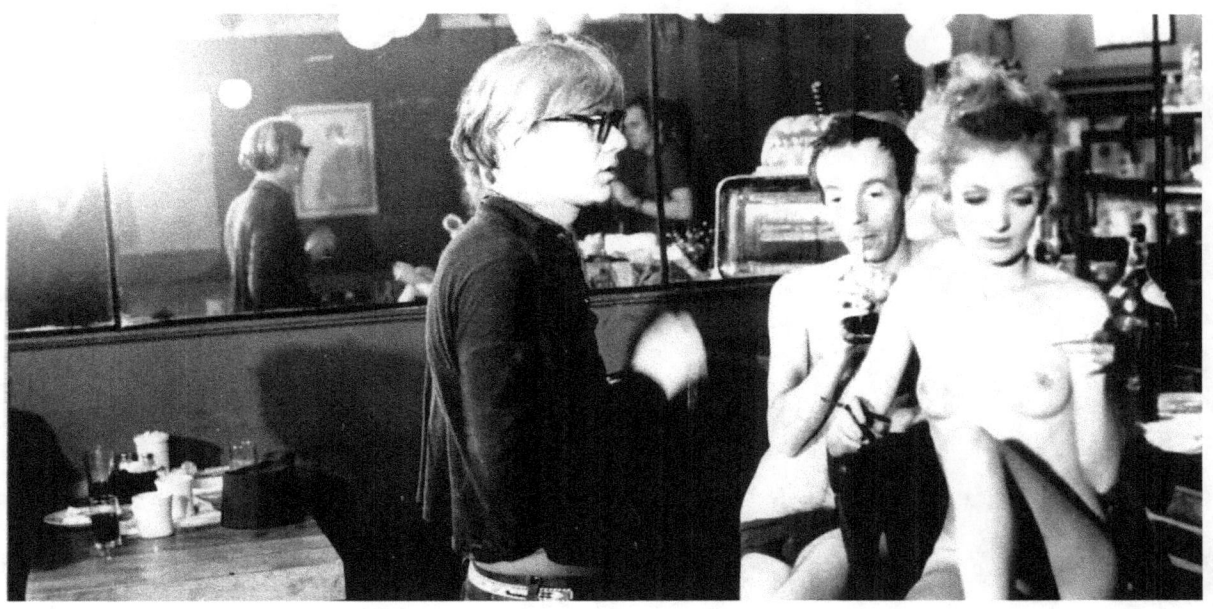

Andy, Taylor and Viva on the set of 'Nude restaurant' (Photos: Billy Name)

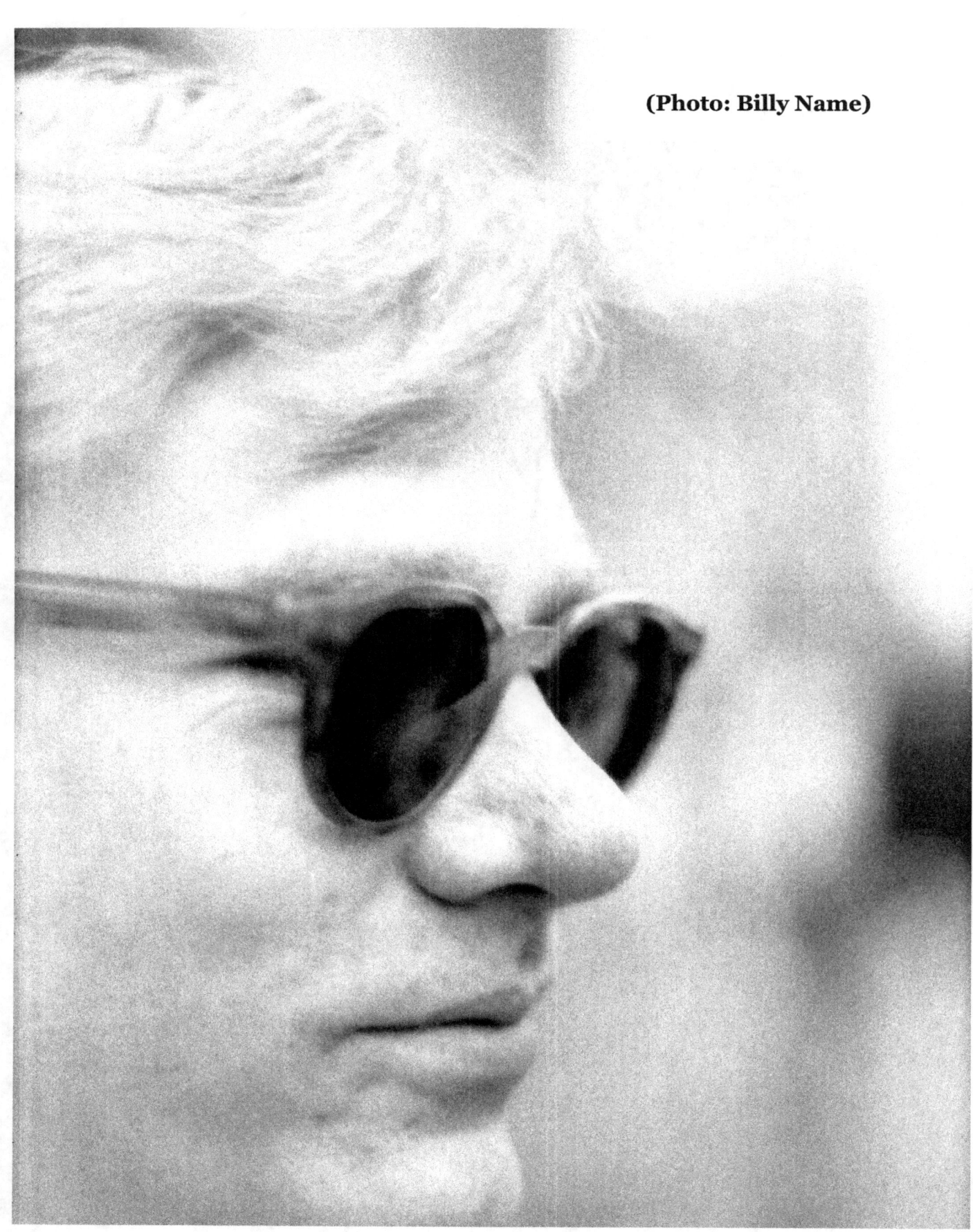

(Photo: Billy Name)

Coming up in Book III . . . 'Your 15 Minutes Are Up!'

Viva's favorite costar Taylor Mead flies back with Warhol from the San Diego filming, his head dancing with exciting possibilities and promises, but he still harbors a nagging fear of being disappointed yet again. . .

Taylor Mead: Super conniving, contriving, promising anything, agreeing with everybody.   Some woman came in representing a Jewish art exhibit benefit in California, and Andy promised her a painting.   When she left, I said, "Andy, are you really going to send her a painting?"   He said, "No, I don't like some of the artists in the show."   He wouldn't tell her that.

Two days after the flight from San Diego, Warhol is shot by a deluded young lesbian "man-hater"with tenuous ties to the Factory.   He is gravely injured, close to death. His shocked acolytes gather at the hospital, keening. . .

Andy Warhol: I never understood why, when you die, you didn't just vanish. Everything should just keep on going the way it was, only you just wouldn't be there.

Warhol does not die, but neither is he really "there" any longer.   According to Billy Name, he has become a fragile "cardboard Andy."   The business suits take over, and The Silver Factory, Warhol's delicate house of cards, with its dancing queens and cocky knights, collapses. . .

www.ingramcontent.com/pod-product-compliance
Lightning Source LLC
Chambersburg PA
CBHW080255180526
45167CB00006B/2541